ARCTIC CIRCLE

North-East Atlantic
Treaty

*LABRADOR
SEA*

*ULF OF
LASKA*

Halibut
Treaty
cific
Salmon
Treaty

Northwest
Atlantic
Treaty

Grand Banks

Georges Bank

*NORTH
SEA*
ICES

MEDIT.

SEA

NORTH

ATLANTIC

OCEAN

TROPIC OF CANCER

*GULF OF
MEXICO*

Inter-American
Tropical Tuna Commission

CARIBBEAN SEA

EQUATOR

GULF OF

GUINEA

SOUTH

ATLANTIC

OCEAN

TROPIC OF CAPRICORN

haling   Commission

In the
Week

severe. The kinds of fish that people are willing to buy represent only a small proportion of the biological materials produced in the sea. And the seas are not uniform in their fertility. As the popular fishing grounds become overcrowded, competition is intensified. This, in turn, can lead to conflict between nations, to depletion of the resource, and to the application of wasteful amounts of capital and labor.

In their examination of the fishery resources of international waters, Dr. Christy and Dr. Scott focus on the economic forces and pressures that will govern present and future use.

The first part of the book discusses the common property aspects of fisheries, and presents background material on the physical productivity and potentials of the ocean, and on supply and demand situations and prospects. The authors then examine the legal principles that guide the present use of the seas and conclude that new formulations, new regimes, and new kinds of regulations are called for if the world's fisheries are to be exploited in an orderly and rational fashion.

FRANCIS T. CHRISTY, JR., research associate with Resources for the Future, Inc., is co-author of *Trends in Natural Resource Commodities*.

ANTHONY SCOTT, professor of economics at the University of British Columbia, is the author of *Natural Resources: The Economics of Conservation*.

Published for Resources for the Future, Inc. by THE JOHNS HOPKINS PRESS

The Common Wealth in Ocean Fisheries

SOME PROBLEMS OF GROWTH AND ECONOMIC ALLOCATION

FRANCIS T. CHRISTY, JR., AND ANTHONY SCOTT

Published for RESOURCES FOR THE FUTURE, INC.
BY THE JOHNS HOPKINS PRESS, BALTIMORE AND LONDON

428468

Copyright © 1965 by The Johns Hopkins Press
All rights reserved
Manufactured in the United States of America

The Johns Hopkins Press, Baltimore, Maryland 21218
The Johns Hopkins Press Ltd., London

ISBN 0-8018-0118-4

Originally published, 1965
Second printing, 1972

SH
331
.C5
1972

Since 1965—
Authors' Preface to the
Second Printing

In 1965, we wrote that the international fisheries situation "will gradually worsen along three lines: through depletion of stocks, through decreased returns per unit of effort, and through increasing numbers of local conflicts" (p. 152). These developments are all taking place, but they are taking place at a rate that is far from gradual. It is now estimated that the rate of increase in world catch will be about half of what it was in the past. Effort, however, continues to grow rapidly, both in the number and tonnage of vessels and in the capability to fish distant waters. The number of local controversies has also increased. But, in addition, these controversies are now being raised in an international context, owing to significant developments in other resources and uses of the sea. A combination of forces has led to a call for a third United Nations Conference on the Law of the Sea and to the necessity for facing directly the problems of the distribution of the sea's wealth.

What the outcome of the third UN Conference will be is far from clear. In fact, at this writing (April 1972) it is not even clear whether the conference will be held in 1973, as initially scheduled, or postponed until 1974 or perhaps even later. And it is certainly not clear what kinds of resolutions might be reached in the many areas of controversy—the extent and kind of jurisdiction over fisheries and sea-bed minerals; freedom of transit through narrow straits; the kind and degree of authority of the agency that will govern deep sea-bed mining; jurisdiction and controls over pollution; the definition of the new concept that high seas resources are the "common heritage" of mankind; ways in which nation-states might share in this common heritage; jurisdiction and control over pelagic fisheries such as tuna, whales, and salmon; the meaning and the limits of the territorial sea; the meaning of preferential rights for coastal states; and many more.

Some of the more important developments that have taken

place in the past seven years are discussed below. With regard to fisheries, there has not been much change in the nature of the problems, but there has been considerable change in their magnitude and severity. In response to these developments there have been a number of unilateral and multilateral actions that have affected the law of the sea. Developments outside of fisheries have also taken place, bringing new pressures to bear upon the resolution of fishery problems. As a consequence, these problems can no longer be dealt with as they have been in the past—i.e., by a small coterie of experts from a few countries reaching agreements on an ad hoc basis and using criteria that are primarily of a biological nature. Instead, fishery problems must now be considered within a global context and fishery values are only one of a number of items that are being traded off.

Fishery Developments

CATCH AND EFFORT

During the 1960's, the rate of increase in the world catch of fish was less than it had been in the previous two decades (see Figure A). In 1969, for the first time since the second World War, the world catch was actually less than it was the year before. It rose again in 1970, but the indications are clear—future growth in the world catch will be at a much lower rate than in the past.

This is borne out by various projections of supply and demand recently made by the Food and Agriculture Organization of the United Nations (FAO)[1] and by economists at the U.S. National Marine Fisheries Service[2] as shown in the figure. The projections, based on different assumptions regarding prices and elasticities of demand, reach different results. But the general conclusions are the same: demand will exceed supplies for several major species, prices will increase, and the future rate of growth of catch for nonfood purposes will diminish sharply relative to the past.

[1] Food and Agriculture Organization of the United Nations, *Agricultural Commodity Projections 1970–1980* (Rome, 1971), pp. 319–29; and *The Prospects for World Fishery Development in 1975 and 1985* (Rome, 1969).

[2] F. W. Bell, D. A. Nash, E. W. Carlson, F. V. Waugh, R. K. Kinoshita, and R. F. Fullenbaum, "The Future of the World's Fishery Resources" (Washington, D.C.: U.S. Department of Commerce, National Marine Fisheries Service, forthcoming).

Million metric tons, live weight

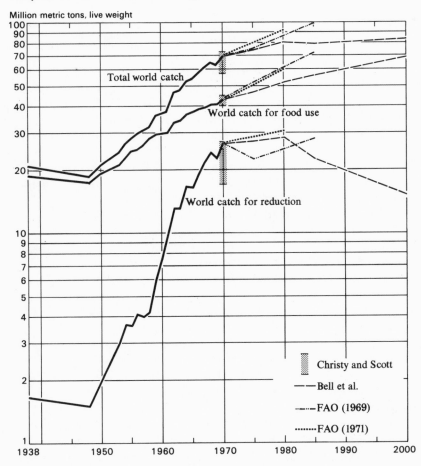

Figure A. World catch of fish, 1938–70, and projections of demand and catch. The FAO (1971) projections to 1980 represent *demand* and are from *Agricultural Commodity Projections, 1970–1980* (Rome, 1971). The FAO (1969) projections to 1985 and the Bell et al. projections to 2000 represent *catch* and are from FAO, *The Prospects for World Fishery Development in 1975 and 1985* (Rome, 1969), and from F. W. Bell et al., "The Future of the World's Fishery Resources" (U.S. Department of Commerce National Marine Fisheries Service, Washington, D.C., forthcoming). The Christy and Scott projection is from Table 7, p. 38.

Overall, the rate of growth is likely to drop from its past rate of about 6–7 per cent per year (a doubling every ten to twelve years) to somewhere between 2 and 4 per cent per year over the next decade or so; and a zero rate of growth seems possible in the more distant future.

The projections refer only to conventional species of fish taken from known stocks and may therefore significantly underestimate future levels of catch. New stocks may be discovered, or there could be shifts to unconventional species. With regard to new discoveries of stocks, FAO has stated that "at the present rate of development few substantial unexploited stocks of fish accessible to today's types of gear will remain in another 20 years."[3]

A shift to unconventional species is indeed possible. Species such as Antarctic krill might be effectively produced and marketed, and world catches might be many million tons more than the projections shown in Figure A. But there are several factors that tend to impede such developments. If an unconventional species is to be used as food for human consumption, it must meet an effective demand, and this requires change in taste preferences or the overcoming of sociological objection to the consumption of certain kinds of fish. These are difficult tasks.

The market for nonfood fish, i.e., fish caught for meal to be fed to poultry and other farm animals, is much more adaptable to unconventional species. It is less flexible, however, with regard to price since substitutes for fish meal are readily available. Thus for an unconventional species to find a market, it must be capable of being caught and processed at a very low cost.

The possibility that the projections underestimate future levels of catch is not really very relevant to the problems of the management and distribution of fishery wealth. What is important is that the supply of most of the world's valuable fish stocks is severely limited; that many of the stocks are already being overfished; and that the demand projections all indicate that even more stocks will be overfished in the future.

The projections also show that there is likely to be little shift in the distribution of catch in favor of the less-developed states. In quantitative terms, the less-developed states now take nearly 40 per cent of the world catch (see Table A). This indicates a major increase over their share in 1958, but almost all of this increase has been due to the phenomenal growth in catch by Peru. For the developing states, excluding Peru, the share of the world catch has remained quite steady at about 22–23 per cent, and the projections indicate that it will be about the same in 1980.

When catch is measured in value rather than weight the figures tell a very different story (see Table B). For example, the value of

[3] *The State of Food and Agriculture 1967* (Rome: FAO, 1967), p. 124.

the Peruvian catch was only about 6 per cent of that of the Japanese catch in 1967, even though Peru took over 10 million tons of fish while Japan took less than 8 million tons. Of the fifteen top states by value, the developing states, including Peru, accounted for only 16 per cent of the total.

Table A. Quantity of Catch by Country Groups as Per Cent of World Total

Country Group	1958	1969
Developed market economies	52	40
Developing market economies		
excluding Peru	22	23
Peru	3	14
Centrally planned economies	23	23
Total	100	100

Source: FAO, *Yearbook of Fishery Statistics.*

Table B. Value of Catch of Fifteen Leading
Countries (excluding China) in 1967

Country	$US (in Millions)
Japan	1,953
U.S.S.R.	1,037
U.S.	439
Spain	326
Philippines	271
France	265
Italy	187
U.K.	175
Norway	166
Pakistan	153
Canada	149
Thailand	146
Peru	124
S. Korea	112
Taiwan	103

Source: F. W. Bell et al., "The Future of the World's Fishery Resources" (Washington, D.C.: U.S. Department of Commerce, National Marine Fisheries Service, forthcoming). The U.S.S.R. figure is a weighted average price of all other countries in the table multiplied by U.S.S.R. landing. This procedure is followed for each species in the U.S.S.R. catch and summed to obtain the total. Original source is FAO, *Yearbook of Fishery Statistics.*

There are no satisfactory overall measurements of fishing effort
—the number and size of vessels, number of fishermen, time spent
fishing, kinds of fishing gear, etc. There are indications, however,
that for many of the particularly valuable stocks of fish, fishing
effort is continuing to increase even though the yields from the
stocks have reached (and in some cases passed) the maximum
yields that can be sustained. There are also indications that the
amount of distant-water fishing effort has been increasing quite
rapidly.

By far the greatest amount of distant-water effort lies in the
hands of the developed states. Table C shows the tonnage of all
fishing vessels over 100 gross tons in size for each of the 15 most
important states for 1970. Almost exactly half of the total for the
world is owned by the Soviet Union. Peru is the only developing

Table C. Fishing Vessels, Factories, and Carriers, Number and Tonnage,
1970, by Rank (Vessels over 100 gross tons)

Country	Number of vessels	Number as % of world total	Tonnage (1,000 gross tons)	Tonnage as % of world total
1. U.S.S.R.	3,055	23.6	3,997	51.2
2. Japan	2,386	18.4	978	12.5
3. Spain	1,364	10.6	433	5.5
4. Great Britain & N. Ireland	577	4.5	235	3.0
5. Poland	176	1.4	231	3.0
6. France	660	5.1	195	2.5
7. Norway	635	4.9	182	2.3
8. W. Germany	182	1.4	147	1.9
9. E. Germany	172	1.3	136	1.7
10. Canada	466	3.6	129	1.7
11. Portugal	158	1.2	110	1.4
12. South Africa	118	0.9	85	1.1
13. Italy	180	1.4	83	1.1
14. Peru	427	3.3	81	1.0
15. U.S.A.	201	1.6	74	0.9
All other	2,028	17.8	708	9.2
World total	12,889	100.0	7,804	100.0

Source: Lloyd's Register of Shipping, Statistical Tables, 1970.

state among the top fifteen, and its tonnage represents only about one per cent of the world total.

In the absence of any changes in the limits of jurisdiction (and perhaps even with such changes), certain of the developing states will probably increase their distant-water effort. Labor costs are becoming an increasingly critical factor with regard to the expansion of distant-water fishing by the developed states, particularly Japan and the Soviet Union.

Because of this, some of the developing states are gaining a comparative advantage that makes their increased efforts more attractive. Capital provided by aid programs and by Japanese investments in joint ventures will tend to shift some of the distant-water effort to the less-developed states. As noted later, however, this may be frustrated by the extensions of fishery jurisdiction and by regional agreements that tend to exclude new entry.

The Soviet Union's response to increasing labor costs is to develop and adopt labor-saving devices. Under the current five-year plan, between 1971 and 1975, the Soviet Union expects to increase its labor productivity by 30 per cent.[4] There are no indications of the extent to which the Soviets intend to increase the size of their fishing fleets. A recent article on fishing industry development in the Ninth Five-Year Plan, suggests that emphasis will be placed on greater development of inland aquiculture, improvements in repair and port facilities, and the development of new gear, including labor-saving devices.[5] The article also states, however, that

. . . research on raw materials of the world's oceans will expand significantly. More new types of vessels will be added to the fishing fleet, production capacities for processing ocean fish into fish products of improved assortment will be increased, and the capacity of refrigerator ships will be enlarged in the present five-year period. During the five-year period, the fishing industry will receive new fishing vessels such as the Atlantik supertrawler, the Altay large refrigerated fishing trawler, special vessels for Barents Sea, and seiner-trawlers for catching pelagic fish.[6]

[4] "Fishing Industry Development in the Ninth Five-Year Plan" (translation of article in *Rybnoye Khozyaystvo* [Moscow], No. 2 [February 1972], pp. 3–5), U.S. Department of Commerce, National Marine Fisheries Service, JPRS 55541, March 27, 1972, p. 9.
[5] *Ibid., passim.*
[6] *Ibid.,* p. 8.

While these statements provide no basis for estimating the future tonnage of the Soviet distant-water fleet, it is nevertheless clear that the Soviets anticipate large increases in their distant-water catch.

CONSEQUENCE OF DEVELOPMENTS IN FISHERIES

Developments in fisheries during the 1960's are marked by two major trends, both of which are likely to continue into the 1970's and to exacerbate the problems in the law and management of the seas. The first of these trends lies in the increasing pressure upon the valuable fishery stocks of the world. The second lies in the growing amount of distant-water fishing effort. The consequences are the growing value of exclusive rights to stocks of fish, the decreasing value of the principle of the freedom of the seas, the increase in depletion of stocks, and more importantly, the speed with which a stock can become depleted. These consequences are accompanied by a growing amount of economic waste through the application of excessive capital and by the increased severity and extension of conflicts.

There are many fishery experts, even today, who continue to estimate the potential biological yield of protein materials from the sea in terms of hundreds of millions of tons and who point out that there are vast stocks of unutilized or underutilized species. While such estimates may have some accuracy in biological terms, they are frequently misused in terms of man's interests and values, tending to offer the prospect of large increases in world catch and to suggest that all nations have opportunities to share in this supposed future wealth. It is implied, and sometimes explicitly stated, that such opportunities can best be realized by the maintenance of the principle of the freedom of the seas, and also that such opportunities will be of particular benefit to the developing states.

But, as shown above, the prospects for large future increases in catch are not particularly good. As this becomes more evident, the option to fish in some future time, which is guaranteed by the principle of the freedom of the seas, becomes devalued. And, simultaneously, the value of exclusive rights to fish stocks becomes greater and greater. Thus, two opposing forces have been set in motion. The major fishing states and the states with rich coastal waters attempt to exclude others from sharing in the exploitation of the resources—the first by agreements that divide up annual yields and the second by the extension of jurisdiction. Opposing forces, however, are found among states that do little or no fishing at present and those that anticipate fishing in waters far from their shores. These states, aware of the decreasing value of the option to fish, want to share more directly in the sea's wealth—the states not presently fishing, by advancing the concept of "common heritage"; and the states developing distant-water fisheries, by insisting upon the preservation of open access.

Thus far in the controversy the condition of open access is still precariously maintained for most of the world's valuable stocks of fish. The growing value of these stocks has provided greater incentives to invest more fishing effort, with the consequence of more rapid and more severe depletion. In addition, the use of highly mobile, distant-water fishing fleets has led to the possibility of "pulse" fishing. That is, a large mobile fleet may be capable of severely depleting a stock of fish in a single season and can then move off to deplete another stock in a far distant area, and from that one to another; eventually returning to the first stock after it has become rehabilitated. While this is probably more of a concept than an actual fact, it does, nevertheless, indicate the rapidity with which a stock can become depleted and also the possibility of a "domino" effect and the need for controls between, as well as within, regions.

With regard to increased number of depleted fish stocks, FAO recently stated that at the time of the first United Nations Law of the Sea Conference in 1958:

> . . . the heavily exploited stocks were limited to some half dozen stocks in the North Atlantic and North Pacific, mostly of the large, valuable and long-lived species (halibut, salmon, plaice or haddock), and the blue whales in the Antarctic . . . [Now] the number of heavily exploited stocks has greatly increased, and includes stocks in all parts of the world. Fortunately only a few stocks have been so depleted that the present yield is only a small proportion of the possible yield. . . . Many more stocks have been sufficiently depleted for the effort expanded in harvesting them to be much in excess of what is necessary, often with some decline in the total yield. In others, the effort is now increasing, or is likely to increase in the near future.[7]

Also, as pointed out by FAO, in previous years the development of a fishery had generally been slow enough to allow for the estab-

[7] *Conservation Problems with Special Reference to New Technology*, FAO Fisheries Circular No. 139 (Rome: FAO, 1972), p. 6.

lishment of some form of conservation measures before depletion became severe. But

> fisheries can now develop in a very few years from the time the first significant catches are made to a stage where management measures are needed. For example, catches of yellowfin sole in the Bering Sea were well under 50,000 tons until 1959, increased to a peak of 450,000 tons in 1961 and dropped to 66,000 tons in 1963. These rapid increases in catches from a particular stock are often due to the activities of long-range fleets, which can easily switch their attention from one stock to another.[8]

The rapidity of depletion may also be a product of the threat of conservation controls or of the establishment of national quotas. When a fishing state believes that a stock of interest to it may soon come under such controls, there is an incentive to invest more heavily and to increase effort. In 1967, for example, it was specifically pointed out that certain Norwegians, aware of excess capacity in the herring fleet, nevertheless saw the need to maintain the fleet and even enlarge it, if possible, because fleet size and catch would be a bargaining basis for national quotas.[9]

This remark, referring to 1967, foreshadowed the dramatic drop in catch of Atlanto-Scandian herring from "well over a million tons in 1967 to a few tens of thousands in 1970."[10] Although this drop was primarily due to the adoption of the technique of purse-seining for herring, the threat of setting national quotas or other kinds of controls did nothing to slow it up.

A prime example of the "domino" effect can be found in the tuna fisheries. In 1967, the Inter-American Tropical Tuna Commission established a total quota on the catch of yellowfin tuna in the region. This was done in spite of the knowledge that a total quota on catch has particularly devastating economic effects.[11] Under this arrangement, each fisherman has an incentive to build a larger and faster vessel in order to get a greater share of the catch for himself before the total quota is reached and the season

[8] *Ibid.*, p. 5.

[9] Giulio Pontecorvo, "Critique: Exploitation of the Living Resources of the High Seas," in L. Alexander, ed., *The Law of the Sea: International Rules and Organization for the Sea* (Kingston: The Law of the Sea Institute, University of Rhode Island, 1969), p. 278.

[10] *Conservation Problems with Special Reference to New Technology*, p. 5.

[11] J. A. Crutchfield and A. Zellner, "Economic Aspects of the Pacific Halibut Fishery," *Fishery Industrial Research*, Vol. 1, No. 1 (Washington, D.C.: U.S. Government Printing Office, 1963).

closes. In the tuna situation, the incentive has clearly been at work. Almost half of the current U.S. high seas tuna fleet (in terms of gross tonnage) has been built since the establishment of the quota—3,809 tons in 1967; 6,032 tons in 1968; 9,185 tons in 1969; and 10,427 tons in 1970.[12] It is reported that an additional 21 vessels with a capacity of about 24,000 tons are now under construction in the United States, and about 32,000 tons elsewhere in the world.[13]

The global repercussions from this artificial stimulus to overcapitalization derive from the fact that the large number of vessels are able to catch the total quota in a short amount of time. Prior to the control, the season was about nine months. It now takes only about three to four months to reach the quota and it will take less as more vessels are added. Since the vessels are large and highly mobile, they naturally turn to other areas of the world after the close of the eastern tropical Pacific fishery. The "domino" effect has already been felt in the Atlantic and may soon reach the western Pacific and Indian Oceans.

The "domino" effect can also come from other kinds of controls and developments. Iceland, for example, has announced that it will extend its fishery limits to 50 miles no later than September 1, 1972. There may be arrangements for a gradual phasing out of foreign fishing vessels. Those vessels that are phased out, whether rapidly or gradually, will have to turn elsewhere. Wherever they turn in the North Atlantic, they will simply add to pressures that are already excessive. This will lead to more controls or more exclusive arrangements or actions and to the displacement of greater numbers of vessels. If the vessels are sufficiently mobile, they may turn to the South Atlantic, adding to the pressures that are beginning to be felt there.

In short, we are now on the brink of precipitous actions and reactions that could, within a year or two, totally change the character of fishery regimes throughout the world. It is not clear that such rapid changes must necessarily be detrimental to the long-run interests of the world community, but it would be preferable for the changes to take place within the deliberation of an

[12] Derived from "American High Seas Tuna Fleet," *National Fisherman, Yearbook Issue 1971,* Vol. 51, No. 13 (April 1971).
[13] "Growing Tuna Fleet Threatens Resource," *National Fisherman,* Vol. 52, No. 7 (April 1971).

international forum rather than through a spate of unilateral and multilateral proclamations and actions.

Developments in the Law of the Sea for Fisheries

The three-mile fishing limit has almost completely disappeared. Most nations, including the United States, which for many years opposed extending limits, have now gone to 12 miles. But extensions much greater than that are becoming more common. In 1958, only six countries claimed more than 12 miles. At the moment, at least sixteen such states have done so, and at least ten of them have made claims to 200 miles.

Even more important in some cases, such as that of Canada and the island states, has been the straightening of base lines and the consequent claim to enlarged internal waters. Aside from Iceland, all claims to fishing zones beyond 12 miles have been made by developing countries, many of them in Latin America. The claims have, at least in part, been stimulated by the appearance of U.S. tuna and shrimp vessels, French lobster vessels, and Soviet trawlers in their nearby waters.

In 1971, Ecuador was particularly active in enforcing its claim to 200 miles. During the year, it made over fifty seizures of U.S. tuna vessels, and collected fines and other fees amounting to more than $2.5 million. The U.S. government has discouraged the purchase of license fees in waters beyond 12 miles because it fears that this would constitute a recognition of the claims and be damaging to its interests (primarily military) in preserving the freedom of the seas. U.S. fishermen can collect the amount of their fines from a special government fund created for this purpose. However, since payment is often a lengthy process and there are other costs borne by the fishermen, such as the time lost on the fishing grounds when vessels are seized, the fishermen do not find this a very satisfactory arrangement.

Ecuador, like most (but not all) of the other states asserting extensive claims, does not prohibit foreign fishing but requires licenses. To obtain a license, a vessel must first pay an annual registration fee of $350, and then buy a trip license for each trip or for a certain number of days.[14] The trip license costs $20 per net register ton of the vessel. This would mean that the *Apollo,* for ex-

[14] Ecuador Law No. 110CL, Ley de Pesca y Fomento Pesquero, Registro Oficial, Year 1, No. 132.

ample, which is one of the largest and newest of U.S. seiners, would have to pay $15,660 per trip (based on 783 net register tons). For comparison, its gross revenue from a trip could be several hundred thousand dollars. If its total capacity of about 2,000 tons were taken up entirely with yellowfin tuna, the value would be over $800,000 at 1971 prices. The *Apollo* was seized twice in 1971 and paid $241,990 in fines.[15]

There is, of course, no guarantee that a vessel will be able to take its full capacity during a trip. More important in terms of the international implications, a tuna vessel may be subject to the license fees of more than one coastal state, since tuna are a highly migratory species and stocks are found over a wide area. This presents complications with regard to the determination of where to fish, the setting of fees, and the sharing of revenues and management. In spite of the complications, however, it is reported that most of the U.S. tuna vessels are purchasing licenses for the 1972 season rather than risk the fines and the fishing time lost during impoundment.

Extensive claims by other states have followed different patterns. In many cases, the claims have not yet been enforced, in part, perhaps, because of the difficulty of patrolling large areas of the sea. In some cases, the claims prohibit foreign fishing entirely or permit it only under certain conditions of investment in the coastal states, as when formerly international seas are claimed as internal waters behind new base lines. And, in certain situations, arrangements may be made for phasing out the foreigners.

Despite the great pressures for extensions of limits, certain factors tend to restrain unilateral actions. For example, there are about fifteen states along the coast of West Africa that have an interest in the coastal fisheries. In the past decade, the share of the catch taken by these states in the waters off their coasts has decreased from 85 per cent to about 40 per cent, with the rest being taken by the vessels of about fifteen foreign states, including Japan, Taiwan, and South Korea.[16] The desire to exclude the foreigners

[15] August Felando, "Statement," in U.S. Congress, Senate, *Fishery Legislation,* Hearings before the Subcommittee on Oceans and Atmosphere of the Committee on Commerce, 92 Cong., 1st sess. Serial No. 92-42 (Washington, 1972), p. 85.

[16] These figures have been derived from some rough estimates presented in FAO Fishery Committee for the Eastern Central Atlantic, "Summary Catch Statistics for the CECAF Area," CECAF/71/5 Sup. 1 (April 21, 1971), Table 4.1.

Preface to the Second Printing

provides a strong incentive for the extension of jurisdiction. But such extensions would necessitate quite complicated arrangements among the coastal states. The problems would include not only the location of the boundaries but also those of co-operating in management, research, and enforcement and in the distribution of fishing rights or of revenues from license fees. Eventually, such complicated arrangements are likely to be necessary, but for the moment they may provide a deterrent to unilateral extensions.

In addition to the growth in unilateral actions, there has been a striking increase in the number of bilateral agreements. The United States, in particular, has adopted such techniques as a means for providing immediate solutions to difficult disputes while avoiding concessions to extensive unilateral claims. Since about 1968, these arrangements have been worked out with the Soviet Union, Poland, and Japan in the Atlantic and the Pacific. Renegotiations occur about every two years and have become increasingly complicated. The agreement with the Soviet Union in January 1971 is typical.

1. In a strip running about 70–90 miles offshore from New York to Maryland, "fishing [is] prohibited with vessels over 110 feet during January 1 through April 15 [except shell-fish]."
2. In a much larger area—from the 12-mile limit out to more than 100 miles from the coast and extending from Montauk Point south to South Carolina—there is to be "no increase above 1967 level in catch of red hake, silver hake, scup, flounders, or black sea bass; no specialized fisheries for scup and flounders (except vessels under 110 feet). No fishing for menhaden January 1 through April 30. Soviet river herring catch limited to 4,000 metric tons annually."
3. In areas off Long Island within the U.S. 12-mile zone, the Soviets are permitted to load fish from November 15 through May 15 and are permitted to fish from January 1 through March 31.
4. The Soviets are also permitted to load fish off the New Jersey coast within the 12-mile zone between September 15 and May 15.
5. And finally, Soviet fishing and support vessels are permitted a limited number of calls into Baltimore and Philadelphia.

Arrangements of this kind, which are designed to meet some of the pressing demands of U.S. commercial and sports fishermen, are, in essence, a primitive barter of goods and services. They provide no basis for determining the value of the items that are being traded. They involve complex exchanges of unlike items, and the complexities are bound to proliferate both in future arrangements with the Soviets and Poles and in arrangements with other nations that will eventually want to participate.

A further indication of the rapid rate of change in fisheries situations is the creation of six new international regulatory fishery bodies in the past ten years. These relate to the Baltic Sea, Japan and Korea, Atlantic Tuna, the Central Eastern Atlantic, the Indian Ocean, and the Southeast Atlantic. As a consequence, almost every area of the oceans is covered by one or more international regulatory agreements, and more than 80 nations are involved.

Certain global solutions to fishery problems have been proposed for discussion at the third UN Conference on the Law of the Sea. In August 1970, the United States put forth a Draft United Nations Convention on the International Sea-bed Area.[17] The only living organisms to which this refers are the "sedentary" fisheries which, according to the 1958 Geneva Convention on the Continental Shelf, are "organisms which, at the harvestable stage, either are immobile on or under the seabed or are unable to move except in constant physical contact with the seabed or subsoil." These resources fall under the jurisdiction of the adjacent coastal state. According to the U.S. Draft Convention, that jurisdiction would extend to the outer edge of the continental margin, not simply to the edge of the continental shelf. And the jurisdiction would be complete in that the coastal state "may, in its discretion, . . . decide whether and by whom the living resources of the seabed shall be exploited."

In August 1971, the U.S. put forward a Draft Treaty containing an article devoted entirely to fisheries.[18] Article III proposes a stock-by-stock approach to fishery problems rather than a zonal

[17] "Draft United Nations Convention on the International Sea-Bed Area," working paper submitted by the United States Government, August 3, 1970.
[18] "Draft Articles on the Breadth of the Territorial Sea, Straits, and Fisheries Submitted by the United States," United Nations General Assembly, A/AC.138/SC.II/L.4 (July 30, 1971).

approach specifying a certain distance or a certain depth. The primary motivation for this is to avoid extensive limits of jurisdiction that, even though restricted to fisheries, might eventually be enlarged to cover other uses of the sea as well. The fear is that the limit might become similar to a territorial sea and thereby interfere with navigation, particularly of military vessels and aircraft.

Article III, however, is not entirely clear. Paragraph 2C states that "the percentage of the allowable catch of a stock in any area of the high seas adjacent to a coastal State that can be harvested by that State shall be allocated annually to it." Paragraph 2E(1) states that "the percentage of the allowable catch of a stock traditionally taken by the fishermen of other States shall not be allocated to the coastal State." In essence, through the criterion of exploitability, this gives everything to the coastal state, but through the criterion of historic rights, takes nothing from the distant-water state. It is also stated that these apparent contradictions would be resolved by the concerned states through negotiation—in short, a continuation of the present approach. The status quo is further reinforced by the provision that paragraph 2E(1) "does not apply to any new fishing or expansion of existing fishing by other States that occurs after this Convention enters into force for the coastal State." It is becoming clear that the arguments are likely to focus on the differences between a stock-by-stock approach, based on concepts of preferential and historic rights, and a zonal approach, based on limits of jurisdiction.

As of this writing, there is no way of anticipating the final outcome of the deliberations within the United Nations. Fishery matters are just beginning to receive the attention they deserve, and many delegations are still in the process of determining and evaluating the nature of their interests in fisheries. Fisheries will have to be balanced against the many other values sought from the sea—values that are quite disparate in both their character and importance. But while the outcome cannot be anticipated, it can be stated with a degree of certainty that fishery problems will never be ultimately resolved and that there will continue to be a very strong need for social science analysis of the problems of management and allocation.

Bibliographic Note

In the past seven years the fisheries economic literature has been fairly un-eventful, devoted to firming up previous notions, but the special literature on *international* fishery matters has been significantly expanded. Perhaps the best source of information on trends and changes in ideas concerning international marine resources lies in the Proceedings of the Annual Conferences of the Law of the Sea Institute at the University of Rhode Island. The Proceedings of these Conferences, which began in 1966, are listed below, followed by three excellent bibliographies published in 1970 and 1971.

Alexander, Lewis M. (ed.). *The Law of the Sea: Offshore Boundaries and Zones.* Columbus: Ohio State University Press, 1967.
———. *The Law of the Sea: The Future of the Sea's Resources.* Kingston: University of Rhode Island, 1968.
———. *The Law of the Sea: International Rules and Organization for the Sea.* Kingston: University of Rhode Island, 1969.
———. *The Law of the Sea: National Policy Recommendations.* Kingston: University of Rhode Island, 1970.
———. *The Law of the Sea: The United Nations and Ocean Management.* Kingston: University of Rhode Island, 1971.
———. *The Law of the Sea: A New Geneva Conference.* Kingston: University of Rhode Island, in press.
Hollick, Ann L. *Marine Policy, Law, and Economics: Annotated Bibliography, the 1960's.* Kingston: The Law of the Sea Institute, University of Rhode Island, 1970.
Koers, Albert. *The Debate on the Legal Regime for the Exploration and Exploitation of Ocean Resources: A Bibliography for the First Decade, 1960–70.* Kingston: The Law of the Sea Institute, The University of Rhode Island, 1970.
Woodrow Wilson International Center for Scholars. *Ocean Affairs Bibliography, 1971.* Ocean Series No. 302. Washington, D.C.: Woodrow Wilson International Center for Scholars, 1971.

Francis T. Christy, Jr.
Anthony Scott

April 1972

Preface

The biological resources of the sea have long fascinated man. The mystery of what lies beneath the surface has stimulated his imagination and nurtured the hope that in this vast area there are resources capable of feeding a growing and a still hungry population for centuries to come. But, at the same time, realization of this hope is impeded by the opacity, instability, and sheer magnitude of the medium itself—by man's inability to see and hold. Fishing—one of man's earliest callings—is still haphazard and subject to the vagaries of weather, ocean currents, and mysterious migrations.

The sea remains a frontier not only in the sense of the lack of scientific knowledge but also in the sense of the lack of co-operation between nations—for the sea is a joint resource of the world community. It belongs to no one—or to everyone—and its biological resources cannot be fenced in and made the property of one individual or one nation. On the high seas there is direct confrontation between nations. Here, nations have the opportunity to co-operate; failing that, the sea's resources become a source of conflict. This common ownership, or alternatively, this absence of individual and national rights, also creates severe problems for management. It is an obstacle to the achievement of an economically efficient system of exploitation and leads to a wastage of the great potential wealth of the seas. These problems of conflict and inefficiency serve to prevent the realization of man's hopes for the sea's resources.

In this book Francis T. Christy, Jr., RFF research associate, and Anthony Scott, Department of Economics, University of British Columbia, have explored the problems to find out what contributions toward solutions could be made by social scientists. A better understanding of the nature of the fisheries of the high seas and the legal and economic problems stemming from the common property characteristic has to be the starting point for improvements in national policy and international co-operation.

Resources for the Future is interested in ocean resources as these may come to play a larger role in feeding people and animals, supplying minerals, providing for commerce, waste disposal, and recreation, and supporting economic growth. RFF's interest extends to the analysis of conflicts that arise over the use of fish and other ocean resources, and to making clear the basis for wider agreement among nations regarding them. This book also carries forward RFF's concern with problems of the flow of natural resources in international markets and the role of resources in underdeveloped economies.

Mr. Christy, whose interest in common property resources began with his dissertation on the Maryland oyster industry, was primarily responsible for the first eight chapters dealing with the factors of supply and demand in international fisheries. Mr. Scott, who has written several outstanding articles on the theory of common property resources, was primarily responsible for the last chapters on the law of the sea and the problems of international agreement. Both, of course, have melded their initial efforts to achieve a joint product.

Joseph L. Fisher, President
Resources for the Future, Inc.

Acknowledgments

The global and comprehensive nature of this book has required us to enter fields of knowledge that are foreign to our background and training as social scientists. We have had much to learn and have stumbled often. If mistakes and misstatements are still evident in the book, the fault is ours and not our tutors', whose generosity and help have been invaluable. We acknowledge very gratefully our indebtedness to the following for their counsel and their comments: Edward W. Allen, International North Pacific Fisheries Commission; Professor John Bardach, University of Michigan; Professor William T. Burke, University of Ohio; Wilbert M. Chapman, Van Camp Foundation; Richard Cooley, Research Center—Alaska Natural Resources; Dean G. F. Curtis, Faculty of Law, University of British Columbia; Professor James Crutchfield, University of Washington; Professor Gerhard M. Gerhardsen, Norwegian School of Economics; Professor L. F. E. Goldie, Loyola University; Herbert Graham, U.S. Bureau of Commercial Fisheries; Robert Hamlisch, Fisheries Division of FAO; William C. Herrington, U.S. Department of State; Columbus O'D. Iselin, Woods Hole Oceanographic Institution; Roy Jackson, FAO; Philip C. Jessup, International Court of Justice; Austen Laing, The British Trawlers' Federation; Peter Larkin, Fisheries Research Board of Canada; George C. Matthiessen, Marine Research Foundation, Inc.; Professor Myres McDougal, Yale Law School; J. Lawrence McHugh, U.S. Bureau of Commercial Fisheries; Donald L. McKernan, U.S. Bureau of Commercial Fisheries; Professor Giulio Pontecorvo, Columbia University School of Business; F. E. Popper, FAO; Milner B. Schaefer, Institute of Marine Resources, University of California; Lionel Walford, Atlantic Fishery Oceanographic Research Laboratory; Donald White, Bureau of Business Research, Boston College; Norman Wilimovsky, Institute of Fisheries, University of British Columbia.

Special thanks are due to Frank Iacobucci and Hugh Ladner for their researches on the multilateral fisheries agreements and the Conventions on the Law of the Sea; and to the Food and Agriculture Organization of the United Nations for permission to adapt figures 9, 10, and 11, and to use figure 12. We are also grateful to the United States Steel Foundation whose contribution of $1,000 stimulated our undertaking.

Our colleagues at Resources for the Future have given much of their time and attention in fostering and guiding the study. In particular we are indebted to Jay Polach for his substantive and useful comments on our interpretations of international law; to Joseph L. Fisher for his stimulus and guidance; and to John Herbert for facilitating the process and mechanics of research.

And finally, we owe a great deal of gratitude to Nora Roots for her perception and care in editing a difficult manuscript; and to Clare O'Gorman Ford for her preparations of the illustrations, charts, and end papers.

Contents

PREFACE TO THE SECOND PRINTING v
PREFACE xxiii
ACKNOWLEDGMENTS xxv

CHAPTER 1
INTRODUCTION 1

CHAPTER 2
THE CHARACTERISTICS OF COMMON PROPERTY
NATURAL RESOURCES 6

CHAPTER 3
THE DEMAND FOR FISH 17
   Patterns of Consumption 18
   Forms of Utilization 22
      FRESH FISH 22
      FROZEN FISH 22
      CANNING 24
      CURING 25
      REDUCTION TO OIL AND MEAL 25
      SUMMARY 26
   Factors Affecting Demand 28
      PERISHABILITY AND PRESERVATION 28
      DISTRIBUTION 31
      TASTE PREFERENCES AND ELASTICITIES OF DEMAND 32
   Projections of Demand 37
      FOOD USE 38
      NONFOOD USE 41
   APPENDIX TO CHAPTER 3
   DEMAND PROJECTION METHODS 46
      FOOD USE 46
      NONFOOD USE 53

CHAPTER 4
THE PRODUCTIVITY OF THE SEAS 56
   Elements of Fertility 56
   The Food Web 65
   Potential Productivity 67

Aquiculture 70
Summary 72

∫ CHAPTER 5
THE FISHERY RESOURCE 74
   Natural Aspects of Fish Populations 76
      DENSITY OF STOCKS 77
      POPULATION FLUCTUATIONS 77
      ECOLOGY 78
   Extinction, Depletion, and Controls 80
      EXTINCTION AND DEPLETION 81
      CONTROLS 84
   Summary 86

CHAPTER 6
THE FISHING PROCESS 87
   Locating the Fish 88
   Catching the Fish 89
   Transporting and Processing Fish 92
   Fish Cultivation 96
   New Developments in the Fishing Process 97
      LOCATING TECHNIQUES 97
      ATTRACTING TECHNIQUES 99
      CATCHING TECHNIQUES 100
      CULTIVATION TECHNIQUES 101
   Conclusion 102

∫ CHAPTER 7
SUPPLY: FISHING EFFORT 104
   Trends in Output 105
   Fisheries in National Economies 114
   Fishing Vessels and Facilities 117
   Fisheries Employment 130
   Summary 136

∫ CHAPTER 8
MEETING FUTURE DEMAND 138
   Sources of Supply 138
      FRESHWATER SUPPLIES 138
      COASTAL FISHERIES SUPPLIES 139
      MAJOR FISHING GROUNDS SUPPLIES 141
   Supplies of Certain Species 143
   National Situations 145
   Outlook for Supply 150
   The Source of Conflict 151

CHAPTER 9
THE ROLE OF INTERNATIONAL LAW 153
 The Freedom of the Seas 154
 Territorial Seas 156
 Treaties before 1945 158
 Developments since 1945 160
 The Geneva Conventions on the Law of the Sea 167

CHAPTER 10
COMPETING DOCTRINES OF INTERNATIONAL LAW OF
THE SEA 175
 The Freedom of the Seas 177
 The Special Position of the Coastal State 182
 The Abstention Principle 187
 Historic Rights 188
 Conservation 188
 Conclusion 189

CHAPTER 11
FISHERY TREATIES AND COMMISSIONS 192
 Fishing Rights Treaties 193
 Research and Management ("Conservation") Treaties 194
  RESEARCH TREATIES 195
  STOCK REGULATORY TREATIES 196
  REGIONAL REGULATORY TREATIES 200
 Observations 203
  THE AUTONOMY OF TREATY COMMISSIONS 204
  THE ORGANIZATION OF RESEARCH 205
  OBJECTIVES OF TREATY COMMISSIONS 208
  NATIONAL QUOTAS AND THE LIMITATION OF ENTRY 209
 Some Problems for Research 211
 Conclusions 213

CHAPTER 12
OBJECTIVES FOR FISHERIES MANAGEMENT 215
 Maximize the Product of the Oceans 217
 Maximize the Rent of the Sea 221
 Reaching Agreement on the Maximization of Rent 225

CHAPTER 13
ALTERNATIVE ARRANGEMENTS FOR THE FUTURE . . . 231
 The Adequacy of Knowledge 232
 The Need for New Arrangements 233
 Management by Regions or Stocks 235
 The Quest for International Economic Efficiency 236

AFTERWORD
SUGGESTIONS FOR RESEARCH 243

BIBLIOGRAPHY 253

APPENDIX A—FAO Classification of Fish 262

APPENDIX B—Classification of Unit Fisheries 267

INDEX 272

LIST OF TABLES

1. Per capita consumption of fish and fish products 19
2. Estimated total consumption of fish, 1957–59 20
3. Changes in per capita consumption of fish, prewar to current period 21
4. Freshwater fish as per cent of total fish catch, 1962 23
5. Catch and projected demand for fish 37
6. Demand for all food fish, 1957–59, and projections for 1969–71 . . 41
7. Peruvian catch of anchoveta, 1955–63 42
8. Growth in Peruvian capacity for production of fish meal 45
9. Projection of demand for food fish, edible weight 47
10. U.S. catch by gear, 1959 92
11. Fish catch by nine countries, 1955–59 and 1963 105
12. Importance of fishery industry in national economies 115
13. Value of national trade as percentage of world trade in fish products, eight countries, 1959 116
14. Foreign trade (exports or imports) in fishery products, selected countries, 1948, 1953, and 1959 116
15. Revenue-expense relationships per boat as fishing effort changes . 128
16. Number of fishermen, four countries, 1938, 1948, and 1958 . . . 131
17. Salient characteristics of the three groups of fishery operations in Japan 134
18. Ratification, as of September 24, 1964, of four conventions passed at the 1958 UN Conference on the Law of the Sea 169

LIST OF FIGURES

Figure 1. Total revenues, costs, and sustainable yields with respect to effort 8

Figure 2. Marginal and average costs and revenues with respect to effort 10

Figure 3. Effect of increased prices on yield and revenue curves . . . 12

Figure 4. Effect of technological innovation on yield and revenue curves 13

Figure 5. Coefficients of income elasticity of demand for fish and animal protein, in terms of quantities 35

Figure 6. Percentage increase in total demand for food fish, low and high estimates for 1969–71 36

Figure 7. Estimated demand for fish, world catch for food use, for reduction, and total, 1938–62, and projections for 1969–71 38

Figure 8. Percentage distribution of total world demand for food fish, 1957–59, and high projection for 1969–71 40

Figure 9. Surface currents of the oceans during northern winter . . 58

Figure 10. The continental shelves of the world 62

Figure 11. Estimation of standing crop of zooplankton biomass in upper 300 meters 63

Figure 12. Food relations in marine ecosystem 64

Figure 13. Effect of changing density, technology, and demand on output levels 82

Figure 14. Total world catch of fish, 1938, 1948–63 106

Figure 15. Annual catch of fish by the United States, Norway, United Kingdom, and Canada, 1938, 1948–63 106

Figure 16. Annual catch of fish by Japan, U.S.S.R., India, Mainland China, and Peru, 1938–63 107

Figure 17. Relative change in volume of catch from 1950 to 1963 (1950 = 100) 108

Figure 18. Change in pattern of catch by groups of species; quantities as percentage of total, 1938, 1948, and 1962 109

Figure 19. Change in pattern of catch by groups of species; quantities as percentage of total, Peru, Japan, India, Canada, and United States, 1938, 1948, and 1962 110

Figure 20. Change in pattern of catch by groups of species; quantities as percentage of total, Norway, United Kingdom, U.S.S.R., 1938, 1948, and 1962 111

Figure 21. Catch of whales, world total and Antarctic pelagic, 1937/38, 1947/48 to 1962/63 113

Figure 22. Catch of whales by Norway, United Kingdom, South Africa, Japan, and the U.S.S.R. as percentage of world total, 1937/38, 1947/48, and 1961/62 113

Figure 23. Japanese overseas joint fishing ventures as of late 1963 . . 120

Figure A1. Division of oceans for classification of unit fisheries . . . 266

The Common Wealth in Ocean Fisheries
Some Problems of Growth and Economic Allocation

Chapter 1

Introduction

IT IS SAID that the last frontier of inner space lies in the oceans of the world, and that man, by thrusting back this frontier, may gain almost limitless resources to feed future generations. Many efforts in many nations are being made to add to our sparse information on the sea and its materials. Even though much still remains unknown, the accumulation of scientific knowledge is well under way and is gathering momentum. But the social scientists have, until recently, given only scant attention to the difficult and intriguing problems that accompany the exploitation and development of the sea's resources. The frontier of the economists and political scientists virtually ends at the margins of the continents.

Aside from a handful of economists, the social scientists have been only vaguely aware that the fishery industries are a source of conflict, physical waste, and economic inefficiency. Though they have looked askance at the claims that oceans are a vast storehouse of resources waiting to be withdrawn, with few exceptions, they have not attempted to analyze the opportunities or the limitations for the development of these resources that are the common property of the world community.

This study is an initial attempt to explore some of the economic and political difficulties that impede the rational development of international fisheries. It is a background study, concentrating, first, on the economic characteristics of the fishery industries and then on the legal and institutional framework within which the industries operate.

Chapter 2 is a theoretical discussion of the fishery as a common property natural resource. This concept is fundamental to an understanding of one of the major reasons for economic inefficiency in the industry. Common property natural resources are those resources that can be used by more than one user at the same time. No single user can control the output of other users, nor prevent the entry of new users. Under these conditions, the industry tends to attract too many producers or to stimulate an overly rapid rate of production.

In Chapters 3 to 8 the discussion focuses on the characteristics of supply and demand for fish, in order to arrive at some feeling for the relative importance of the industry and to anticipate the location and severity of problems that may emerge in the near future. The worldwide demand for fish is growing very rapidly. In 1962, about 33 million metric tons, live weight, of fish were caught for food use. By 1970, the demand may be between 40 and 45 million tons. In addition to fish caught for direct use as food, a large quantity of fish is caught for reduction purposes, most of it for feed for farm animals. This use of fish has been growing at extremely rapid rates in recent years. In 1958, the catch of fish for reduction was about 4.3 million metric tons, live weight. In only four years, this amount had almost tripled, reaching a total of 11.9 million tons. In view of this extraordinary increase, any attempt to estimate future growth is very difficult, and figures must be used with caution. It may be that by the year 1970 the demand for fish for reduction purposes will be between 17 and 27 million tons. This would mean that total world demand for fish for all purposes may be between 57 and 72 million tons in 1970.

The growth in demand will not be uniform, either as to nation or as to the kind of fish. In most of the developed countries of the West, the *per capita* consumption of food fish has been relatively stable or slightly declining, because increased incomes in these countries are often accompanied by greater consumption of some of the more expensive meats, and a shift away from fish. But the population increases that have occurred and that may be expected in these nations are sufficient to overcome this effect, so that total demand will still increase. In 1970, therefore, the demand for food fish in Western Europe and North America may be 20 to 30 per cent higher than it was in 1957–59.

In the Soviet Union and Eastern Europe the growth in consumption may be considerably greater. The U.S.S.R. is making a deliberate and concerted effort to increase its domestic consumption of fish. By 1970, the quantity sought by Russia and Eastern Europe is likely to be 60 to 90 per cent above that of 1957–59. Similar growth rates may also occur in Japan, whose fishing fleets are now in all the major seas of the world. It is to be expected that these two nations will become even more dominating influences in international fisheries than they are now.

In reality, the demand is not for fish as such but for specific items, which may be as different as fresh shrimp is from salt cod. The consumer discriminates between species of fish and between kinds of processing. Thus the fact that there may be billions of tons of fish organisms in the ocean is not relevant to the fishing industry which seeks to maximize the net economic returns from its sales to the housewife. The fishermen of the world must still compete for the relatively few species for which there is a known market and clear demand.

This raises questions as to the characteristics of supply. A review of the nature of the resource points out that the desired fish are not uniformly distributed throughout the oceans. Differences in fertility are as great in the sea as they are on land, ranging from virtual deserts in mid-ocean to the fantastic abundance off the Peruvian coast. In general, the coastal waters and continental shelves yield the greatest quantities of fish that are currently in demand, but even among these areas there are wide differences. Thus fishermen tend to concentrate in areas of known productivity such as the North Sea and the Grand Banks, off the coast of Newfoundland. The Grand Banks, for example, attract fishermen from more than a dozen nations, including those from Japan who travel some 10,000 miles.

There are not only differences in the fertility of ocean regions, but there are also wide differences among fish species in their vulnerability. For some species, and in some areas, the concentration of sustained fishing effort over a number of decades has led to depletion of the fish stock. Indeed, where demand increases and where there are no controls on fishing, some depletion of the resource over the long run is inevitable. Salmon in both the Atlantic and the Pacific, the blue whales of the Antarctic, the North Sea herring, Pacific sardines, and many other species of fish are becoming less plentiful.

Such problems are likely to become more severe in the future, as world demand increases and as the technology of location, capture, and distribution improves. In order to gauge the severity of these problems, it becomes important to know the kinds and amounts of investments that nations are making in their fishery industries, not only with respect to capital and labor but also with respect to training and research. Unfortunately, in spite of the major efforts by the Food and Agriculture Organization of the United Nations, statistics on investment are still inadequate. Nevertheless, some of the major differences in amounts and kinds of operations can be described, such as the development of large fleet-type operations by the Russians and the use of extensive foreign bases by the Japanese. These developments, together with the general improvements in technology, are placing greater strains on the resources than have existed heretofore. They are also accompanied by problems of congestion and by increasing conflict.[1]

The conflicts are the result, not only of increased competition for scarce resources but also of the extension of effort by foreign fishermen into areas that have historically been fished only by the vessels of the adjacent state. In order to understand the problems of resolution of conflict, it becomes necessary to understand the legal framework within which resolution can take place. This is the subject of Chapters 9 to 13, which deal with the principles of the law of the sea, the kinds of international agreements that are in effect, and criteria for economic efficiency.

Perhaps the most immediate area of conflict lies in the definition of the extent of exclusive fishing rights. Some nations claim three miles; others claim six, ten, twelve, or even 200 miles. Generally, the pressures are for the wider extension of exclusive fishing zones. Some nations are in an ambivalent position, however, be-

---

[1] Some typical headlines are: "Spanish Warships off N. Africa," *Washington Post,* Sept. 9, 1962; "Boat is Seized on Sea of Galilee," *Washington Post,* Feb. 11, 1963; "U.S. Bids Ecuador Free Tuna Boats," *New York Times,* May 30, 1963; "42 Japanese and 5 Boats Released by South Korea," *New York Times,* June 20, 1963; "2 Soviet Vessels are Driven Off," and "3 French Ships Will Face Greedy Soviet Fish Fleet," *Washington Post,* Nov. 24, 1962; "Alaska Halts Japanese Fishing; Seizes Boat and Holds 2 Men," *New York Times,* April 16, 1962; "Alaskans Charge Russians Foul Up Fishing Gear," *Washington Post,* Sept. 8, 1963; "The World 'Fish Fight' Gets Hotter," *Milwaukee Journal,* Aug. 25, 1963; "Japan, Korea Break Off Fish Parley," *Washington Post,* April 5, 1964; "Rio Lobster War Alerts Two Navies," *Washington Post,* Feb. 8, 1963.

cause they wish to protect their coastal fisheries from foreigners, and at the same time protect the rights of their fishermen in waters adjacent to other nations.

This desire to extend national limits is understandable among coastal fishermen who suddenly find themselves in competition with many fishermen of other nations. When, as is frequently the case, the efforts of the foreigners are well organized and unified in fleet-type operations, the local fishermen not only resent this "invasion" but also become apprehensive about the capacity of the resource to bear the efficient catching techniques of the foreigners. In other waters, where coastal fisheries have been shared for many years and "invasion" is not an element, the growing demand for fishery products together with indications of faltering supplies gives the coastal fishermen strong economic incentive to put pressure on their government to evict the foreign fishermen.

Even on the high seas where it is clear that all nations have equal legal rights, problems arise because of congestion of vessels or because of conflicting methods of catching. There are arguments not only over the size of mesh that should be used but also over the effects of discarded nets on trawling activities; over tangling of different kinds of gear; and over other differences in operations and kinds and sizes of fish being sought. An additional source of conflict lies in the differences of opinion as to rights of a nation to the "sedentary" fishes of the continental shelves far outside any recognized exclusive fishing zones.

The resolution of such conflicts over fishery resources is difficult. The international law of the sea is slow to adjust to the changing balance of international maritime power, to the new maritime technologies, and to the recent increase in competition for scarce resources. It is suggested that economic objectives should play a stronger role in the decisions on international arrangements than they have in the past. One possible arrangement, discussed in the final chapter, is an international fishery authority that would be able to make use of the lowest cost labor and vessels and sell its product to the highest bidder. But for any improvement to occur in the management and exploitation of international fisheries, there must be more information. The need for social science research—apparent throughout this study—is discussed in an Afterword. It is hoped that this study will attract increased attention by economists and political scientists to the critical problems of these internationally shared resources.

Chapter 2

The Characteristics of Common Property Natural Resources

🐟. 🐟. 🐟. 🐟. 🐟. 🐟. 🐟. 🐟. 🐟. 🐟. 🐟 🐟. 🐟. 🐟. 🐟. 🐟. 🐟. 🐟. 🐟. 🐟. 🐟.

A BASIC characteristic of all fisheries is that they are common property natural resources. Like other such resources—the air we breathe; outer space and the upper atmosphere; wildlife and game; oil pools in the United States; outdoor recreational resources; flowing streams and large bodies of water; and many more—they can be used simultaneously by more than one individual or economic unit. No single user has exclusive use rights to the resource nor can he prevent others from sharing in its exploitation. An increase in the number of users affects each user's enjoyment of the resource.

One of the major reasons why these resources are classified as *common* property is that the costs of appropriating and defending exclusive use rights are felt to be higher than the added returns that such appropriation might bring. The costs are high mainly because most of these resources extend indivisibly over very large areas, due to their mobility or fluidity. It is difficult, for example, to maintain wildlife within small boundaries. Some fish species, such as bluefin tuna, range over the entire Pacific, from Mexico to Japan. And the salmon that spawn in the streams of Northwest America are found as far west as the middle of the Pacific Ocean. Migratory birds freely cross continents. Oil fields also extend over very great distances, as do flowing streams.

And, in addition to the private costs, there are social costs as re-vealed by customs and laws that prevent the acquisition of exclusive rights to the resources. It has been a firmly based American tradition, for example, that all citizens should have an equal right to hunt game or go fishing. A modern derivation of this tradition is that every citizen should be able to enjoy the scenic wonders of our country, or participate in outdoor recreation.

For other resources, common property is perpetuated less by the high costs of appropriation and defense than by the low, extra returns anticipated. This occurs for resources that are apparently bottomless, or of such vast abundance that use by one individual does not diminish use by others. In such cases, there is, so far, little advantage in owning a portion of the resource or restricting the freedom of use. Three hundred years ago the apparent abundance of ocean resources was a partial reason for the establishment of the doctrine of the "freedom of the seas."

One of the unique characteristics of a common property natural resource, such as a fishery, is that the amount of effort applied is not subject to the restraints that govern the exploitation of a solely owned resource. The individual user of a common property resource is usually in physical competition with all others in his attempt to get a large share of the product for himself. It is unreasonable to expect an individual producer to willingly and one-sidedly restrain his effort; anything that he leaves will be taken by other producers. Furthermore, in the fishery there is no limit on the number that can participate so that as long as there is any profit to be gained, additional producers will enter the industry until all true profit (or rent) is dissipated. With such conditions, with demand increasing, and without controls, it is inevitable that the fishery will not only become depleted but also that the exploitation of the fishery will become economically inefficient in its use of labor and capital.

In an unexploited fishery, natural mortality tends to balance additions to the population so that the population remains fairly stable over the long run, although short-term natural fluctuations do occur and sometimes can be very severe.

Fishermen are simply another kind of predator. To a certain extent, they replace natural mortality by taking fish that otherwise would have died from "natural" causes. But beyond this level, fishing will reduce the population and, usually, the amount of recruitment.[1] Levels of catch can be sustained indefinitely if the

[1] This is an oversimplification since catch may, by thinning the population

catch, together with natural mortality, is balanced by the recruitment. The yield that can be sustained depends upon the level of population and so upon the amount of fishing effort that is applied. With low levels of effort, the catch will be low, while the population, recruitment, and natural mortality each will be high. For higher levels of effort, there will be higher sustainable yields and lower populations until a population is reached at which the sustainable yield is at a maximum. For levels of effort that are

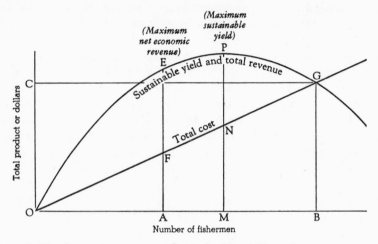

Figure 1. Total revenues, costs, and sustainable yields with respect to effort.

greater than this, the sustainable yields will be lower because of lower population levels and lower amounts of recruitment.[2] Sustainable yield as a function of effort is shown by the curve in Figure 1.

The general pattern of exploitation of a new fishery, however, does not follow the path of sustainable yield. As the fishery develops and the market for the product expands, more effort is attracted

---

and reducing the competition for food, permit the remaining individuals to grow faster and reproduce more successfully.

[2] According to the eumetric yield theory, the maximum sustainable output of certain species, in terms of weight, not numbers of fish, will be reached only at an infinity of effort. This requires that the age (and weight) at which the fish are harvested be adjusted (by changes in size of mesh) with respect to the amount of effort applied. See page 85.

into the industry. Eventually, it is likely that the catch, together with the natural mortality, will be greater than recruitment so that the stock will begin to decrease. But as the stock decreases, the task of catching the remaining fish becomes more difficult. Cost per unit of product will begin to rise; some producers will leave the industry, effort will be somewhat reduced, and the stock may begin to replenish itself. The resultant lower costs of catching may attract more fishermen and more effort, which will again reduce the stock. Eventually, the fishery may arrive at an equilibrium of population and effort, which is likely to be marked by a relatively large amount of effort, a low population, and a low sustainable yield. This will be at some point along the sustainable yield curve.

After a stock is reduced in size, the difficulty of finding the remaining fish serves as a safeguard preventing the extinction of the species. But it should be pointed out that this safeguard is by no means guaranteed. If demand for the product rises, and the consumer is willing to pay higher prices, the fisherman will have an incentive to increase his effort, and there will be additional pressure upon the stock. It is also possible that more efficient catching devices will be developed, thereby lowering the cost of catching the fish. This will also attract additional effort and serve to reduce the population even further.

It is unlikely, however, that the process will be carried to the point of resource extinction. Rather, the generally growing demand and improving technology will work to deplete the resource and reduce the yield well below the maximum level that could be sustained indefinitely. When "depletion" in this sense becomes severe, the fishermen, or the nations from which they come, usually accept forms of control designed to prevent further depletion or to rehabilitate the stock to the point where it produces a higher sustainable yield.

The tendency of a common property resource, such as a fishery, to become "depleted" is therefore a consequence of the absence of any economic restraint on effort. There is also a severe economic consequence. This is that there will tend to be an excessive amount of capital and labor applied to the fishery. The fishermen are operating as individuals, each seeking to maximize the difference between his revenues and his costs. But because there are no restrictions on the number of fishermen that can enter the industry, *any* true profit will attract additional fishermen. This will mean that the total revenues will be shared by more and more producers until no true profit at all remains to be distributed. For the entire fishery, the fleet's revenues will just equal costs, so that the revenues and costs of the average fisherman will also be equal.

In Figure 1, total costs and total revenues are shown with respect to the number of fishermen engaged in the fishery.[3] Certain simplifying assumptions have been made. It is assumed that there are no fixed costs for the whole fishery and that fishermen experi-

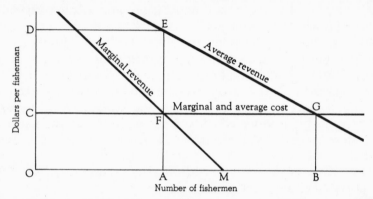

Figure 2. Marginal and average costs and revenues with respect to effort.

ence identical operating costs. The total cost curve, therefore, is shown as a straight line. (This would not, of course, be true where congestion becomes significant because large numbers of fishermen operating in a small area would create additional costs for each other.) Prices of fish are assumed to be constant, so the sustainable yield curve also represents the reaction of total revenues as effort is increased.

In Figure 2, the same variables are shown but in terms of revenues and costs *per* fisherman rather than for all fishermen together. *OC*, for example, represents the amount of operating costs incurred by the average and marginal fisherman, and is the same no matter how many fishermen are engaged. But as the number of fishermen increases, both the average and marginal revenues per fisherman decline. Thus, where there are *OA* fishermen engaged, each receives an average revenue of *OD*, and where there are *OB*

[3] Each fisherman is assumed, for the moment, to be operating throughout the season, and the number of fishermen engaged, therefore, represents total effort.

fishermen engaged, the average revenue declines to OC. With OA fishermen, the *additional* revenue to the industry would equal the costs that each fisherman bears. This is the point where marginal costs and marginal revenues are equal and where the industry will produce the greatest net revenue, profit, or rent. In Figure 1, at this point, the total costs are equal to AF, total revenues are AE, and net revenues (EF) are at the maximum (the slopes of the revenue and cost curves are equal). In Figure 2, the difference between average costs and average revenues (EF) constitutes the average net revenue per fisherman which, when multiplied by the number of fishermen engaged (OA), produces the maximum net revenue to the industry as represented by the rectangle $CFED$.

At this point a sole owner of the fishery resource would stop hiring additional fishermen, because at this point the profit to the owner is maximized. But in the absence of sole ownership, the profit is shared by all the fishermen and, as long as there is some profit to be shared, additional fishermen will be attracted into the fishery. Therefore, in the absence of restrictions on entry, OB fishermen will eventually enter the industry; total costs and total revenues will be equal; and the profit will be dissipated by both rising costs and falling revenues. Not only will the output per unit of input be lower than under conditions of sole ownership, but the exploitation of the fishery will be economically inefficient. The goal of economic efficiency can be approached by preventing excessive entry into the industry, so that those who fish would be producing the maximum net economic revenue (to be shared by them, or appropriated by the public) and so that those who are prevented from participating will be able to produce other goods and services valued by the community.[4]

It is important to point out that the misallocation of labor will still be present even if demand for the product rises or if technological innovation takes place. Increasing prices, with increased demand, will raise the total revenue curve so that it will intersect the cost curve further away from the origin. In Figure 3, prior to the in-

---

[4] Theoretically, at least, it is possible to question whether or not society would be better off by restricting entry. The costs of enforcement; the possibility of raised prices to the consumers, because of oligopoly and a disincentive to innovate; high movement costs; plus lack of outside employment may mean that the other goals and services produced are more than offset by the costs of displacement. See Anthony Scott, "Optimal Utilization and the Control of Fisheries," ed. Ralph Turvey and Jack Wiseman, *The Economics of Fisheries* (Rome: FAO, 1957), pp. 44–45.

creased demand, *OA* fishermen are engaged in producing a total
revenue and incurring total costs of *OF*. With the price increase,
the total revenue curve is raised and the *OA* fishermen receive, at
first, a total revenue of *OH* but at no greater cost than before.
This produces a profit of *FH* to be distributed among the fishermen. The profit will attract additional fishermen into the industry, thus increasing the total cost, until total costs and total
revenues are once again equal. Total revenue to the industry will

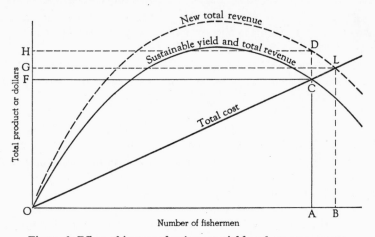

Figure 3. Effect of increased prices on yield and revenue curves.

be higher (by *FG*) but so will total costs and there will again be
no profit. Furthermore, total output (the quantity of fish produced) is likely to be *lower* than it was before the price increase.[5]
If it is assumed that the first revenue curve also represents the
product curve (prices unaffected by output levels and equal to
one), then when there are *OB* fishermen the quantity produced
by them is less than the quantity produced by *OA* fishermen.
Higher prices will attract more fishermen and tend to further deplete the fishery, and, at the same time, will not benefit the fishermen over the long run.

In Figure 4, the consequences of an innovation in the technique
of catching fish are shown. It is assumed that this innovation
changes the yield function with respect to effort, that is, that each
fisherman can take a larger quantity of fish per haul or per day

[5] This depends upon whether or not the slope of the yield curve is increasing
or decreasing when intersected by the revenue curves.

than previously.[6] The resulting redrawing of the yield curve is equivalent, on the same effort scale, to a total revenue curve at unchanged prices, that will rise more steeply, peak sooner, and fall more quickly than before. The initial application of the technological device will improve each fisherman's catch during the early part of the season. But it will, at the same time, serve to reduce the stock of fish more severely. Before long, the average revenues per

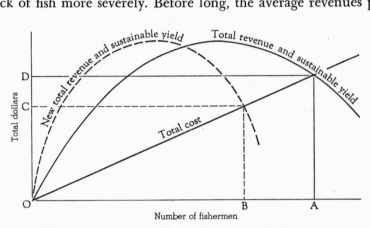

Figure 4. Effect of technological innovation on yield and revenue curves.

fisherman will be reduced, and some fishermen will leave the industry. As a consequence, there will be only *OB* fishermen instead of *OA,* and the total catch and total revenue will be diminished by the amount *DC.* The costs and returns per remaining fisherman will be no different than before, and there will still be no profit produced by the industry. If the technological innovation were to lower the costs incurred by each fisherman for a season of effort (lower fuel consumption, for example), the total revenue would also be likely to decline although the number of fishermen would increase. Average revenues would be lower to match the lower average costs, and there would still be no profit.

To some extent, the description of these changes has been oversimplified. Prices are not unaffected by output levels; there are variations in length of season as well as in number of fishermen; costs are unlikely to be uniform; and equilibrium conditions with sustained yields are not generally achieved. In reality, there may

[6] The fishermen are still assumed to be working a full season. Therefore the horizontal axis properly measures fishermen-seasons. Actually, either the number of fishermen or the length of the time that each works could be varied.

be long periods of high economic returns per unit of input. This is particularly true during the initial stages of exploitation of a new fishery. However, as equilibrium conditions are approached, the excessive application of capital and labor will become more severe and exploitation will be economically inefficient.

Most of the changes that are actually occurring (growth in demand and improvements in technology) are likely, therefore, to have a depleting effect upon the fish stock. As depletion becomes severe, and the fishermen experience declining physical yields, social pressures are built up in the industry to establish some measures of control on use. Usually, the forms of control that are adopted are designed to prevent further depletion or to promote rehabilitation. The physical objective of maximizing the sustainable yield provides the basis for most international fishery agreements (as well as for most intra-national forms of control).

This point of maximum sustainable yield, however, will never correspond to the point of maximum economic efficiency.[7] The greatest net economic return will always be at a point closer to the origin (where less effort is engaged), under the equilibrium conditions that are assumed.[8]

In Figure 1, for example, the maximum sustainable yield is at point *P* on the total product curve. The slope of the curve at this point is horizontal, changing from a positive to a negative slope. At this point the marginal product with respect to effort is zero (as shown by point *M* in Figure 2), which means that the total catch is the same as it was before the last fisherman entered the industry.

Nevertheless, for various reasons, international treaties are almost always formed on the basis of achieving and maintaining maximum physical yields. The methods that are chosen to achieve this objective are varied. The most direct form of control is the imposition of a quota—a limit on the total quantity of fish that may be taken during any one season. When the quota has been caught, no more fishing is permitted until the next season. Under a system of this sort, the Pacific halibut fishery has recovered from an annual output of about 45 million pounds in the early 1930's, to about 65-70 million pounds in recent years.[9] However, the imposition of

[7] Except by the coincidence of unusually shaped curves.

[8] For maximum physical sustainable yield to require equal or less effort than maximum net economic revenue, the additional labor would have to have zero or negative costs, or the revenue curve would have to be kinked.

[9] James Crutchfield and Arnold Zellner, "Economic Aspects of the Pacific Halibut Fishery," *Fishery Industrial Research*, Vol. 1, No. 1 (Washington: U.S. Government Printing Office, 1963), pp. 1–173. Crutchfield and Zellner present

the quota forces each fisherman to engage in intensive fishing activity when the season opens in an attempt to get the greatest share of the quota before the total limit is reached and the season is closed. And since all fishermen will operate on the same basis, the quota will be filled rapidly and the season will end quickly. In the Pacific halibut fishery, between the early 1930's and the mid-1950's, the length of the season dropped from nine months to less than two months in one area, and from seven months to about three weeks in another area. Such drastic shortening of the season has economic impact not only upon the fishermen but also upon the processors and distributors. The fishermen must find other employment for their vessels and for themselves during the long periods when halibut fishing is prohibited. This leads to costly adaptations or to compromises in design of vessels and gear.[10]

Under the short season, the processing and distribution facilities are strained. In the early 1930's, for example, the market received only an average of about 100,000 pounds of halibut per day. In the mid-1950's, however, somewhat higher total output and much shorter seasons led to an average of about 600,000 pounds per day for less than two months. This tended to depress the price received by fishermen and to impose greater costs for freezing and storage. There is also evidence of a decline in quality of the product because of the longer average storage required.

Since the mid-1950's the fishermen have voluntarily agreed to spread their effort over a longer period by remaining in port for a certain length of time between each trip to the grounds. This voluntary layover program has ameliorated some of the difficulties described above and has about doubled the length of the season over what it was in the middle 1950's. But a layover itself is wasteful; there is still an excess of labor and capital applied to the fishery.

Some forms of controls such as the establishment of nursery areas or of size limits on fish, may help the fish stocks to recover and lead to higher quantities of catch. Others, such as gear restrictions, may reduce the catch of the individual fisherman, but, if more fishermen enter, the total catch may still be beyond that of the maximum sustainable yield.[11] None of these controls will improve

---

a thorough analysis of the economic consequences of the quota control system as applied to the Pacific halibut fishery.

[10] It also places additional pressures upon the stocks of the other fisheries to which the halibut fishermen turn.

[11] In the United States the prohibitions against salmon traps in Alaska and power dredging for oysters in Maryland are outstanding examples of controls

the net economic returns to the fishery in the long run, because
none of them prevents the excessive application of effort.[12] If
economic efficiency is to be considered a valid goal for management of fisheries, then it can only be approached by restricting the
number of producers.[13]

---

that impose heavy costs upon the producers. The fishermen required to use
technologically inefficient devices cannot compete effectively with the producers
in other states or with the producers of competitive commodities. These
controls, established to protect the fishermen in the short run, may work to the
destruction of the industry in the long run. See Richard A. Cooley, *Politics
and Conservation, The Decline of the Alaska Salmon* (New York: Harper and
Row, 1963); F. T. Christy, Jr., "The Exploitation of a Common Property
Natural Resource: The Maryland Oyster Industry" (Ph.D. dissertation, University of Michigan, 1964).

[12] Some of them, by increasing the quantity of catch, may lead to a decline
in the price of fish to the public. This may be a minor source of gain to the
public. See Ralph Turvey, "Optimization and Suboptimization in Fishery
Regulation," *American Economic Review*, Vol. 54, No. 2, Part 1 (March 1964),
p. 75.

[13] See Chapter 12 for discussion of the problems underlying the choice
between maximizing physical yields and maximizing economic yields.

Chapter 3

The Demand for Fish

꿿. 꿿. 꿿. 꿿. 꿿. 꿿. 꿿. 꿿. 꿿. 꿿. 꿿 꿿. 꿿. 꿿. 꿿. 꿿. 꿿. 꿿. 꿿. 꿿. 꿿. 꿿.

CURRENTLY, about 75 per cent of the weight of the world catch of fish is used as food. It is a highly nutritious commodity with a large percentage of readily digestible animal proteins. Its fat content, which varies from about 1 to 20 per cent or more of the weight, is made up of a large proportion of polyunsaturated fatty acids. Many of the essential vitamins and minerals are also present. It is quite natural, therefore, to think of fish, that are free for the taking in the marine waters, as an attractive solution to the world problems of malnutrition.

The demand for fish, however, is determined by many factors other than those relating to its potential supply of necessary food elements. As for all food commodities, the demand for fish is the net result of the complex intermixture of such factors as perishability, distribution, marketing, price, competition with other foods, taste, income, etc. Refined economic analysis, which would take all these factors into account, is beyond the scope and time limitations of this study. In order to anticipate future changes, therefore, we have relied primarily upon rough estimates of demand elasticities made by the Food and Agriculture Organization of the United Nations and upon estimates of present patterns of consumption.

Measures of consumption are derived indirectly from estimates of production and foreign trade, and such estimates are beset by difficulties unlike those for any land-based commodities. Production does not occur on specific sites but ranges from inland ponds to the coastal surf to areas many thousands of miles from the home port. Fish may be transferred to vessels of different nations while on the high seas, or they may be landed directly in foreign ports. Some fish are used for bait, and some are consumed by the vessel's crew. Fish that are thrown overboard as trash by one nation's fishermen may be kept for food by another's. They may be returned to port as whole fish, as decapitated and gutted fish, as fillets, as fish meal, or even as frozen and packaged fish products. There are considerable variations in the proportions of fish that are considered edible, as well as in oil and fat content. In international trade, fish may be transferred in any form from whole fresh fish, through cured fish (salted, smoked, marinated), to canned, frozen, or specialty products.

The problem of estimating demand is made even more difficult by the lack of comprehensiveness and uniformity in the reporting of fish production and consumption statistics. In most of the fishing nations, a considerable proportion of the total catch is landed in small local ports. This is particularly true for the coastal fisheries of India and Southeast Asia which supply local, rural populations and provide sustenance for the fishermen. It is difficult to get satisfactory tallies from such small and scattered producing areas. Furthermore, fishermen the world over are notoriously reticent about the location, size, and price of their catch.

Fortunately, for most of the major fishing nations the figures are satisfactory enough to enable us to see some of the changes that are occurring and to anticipate some rough magnitudes of demand. This is only possible because of the considerable efforts of the Food and Agriculture Organization of the United Nations, which compiles statistics from all fishing nations, encourages the adoption of standard measures, and publishes the annual *Yearbook of Fishery Statistics*.

Patterns of Consumption

Countries where per capita consumption of fishery products is high are listed in Table 1. The list includes both high- and low-income countries, industrial nations and raw material producers, and countries in each of the hemispheres. If any generalization can be made, it would be that each of these nations has a relatively long coastline in proportion to its total area, and high population densities in close proximity to the seas—an indication of the effect of supply availability upon consumption.

For the nations that are listed, fish make up anywhere from a tenth to three-quarters of the animal protein intake per person. The typical Portuguese and Norwegian each consumes about the

Table 1. Per Capita Consumption of Fish and Fish Products [a]

Country	FAO, 1957–59 Edible weight	USDA, 1957–58 Landed weight	As per cent of total animal protein 1954/55–1956/57	As per cent of total calories 1958
	(kg./yr.)	(kg./yr.)	(per cent)	(per cent)
Japan	22	40	72	3.0
Portugal	20	35	59	2.4
Norway	19	44	19	2.3
Sweden	18	20	12	1.2
Philippines	15	24	n.a.	1.9
Denmark	15	22	13	1.2
Taiwan	11	22	54	1.5
Finland	11	14	11	0.8
Spain	11	21	n.a.	1.4
United Kingdom	10	19	9	1.0
Thailand	9	28	n.a.	6.2 [b]
Greece	8	14	16	0.9

n.a. Not available.

[a] This table gives per capita estimates for most of the countries with high rates of consumption. Figures are not available for some of the small island countries, such as Iceland, Faroe Islands, Greenland, etc., for which per capita consumption of fish is undoubtedly very high.

[b] This estimate appears to be based upon an error. In all other countries one kilogram of fish per year, landed weight, supplies from 1.5 to 2.0 calories per day. For Thailand, however, one kilogram provides 5 calories per day, according to the implicit relationship.

Sources: Col. (1): *Agricultural Commodities—Projections for 1970* (Rome: Food and Agriculture Organization of the United Nations, 1962), p. A-12. Col. (2) and (4): *Food Balances in Foreign Countries,* Parts I and II, FAS-M-100 and FAS-M-101 (Washington: Foreign Agricultural Service, U.S. Department of Agriculture, 1960). Col. (3): *Food Supply, Time Series* (Rome: FAO, 1960).

same amount of fish, but this food provides about 60 per cent of the former's animal protein consumption and only about 20 per cent of the latter's. In this sense, the Chinese (Taiwan) are far more dependent upon fish than the Norwegians, even though per capita consumption of fish is higher in Norway.

The major fish-consuming nations, in terms of *total* disappearance of fish in 1958, are shown in Table 2. Because of the lack of

Table 2. Estimated Total Consumption of Fish, 1957–59

Country and region	1,000 metric tons, edible weight
Country:	
Japan	2,000
United States	900
United Kingdom	500
Indonesia	500
India	400
Philippines	400
W. Germany	400
Spain	300
France	250
Thailand	200
Italy	200
Portugal	200
Pakistan	200
Region:	
Asia and Far East (excl. Mainland China)	4,200
Western Europe	2,400
Africa	1,200
North America	1,000
Latin America	600
Near East	150
Oceania	50

Source: FAO, *Agricultural Commodities—Projections for 1970,* Rome, 1962; per capita consumption estimates times population.

readily available statistics, this table does not include two countries that would rank close to the top in total consumption: U.S.S.R. and Mainland China, which at that time may have been consuming on the order of 1.2 million and 2 million metric tons of fish, respectively, in terms of edible weight.[1] Total world con-

---

[1] Consumption figures are generally presented in terms of edible weight which is the weight of the fish after gutting and decapitating. Total demand figures, presented later in this chapter, convert edible weight to live weight in order to be consistent with the statistics presented in the rest of the text.

sumption in 1958 may therefore have been about 14 million
metric tons of edible fish products. About half of this was consumed by the people of Asia and the Far East, about 30 per cent
by Europeans, and the balance by the rest of the world.

Looked at another way, Mainland China, Japan, Russia, and the
United States together accounted for about half of the world's
food use of fish. Although each of these four has a high level of
population (accounting for about two-thirds of the world's peo-

Table 3. Changes in Per Capita Consumption of Fish,
Prewar to Current Period [a]

Minus 10 per cent or more	Plus or minus 10 per cent	Plus 10–30 per cent	Plus 30 per cent or more
United Kingdom	United States	France (?)	Japan
Spain	West Germany	Italy (?)	India-Pakistan
France (?)	France (?)	Portugal	Mainland China
	Italy (?)	Thailand	U.S.S.R.
		Indonesia	Philippines

[a] The use of four gross categories is necessitated by the inadequacy of the statistics.
For example, estimates of change for France, as given by three different sources,
show decreases of 26 per cent and 2 per cent and an increase of 28 per cent. Some
of the marked increase in per capita consumption in the low-income Asian countries
may be due to significant underreporting in the prewar period, but this is not
believed to be sufficient to affect the placing of these countries.

Sources: FAO, *Food Supply, Time Series*, Rome, 1960; R. Hamlisch and R. A.
Taylor, "The Demand for Fish as Human Food," Paper No. R/V.1/1 presented to
FAO International Conference on Fish in Nutrition, Sept. 1961; J. Frederic Dewhurst,
et al., Europe's Needs and Resources (New York: Twentieth Century Fund, 1961),
p. 557; changes for Mainland China, U.S.S.R., Indonesia, and Philippines were estimated from production and population figures.

ple), they differ in many other respects, as do the rest of the countries on the list. Such differences begin to show a pattern when we
look at changes in rates of consumption.

The changes in per capita consumption in the fifteen most important fish-consuming nations, as expressed in Table 3, show a
split between the western and eastern nations. There have been
marked increases in consumption rates in Japan, Russia, and the
low-income countries of Asia, but only moderate increases or decreases in the United States and the countries of Western Europe.
When these per capita rates are measured with population
changes, the total effect is even more significant.

Forms of Utilization

The patterns of consumption, described above, refer to fish as if it were a single undifferentiated commodity. But there are wide variations in the product, not only in species consumed but also in the form in which they are consumed. One major difference in use is between the foods and the nonfoods, and, within the former category, fish can be used fresh, frozen, canned, or cured.

FRESH FISH

The major constraint on the marketing of fresh fish is perishability. Even in the temperate zones, icing will maintain fresh quality for no more than ten days to two weeks. The countries where the use of fresh fish is important are generally the ones where supply is readily available to the large population centers. This, in turn, depends upon geographical characteristics such as a long coastline in proportion to area; marketing and distribution facilities; or the presence of an inland fishery culture. Italy and the United Kingdom quite clearly fit the first requirement, and the latter country is aided by a relatively well organized marketing and distribution system that makes fresh fish available in inland metropolitan markets. In the United States, rates of consumption of fresh fish are noticeably higher in cities close to the producing areas.

In the tropics and subtropics, fish must generally be treated if they are not to be eaten the same day they are caught. Thus the consumption of fresh fish in these areas (which are generally coincident with the low-income countries of the world) is even more limited than in the temperate zones. And yet many of these countries have high rates of catch for the fresh market. This indicates a relatively high proportion of inshore daytime fisheries, where fish can be caught and brought to market in the same day, or a high proportion of inland water fisheries. Evidence of the latter is shown in Table 4.

For the world as a whole, the catch for the fresh market increased from 9.8 million metric tons in 1948 to 16 million in 1962, an increase of 60 per cent. However, since total catch has almost doubled over this period, the relative importance of fresh market fish has decreased from 51 per cent of the total to 36 per cent.

FROZEN FISH

The development of freezing techniques has had considerable influence on consumption in the industrialized countries and almost none in the rest of the world. Freezing techniques overcome the problem of perishability and yet permit the product to compete directly with fresh fish. In several countries, it is difficult to estimate the differences in demand, primarily because frozen fish is frequently thawed and sold or served as "fresh fish." This direct competition usually occurs where the frozen products are sold as

Table 4. Freshwater Fish as Per Cent
of Total Fish Catch, 1962

Country	Per cent
Mainland China (1959)	40
Indonesia	43
Pakistan	66
India	34
Thailand	20
Philippines	3
Japan	1
U.S.S.R.	10
United States	2
West Germany	2
Italy	6

whole fish (usually beheaded and gutted) or as fish fillets. Freezing, however, has also been accompanied by the production of a more highly processed commodity which is generally designed to facilitate home preparation. This processing, together with the fact that freezing widens both geographic and seasonal distribution, has led to dramatic increases in the consumption of certain products in the United States. The production of frozen breaded shrimp, for example, rose from 17 million pounds in 1952 to about 70 million pounds in 1959. Fish portions such as fish cakes and fish bits rose from 22 million pounds in 1958 to 60 million pounds three years later.

The freezing of fish carries with it significant implications for supply. These will be discussed in more detail later, but two effects might be mentioned at this time. First, freezing has permitted the marketing of new species. For example, ocean perch (redfish, rosefish) were generally discarded as trash fish before 1933 in the United States. In that year, however, it was found that they could be easily filleted and frozen, and that the product was readily marketable in the Midwest. In response to this, U.S. production rose from about 200,000 pounds in the early 1930's to more than 200 million pounds in recent years. The second effect of freezing has been the development of distant-water fisheries that depend upon freezing vessels that are capable of immediate preservation of the catch or that make use of freezing facilities in foreign ports. Thus the limitation of perishability has become less important. As a result, Russian factory ships can, and do, operate successfully off the New England coast and California tuna vessels off the coast of Ecuador.

For the world as a whole, the catch of fish for freezing rose from 1 million to 4.2 million metric tons, live weight, between 1948 and 1962. This represents an increase of over 300 per cent and a shift in relative importance from 5 per cent to 9 per cent of total world catch.

CANNING

The consumption of canned fishery products is also primarily a characteristic of high-income countries. By far the major amount of production is restricted to four kinds of fish—salmon, tuna, herring, and sardines. The major exceptions to this are the miscellaneous species of low unit value that are packed for animal food in the United States and the growing production of canned molluscs in Japan.

The United States is the chief consumer of canned salmon and tuna. These have a relatively high unit value and compete directly with meat and poultry. They are highly palatable, convenient to use, and storable over long periods. Largely because of changes in the supply situation, there has been a marked shift from canned salmon to canned tuna in the United States. Since the early 1930's the per capita consumption of the former has dropped by more than 50 per cent, while that of the latter has increased about five-fold.

The consumption of canned herring and sardines is more widely distributed throughout the countries of North America and Western Europe, but is still negligible in the low-income countries of Asia and the Far East.

The catch of fish for canning in all countries increased from 7 per cent of total utilization in 1948 to 9 per cent in 1962.

CURING

The oldest and the least expensive form of preserving fish is curing, which includes salting, drying, smoking, pickling, and fermenting. The choice of method is primarily dependent upon climate and the availability of preservative materials; these factors, in turn, have tended to induce enduring patterns of consumption.

Production of salt fish is generally restricted to the countries of Northern Europe, North America, U.S.S.R., and Japan, which have favorable climatic conditions and a relative abundance of salt. Cod and herring are by far the most important species in this category. In Southeast Asia, a highly nutritious fermented sauce prepared from fish and practically saturated in salt has been a commodity of considerable importance for a long time. In most of Asia and the Far East, as well as in Africa, preservation is accomplished primarily by either smoking or drying and covers a wide variety of fresh and marine species.

Curing of fish has remained important to low-income countries, but it has declined considerably relative to the other forms of utilization in North America and Western Europe. For the world as a whole, curing dropped from 24 per cent of total utilization in 1948 to 17 per cent in 1962.

REDUCTION TO OIL AND MEAL

The most significant increase in the utilization of fish has occurred in production of fish meal and oil and fertilizers and other industrial materials. The quantity of fish caught primarily for reduction increased from 1.5 million metric tons, live weight, in 1948, to 11.9 million tons in 1962—an increase of almost 700 per cent. In the latter year, this catch accounted for about 27 per cent of total world take. Since these figures represent only the fish caught directly for reduction and not the by-products of other processes that are included in the production of oil, meal, etc., they underrepresent the relative importance in terms of consumption.

Fish meal is a protein concentrate that is taken from raw fish by the process of cooking, pressing, and drying, and is used principally as an additive for poultry and hog feeds. If ways are found to remove the unpleasant fish odors and tastes, which now make fish meal unattractive as a food additive and limit its use for feed, demand should increase significantly.

Other products of reduction are stickwater and fish oils. Stick-water is evaporated and reduced to a fish soluble; like fish meal it is used as a protein additive for animal feed. Fish body oil repre-sents the fatty portion of raw fish and is used for margarine, paints, floor coverings, soap, etc. Fish liver oil has long been valued be-cause of its high vitamin A and D content. Whale oil, of historical importance for illumination, is now used for candles, soap, and lard substitutes.

Most of the world's production of fish meal and oil is consumed by the United States, Western Germany, the United Kingdom, and Japan. Other Northern European countries, Canada, and Russia take almost all the rest.

These materials are derived mainly from a few species of oily fish. Within the United States, menhaden provides about three-quarters of total fish meal production and 85 per cent of fish oil. Peru, the world's largest producer, depends upon anchovetas, and Japan, upon the saury and whale.

SUMMARY

Certain significant patterns of consumption of fish and fish products emerge from the discussion above. There is, first, a no-ticeable—and not unexpected—tendency for the industrial coun-tries of the West to consume highly processed products. Fresh fish is giving way to frozen. The consumption of cured fish has been falling, while consumption of canned fish has been increasing. Per capita consumption of all fish for food has remained relatively stable, but the use of fish for reduction to meal and oil for hog and poultry feed has grown rapidly. These shifts are readily apparent in the United States and the countries of Northern Europe. They are less evident but still valid for Scandinavia and Southern Europe. Although there are no satisfactory measures for the Soviet Union and Eastern Europe, the rapid increase in production and use of factory ships indicates that the same general trends hold true, with the exception that per capita consumption of all fish is probably increasing.

It is generally misleading to talk about the demand for fish as a whole. There is actually a very wide and significant variation in the types of fish products consumed and demanded. This is true not only for species of fish but also for forms of utilization. The differences in patterns of demand between countries are also ex-tremely varied.

For food purposes, it is apparent that the West values a relatively small number of species—shrimp, tuna, salmon, cod, haddock, halibut, ocean perch, and a few others. This is mostly due to
the fact that the waters of the North Atlantic and North Pacific do
not contain the extremely wide variety of species found in more
southern waters, and to the general tendency to seek out the
known and accepted kinds of fish. Taste preferences for certain
kinds of fish have been relatively strong and difficult to change. Increased availability, with a lowering of price may, over time,
induce change. Market promotion may also have some effect, but
this is very difficult to measure. More significant, however, at least
for the United States, may be the high degree of processing and
the development of breaded fish products which tend to obscure
flavor and consistency differences and permit greater substitution
among species.

Fish consumption in Japan is more closely patterned after that
of Asia and the Far East than after the industrialized countries of
the West. The growing amounts of fish caught for freezing and
canning are primarily for the export market, and domestic consumption is still chiefly restricted to fresh and cured fish, as it is
for India, Indonesia, the Philippines, and other Far Eastern nations. The per capita food use of fish products is generally increasing rapidly throughout this area, and fish is becoming a more significant item in the diet. It is also generally true that a much wider
variety of species are demanded than in the West, where certain
kinds of fish are considered as "trash fish" and are returned to the
water or avoided completely.

As will be seen later, the possibility of international management agreements is complicated by these different patterns of
consumption. Even now, if two or more nations fishing the same
stock demand different sizes of fish, agreement on the size of mesh
is difficult. Difficulties are also apparent when one nation places a
high value on one species that is a predator or competitor of another species which is preferred by a different nation. In such a
case, how is a decision reached that leads to the conservation of one
species at the expense of another species? It may be that such problems are less intractable than they now appear, but this can only
be determined after careful economic analyses of the structure of
demand.

Factors Affecting Demand

It is frequently pointed out that there is a severe protein deficiency facing most of the low-income and highly-populated countries of the world. It is also assumed that the annual production of fish could be increased many times. The popular and attractive conclusion is that fish production should be stimulated in order to provide the needed protein. While this is a worthwhile goal, the fact remains that consumption of fish depends upon demand, and therefore, upon taste preferences, marketing distribution facilities, prices, competition with other foods, and income levels. Estimating the feed requirements for meat animals is a relatively simple matter of balancing feed content with cost. In feeding himself, however, man adopts a much more complex approach. His demand is generally not for protein, as such, but for milk, meat, fish, poultry, etc.; and it may not be for fish, as such, but for salt fish, dried fish, fresh fish, etc., or for lobster, cod, salmon. Furthermore, his demand is not determined primarily by the fact that fish may provide the necessary food elements, but by tastes, prices, and income.

Nevertheless, the facts of malnutrition and of the presence of significant quantities of animal protein in the seas justify studies of methods for reconciling taste and hunger. Although there has been much basic research directed toward increasing the supply of fish, relatively little thought has thus far been given to the economic aspects of demand, and to the amount that people are willing to consume at various prices, or the amount that people are willing to pay for various quantities. The schedule of demand reflects a whole host of separate and related factors, which are discussed in the following pages.

PERISHABILITY AND PRESERVATION

Taste preferences, as reflected by price and income elasticities of demand, have been conditioned by the availability, and regularity and form of fish supplies over a very long period. And these, in turn, have been considerably affected by the factor of fish perishability. Fish tend to deteriorate immediately after being caught. One of the earliest changes that takes place is autolysis, during which certain enzymes digest the tissues causing a softening or partial liquefaction of the tissues and a change in flavor and odor. In red meats, this process is called ripening and is desirable in that it produces a tender juicy meat of good flavor. In fish, however, the results are highly disagreeable to the human palate. The speed of deterioration depends primarily upon temperature, but also varies for different kinds of fish and different methods of handling. This time limit has had a significant effect upon the seasonal and geographical distribution of the product and upon the form of utilization. Techniques of preservation have been developed and maintained for many hundreds of years, so that the consumer has come to depend upon, and to demand, the products with which he is familiar and which he knows by experience to be satisfactory. Changes in the availability of supply (through improved and less expensive processing or marketing techniques) can lead to a greater satisfaction of the well-established taste preferences, so that per capita consumption of these products will rise.

However, consumer habits, even though well established, can change over the long run. Shifts in taste preferences and demand occur when a new condition of supply availability persists over a long period or when the consumer becomes acquainted with a new product. The latter factor depends upon advertising or market promotion and has its greatest effect in the high-income countries. The rapid acceptance of frozen breaded fish sticks and portions in the United States is an example. Wide publicity about the occasional association of disease with shellfish is an illustration of a negative force on demand.

Processing techniques, therefore, can have two separate effects on demand. First, they can lead to increased satisfaction of present demands by providing the same or similar products at reduced prices, and, second, they can induce changes in demand by providing new products that come to be accepted by the consumer. These effects cannot always be easily separated, and the same technique may have different impacts upon different patterns of consumption. Of the significant technological innovations on the horizon, two (freeze-drying and irradiation) will lead to products similar to those consumed in high-income countries and one (reduction to a high-protein concentrate) will lead to a product that is strikingly different.

Frozen fish, which have already been well accepted in high-income countries in the West, generally compete with fresh fish and, in some areas, are preferred because of the greater assurance of quality. While freezing preserves fish for long periods and per-

30   The Common Wealth in Ocean Fisheries

mits wider distribution, its cost keeps the price of the product relatively high and thus inhibits greater consumption in the low-
income countries of Asia and the Far East. Furthermore, it
requires a "cold chain" from processing plant to market which is
unlikely to be established solely for the distribution of fish
products. Cost-reducing refinements in the technique may be expected, but it is unlikely that they will be significant enough to
affect consumption rates materially in low-income countries.

Freeze-drying and irradiation represent two new processes for
overcoming perishability and producing a commodity that may
compete widely with fresh fish. In the former method, the water is
almost completely removed, so that the product loses about five-
sixths of its original weight. When wrapped tightly or canned to
keep out the air, the product can be stored for years at normal
temperatures. When immersed in water, it is quickly restored to
its original form and compares well with fresh fish. The reduced
weight of the product and the fact that it does not require cold
storage means that transportation and marketing are greatly facilitated. At present, however, such savings do not appear to be sufficient to overcome the high costs of the processing, although at
least one commercial plant is now producing freeze-dried shrimp in
the United States. Irradiation of food, which is still highly experi-
mental, reduces the bacterial population of micro-organisms by
90–99 per cent without damage to flavor or texture and thus preserves the product for extended periods.

A quite separate technique of preservation which may have a
greater impact upon low-income countries than freezing or irradiation is the reduction of fish to a material with a high concentration of protein. This is sometimes referred to as "fish flour," although more properly as fish protein concentrate or FPC.
Although the possibilities of producing such a concentrate for human consumption have been studied by many countries for 20–25
years, it is only during the past 10 years or so that intensive in-
vestigations have been under way. The major motivation for these
studies lies in the growing alarm over rapidly increasing population
and over continued protein deficiencies, in combination with the
feeling that ocean fisheries are being "underutilized."

The basic aim is to produce, from either whole fish or fish
wastes, a commodity that is bland; has a high concentration of animal protein; can be stored at normal temperatures for extended
periods; can be added to other foods (cereal flour in particular)

without affecting taste or appearance; will be accepted by the consumers; and can be produced at low cost. Several processes have been developed but they do not meet all the criteria satisfactorily. Nevertheless, there is reason to believe that a satisfactory commodity can be produced at low cost, and that consumer acceptance and demand will develop. This product will satisfy the demand for protein rather than for fish, and thus reflects an entirely different set of price and income elasticities and taste preferences. It is more analogous to the demand for vitamin pills and concentrates than it is to the demand for food.

The development of a widespread demand for FPC would have significant implications for the fisheries industries of several nations. Among Western countries, for example, there are plentiful stocks of fish that are considered "trash" and that are either avoided by the fishermen or returned to the water. If these fish were suitable for FPC and if demand for them developed, a new industry would be opened up for the fishermen. Such a development may also, as mentioned in Chapter 5, have an effect upon the ecological relationships among the species in the area. First effects of FPC might be found in countries with well-developed fish meal industries that could be readily converted to fish protein production.

DISTRIBUTION

The availability of fish and fish products also affects demand patterns. Seasonal distribution can be evened out by some of the preservation processes described above and, given time, the demand for off-season produce will build up.

Geographic distribution is affected not only by changes in preservation techniques, but also by the general availability of transportation and marketing facilities and institutions for all types of food products. The presence of such facilities is related to the total economy, and in low-income countries, where these facilities are missing, fish is eaten only in areas where it is caught. Improved lines of communication are important to the stimulation of demand, but in most areas it is unlikely that roads and railroads will be built exclusively for fisheries. In high-income countries, the problem of transportation is of less significance, even for fresh fish, as certain luxury items are distributed far inland by air carrier.

Marketing organization in low-income countries is frequently a very important impediment to the development or full satisfaction of demand. In some cases—in both low-income and high-income countries—the fishermen themselves restrict output in order to ensure high prices. And in other cases, the marketing agents discourage the development of increased supplies so that they can keep risks down and profit margins high. Governments, international agencies, and industry are all making strong efforts to improve the situation, but the tradition of centuries is difficult to change.

TASTE PREFERENCES AND ELASTICITIES OF DEMAND

The consumer's taste for fish and fish products is conditioned not only by the supply but also by his taste for other foods that compete for his dollar and for a place in his diet. The relevant question is not whether fish are liked or disliked, but whether they are liked or disliked more than some other food commodity. In certain cases, it may appear that there is an intrinsic distaste for a specific commodity, and the commodity is considered to be non-competitive. Usually, however, this distaste simply reflects unfamiliarity with the product. With changes in consumer income and in knowledge of the product, the demand pattern can change. Superstitions and taboos, for example, tend to become ineffective when they are exposed and when the questionable commodity becomes readily available.

These superstitions and taboos are relatively less important than other factors in the determination of demand. In most cases, tastes for fish occupy the middle area of the consumer's preference map where they compete directly with tastes for other foods. The characteristics of such competition differ widely between the high- and low-income countries and even between regions in the same country.

In high-income countries, the significance of per capita income levels and of relative prices, while still important, is less important than in the low-income countries. The physical quantity of *all* food consumed per person, for example, is relatively fixed in high-income countries because additional pounds, proteins, calories, vitamins, etc., are not required or demanded, and in some cases are actually avoided. This means that total food consumption may be expected to increase at about the same rate as population. Furthermore, present taste preferences can be satisfied more easily in high-income countries, and consumption rates will respond less rapidly to increases in per capita income than to other factors, such as convenience in home processing, awareness of healthful or unhealthful qualities of food, etc. While demand for total quantity of foods per capita will not increase, we can still expect shifts in demand and in the pattern of consumption among the various components of the food diet.

It is generally believed that, as per capita incomes increase, the quantity of fish consumed *relative* to the quantity of meat consumed tends to decline; that is, the income elasticity of demand for fish is lower than that for meat. The substitution of meat for fish, however, is limited by the consumer's demand for *variety* in his diet. The preference for meat will never lead to an exclusive meat diet, but will be tempered by the desire to vary the kinds of food consumed. In other terms, as incomes increase, the income elasticities of demand for specific foods tend to become equal and to approach zero, so that the per capita consumption of fish as a whole will become fixed in quantitative terms.

The more significant changes in the high-income countries will be associated with the forms of utilization, the kinds of products, and the expenditures on food commodities, rather than with the quantities. Thus, a 10 per cent increase in income may lead to a 10 per cent increase in *expenditure* on food (unit elasticity) but no increase in quantity consumed. The higher expenditures will go toward the luxury items and toward more highly processed commodities. This trend has been apparent in the United States for many years. There is, for example, a high demand for fresh lobster, crabs, oysters, and scallops, all of which are relatively high-priced foods. There is also a noticeable growth in the per capita consumption of canned fish (particularly tuna), frozen fillets, and breaded fish sticks and portions—the commodities that can be easily prepared for the table. Similar trends in consumption are likely to evolve in the countries of Western Europe.

A study[2] of income elasticities of demand for fish in Great Britain shows a situation similar to that in the United States, and also points out the heterogeneity among fish products. It was found that for 1958 an increase in income of 10 per cent would lead to an increase of 2 per cent in the quantity of all fish consumed. This total, however, hides the fact that the same increase in income would lead to an increase of 11.5 per cent in consumption of

[2] National Food Survey Committee, as reported in R. Hamlisch and R. A. Taylor, "The Demand for Fish as Human Food" (Paper No. R/v.1/1), FAO International Conference on Fish in Nutrition, September 19–27, 1961.

shellfish and a decrease of 1.9 per cent in consumption of cooked fish, as served in fish and chips.

In the foreseeable future, the pattern of consumption in the low-income countries of Asia, Africa, and Latin America, and to a lesser extent in Japan, will follow markedly different trends than those described above. Taste preferences cannot be readily satisfied in most of these areas, and the quantitative consumption of food per person can still increase. Income levels of consumers and price of product are of overriding importance in the determination of consumption. In Figure 5 the income elasticities of demand for fish and for animal protein are shown for a number of countries. It is quite evident that the low-income countries have a much greater expected response to increased income levels than the high-income countries. The comparison between the elasticities for fish and for animal protein indicate the relative degree of preference for fish as against other sources of protein. In India and Pakistan, for example, fish is only slightly less preferred than eggs, milk, and meat, while in Ceylon, Japan, and the Philippines, fish is much less in demand as a source of animal protein. Where meat is inexpensive and plentiful, and where meat consumption is high (as in Argentina and Uruguay), the demand for a variety of foods leads to a higher income elasticity for fish than for other sources of animal protein. In such cases, increased incomes will result in greater percentage increases in consumption of fish than of red meats.

In the low-income countries, the high demand for fish and animal protein is balanced by a low demand for cereals, starchy roots, pulses, and nuts. As incomes increase, therefore, consumption will shift away from the latter and to the former. Changes in income, however, are actually projected to be quite gradual and will, consequently, have little immediate effect upon the utilization of fish.

Therefore, the most immediate change can be expected from shifts in the relative prices of the food commodities. These, in turn, depend upon institutional changes and technological developments that affect the costs of one food more than of another. Overcoming transportation and marketing impediments is more likely to affect all food equally than any single food individually, so that, while the price of all foods may drop, the price of one food compared to another may remain about the same. In such a case, the pattern of consumption will change only to the extent that lower food prices mean greater relative income. Technological de-

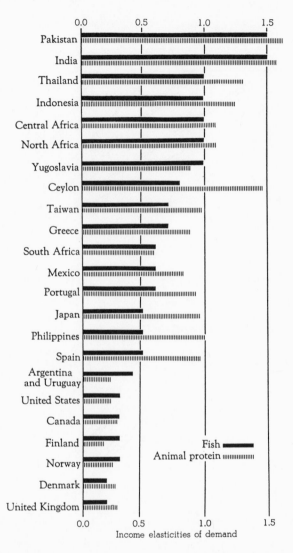

Figure 5. Coefficients of income elasticity of demand for fish and animal protein, in terms of quantities. Income elasticities of demand show the change in consumption of a commodity in response to the change in consumer income. For example, a 10 per cent increase in per capita income would be accompanied by a 15 per cent increase in the quantity of fish consumed in India and a 3 per cent increase in the United States. It should be noted that the coefficients for fish and animal protein are not strictly comparable, since the elasticities for fish have been rounded off to tenths and those for animal protein to hundredths. (*Source:* Food and Agriculture Organization of the United Nations, *Agricultural Commodities—Projections for 1970*, Rome, 1962.)

Figure 6. Percentage increase in total demand for food fish, low and high estimates for 1969–71.

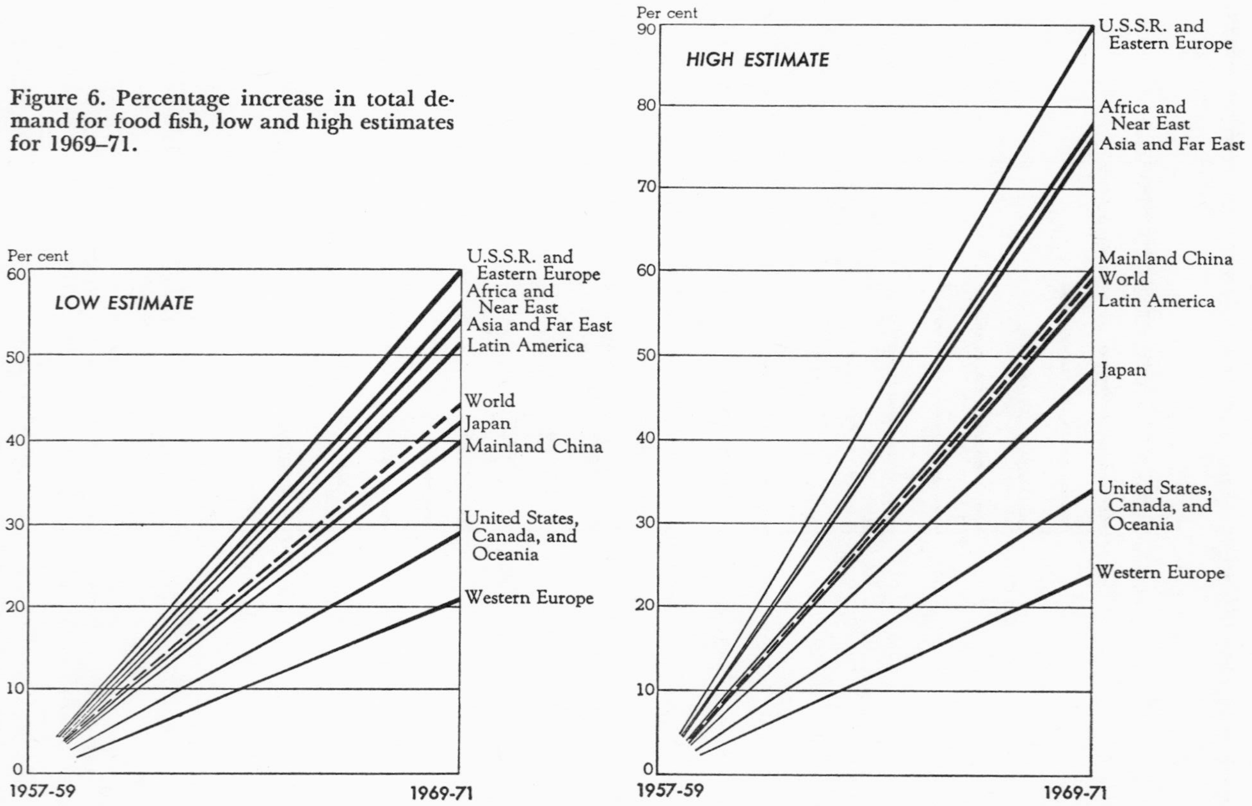

velopments in production and processing, however, may significantly affect the costs of a single food industry and, assuming that the lower costs are translated into lower prices to the consumer, may lead to a marked shift in consumption patterns. The development of a low-cost "cold chain" or freeze-dried or irradiated foods may affect all sources of animal protein equally, or lead to only slightly different competitive advantages. The development of a low-cost fish protein concentrate, on the other hand, would create unique advantages for fish that might not be matched by technological changes in protein concentrates from milk. It would seem, therefore, that per capita consumption of fish in low-income countries would increase more rapidly in response to fish protein concentrate developments than in response to any other technological or institutional changes that are on the horizon.

Projections of Demand

We estimate that the demand for all fish in the year 1970 will range between 57 and 72 million metric tons, live weight. The

Table 5. Catch and Projected Demand for Fish

(million metric tons, live weight)

Use	Catch		1970 Demand	
	1957–59	1962	Low	High
Food use	28.0	32.8	40	45
Nonfood use	4.8	11.9	17	27
Total	32.8	44.7	57	72

wide range in this estimate should serve as a warning that our estimate is not to be considered a definitive projection of the future situation. The derivation of the estimate, and the difficulties involved, are described in the appendix to this chapter. The summary of the results is shown in Table 5.

These estimates are shown in Figure 6 in terms of percentage increases applied to world production estimates. The total world catch has been growing at a fairly steady rate of about 6 per cent per year since World War II (see Figure 7). According to our estimates of the future, the demand may continue to increase at about the same growth rate but may be as low as 5 per cent or as high as 7 per cent per year, using 1957–59 as a base.

But these are very rough estimates. We have some confidence that the 1970 picture of food use will be about as projected. We have very little confidence, however, in our estimate of the demand for nonfood use of fishery products, largely because of the phenomenal recent growth.

FOOD USE

In North America and Western Europe the per capita consumption of fish has changed very little in recent years, and there is no reason to expect any significant change in the future. Increasing per capita incomes in these countries will involve greater relative

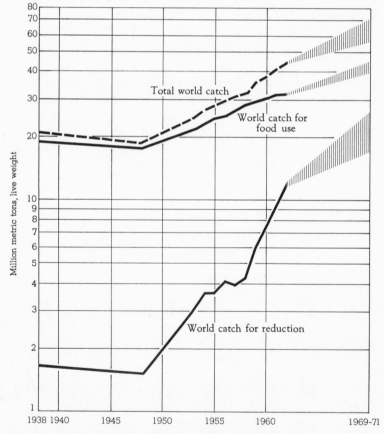

Figure 7. Estimated demand for fish, world catch for food use, for reduction, and total, 1938–62, and projections for 1969–71.

consumption of meat than of fish, and will also lead to greater relative demand for certain kinds of fish than for others. The consumption of canned and fresh and frozen fish may increase in response to improved technology and distribution facilities. On the other hand, the consumption of cured fish is likely to decrease. This may mean continued high demand for tuna, shrimp, salmon, halibut, and molluscs and a lower demand for herring, cod, and other species that are generally cured.

Japan's increase in demand is also expected to be below that of the world average. Although per capita incomes are expected to increase rapidly, these will lead to higher consumption of other foods than of fish. Taste preferences for different species of fish in Japan do not vary as widely as those in North America and Europe. Consequently shifts in patterns of consumption among species will probably respond more to changes in relative availability than to the increases in income.

In Asia and Africa, by 1970, there will be over 500 million additional people, almost four times the increases expected in Europe and North America. This, combined with high income elasticities of demand for fish, will lead to large increases in total demand even though per capita income growth will be relatively small. Because, in most of these countries, the demand for animal protein is higher than the demand for fish, the development of a cheap fish protein concentrate would be likely to increase the total demand for fish well beyond that expected. There is no way of gauging the effect of such a development, not only because it is still unproven, but also because protein demand is conditioned by nonmonetary values as well as by price and income. The strong goal of overcoming the severe problem of malnutrition that exists in areas of Asia and Africa is stimulating more and more research on fish protein concentrate. If the research effort is successful, it could be followed by a rapid growth in demand.

Speculation about demand for fish in Mainland China is difficult. No consumption estimates are available and our only guide lies in production figures that are difficult to accept. Output, in the past ten years, has reportedly increased ten times, and, on this basis, output per capita amounted to about 3 kg., edible weight, in 1957–59. Our 1970 estimates, which show an increase to between 3½ and 4 kg. per person, are about the same as for most other countries of Asia and the Far East, excluding Japan. Growth in total demand, however, is less, because China's population is expected to increase only about 20 per cent, while population in the other countries will increase about 32 per cent.

The largest increase in demand that is expected is that of the U.S.S.R. In an interesting paper presented to the 22nd Congress of the Communist Party of the Soviet Union,[3] some light is shed upon the motivation behind the current expansion of Russian fishery operations. This paper attempted a comparison between the efficiencies in the production of fish and those of meat, and concluded that fish can be supplied with fewer man-hours and smaller capital investment. It was stated that the major reason for the difference was the fact that fish are a free resource requiring no inputs of feed,

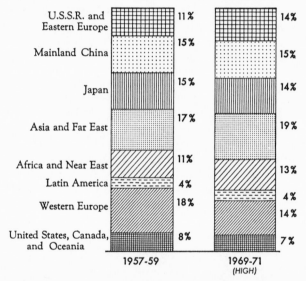

Figure 8. Percentage distribution of total world demand for food fish, 1957–59, and high projection for 1969–71.

cultivation, etc. Although the analysis is hampered by the absence of meaningful price data, the conclusions are significant because of their implications for the investment of effort in fisheries. It indicates that at least part of the growing effort may be a reflection of cost analysis rather than a response to individual taste preferences.

In the 1958 seven-year plan, Russia announced a target for 1965

[3] S. V. Mikhaïlov, "On the Comparative Efficiency of Production of Some Products of the Land and Sea," *Okeanologiĩa*, Vol. 2, No. 3 (1962), pp. 385–92; translated by W. G. Van Campen, Bureau of Commercial Fisheries, Honolulu, Hawaii, October, 1962.

of about a 50 per cent increase in production. This represents a continuation of their past growth rate of 6 per cent per year which, if extended to 1970, would indicate a doubling of output over the 1957–59 level. Consumption which in 1957–59 was about 6 kg. per person, may increase to between 8 and 10 kg. by 1970.

The projected changes in demand and shifts among major regions of the world are shown in Figure 8 and Table 6.

Table 6. Demand for All Food Fish, 1957–59, and Projections for 1969–71

Area	Quantity (edible weight)			Per cent of world total			1969–71 relative to 1957–59	
		1969–71			1969–71		1957–59	
	1957–59	Low	High	1957–59	Low	High	Low	High
	(1,000 metric tons)			*(per cent)*			*(1957–59 = 100)*	
U.S., Canada, and Oceania	1,010	1,300	1,360	8	7	7	129	134
Western Europe	2,370	2,860	2,950	18	15	14	121	124
Latin America	570	860	900	4	5	4	151	158
Africa and the Near East	1,500	2,340	2,650	11	12	13	156	177
Asia and Far East (excl. Japan and Mainland China)	2,200	3,400	3,900	17	18	19	154	176
Japan	2,000	2,800	3,000	15	15	14	142	148
Mainland China	2,000	2,800	3,200	15	15	15	140	160
U.S.S.R. and East Europe	1,500	2,400	2,850	11	13	14	160	190
World Total	13,100	18,800	20,800	100	100	100	144	159

Source: See Table 9, in appendix to this chapter.

NONFOOD USE

Our estimate of the demand for the nonfood use of fish is basically a guess as to what might reasonably be expected in the future. The situation has been changing so rapidly recently that economic analysis is of little or no value in looking as far ahead as 1970. The changes can be seen by reference to Figure 7, showing the growth in catch of fish for reduction. Output between 1948 and 1962 increased almost 8 times, at the rate of 16 per cent per year. Growth slowed up in the mid-1950's but since 1958 has been increasing at the phenomenal rate of 30 per cent per year. Most of this is accounted for by the remarkable growth in the Peruvian catch of anchoveta (Table 7). The first signs of a retardation in this growth rate appeared in 1963, when the catch was slightly less than in the previous year. In the first ten months of 1964, however, fish meal production was up 32 per cent over that of the first ten months of 1963.*

Table 7. Peruvian Catch
of Anchoveta, 1955–63 [a]

Year	1,000 metric tons, live weight
1955	58.7
1956	118.7
1957	326
1958	737
1959	1,909
1960	2,943
1961	4,580
1962	6,690
1963	6,630

[a] Data for 1955–61 from Instituto de Investigación de los Recursos Marinos, *La Industria Pesquera de la Anchoveta,* Informe No. 11, La Punta, Callao, Peru, 1963. Data for 1962–63 from FAO *Yearbook of Fishery Statistics,* Vol. 16, 1963.

In the face of such rapid changes the view of the future is obscured, and our estimates simply represent the assumption that this recent growth rate must eventually slacken off. We can, however, discuss some of the pertinent elements that make up the demand for fish for reduction, even though we cannot ascribe weights and values to these elements.

Most of the fish that are caught primarily for reduction come from the herring group and include the herrings, the menhadens, anchovies, sardines, pilchards, etc. Since some of these are also used as food, and since some products of reduction are also derived from the waste products of food fishes, the category of "catch for reduction" does not exactly equal the nonfood use of fishery prod-

* Since this has gone to press, an estimate for 1964 has become available showing catch at over 8 million tons, which is more than 25 per cent greater than the 1963 figure.

ucts. The difference, however, is probably a negligible proportion of the total.

Fish that are caught for reduction are processed into fish meal, fish oils, and solubles. Although there are a variety of uses for the end products (fertilizers, feed, drying oils in paints, etc.) the most important use at present is as a high protein concentrate feed for poultry and pigs. A fish protein concentrate for human use will probably not be developed in time to have significant implications for the 1970 demand for fish caught for reduction, and we have therefore made no specific allowances for it in our estimates of the 1970 situation.

Fish meal is becoming an increasingly important constituent of the rations fed to poultry and swine. This accompanies the shift from a farm-type to a factory-type production, exemplified in the United States by the development of the commercial broiler. Such production depends heavily upon purchased formula feeds rather than upon home-grown grains. The formula feeds, in turn, make use of high protein concentrates, such as fish meal, soybean meal, meat scraps and tankage, feather meal, blood meal, etc. One advantage that fish meal has over the others is that it contains an unidentified growth factor (called UGF) that stimulates rapid growth. This fish factor is of considerable value up to a level of $2\frac{1}{2}$ per cent of the total feed ration of commercial broilers. Beyond that level, little additional growth stimulus is obtained, but fish meal continues to be an important source of amino acids up to a level at which fish meal makes up about $7\frac{1}{2}$ per cent of the broiler diet. At this level, the broiler does not need more amino acids, but can continue to receive other values from fish meal including energy, minerals, and vitamins. However, a negative factor begins to develop at higher levels of fish meal in the ration. For broilers, more than 10 per cent of fish meal in the ration tends to lead to fishy flavors in the meat and to an unacceptable product, although this varies quite a bit for kinds of fish, methods of processing, and methods of feeding.[4] This same pattern holds true for swine and for raising egg producers, although the levels of significance may be different.

Fish meal is of relatively little importance at present for beef cattle and milk cows, although there are indications that it can be

[4] See the papers in Food and Agriculture Organization of the United Nations, *Future Developments in the Production and Utilization of Fish Meal*, Vol. II, Rome, 1961.

used in fairly heavy proportions. Some recent tests have indicated that milk cow rations containing up to 30 per cent fish meal do not taint the milk.[5]

Competitive high protein feeds are also developing rapidly. Some of these are by-products of the meat industry, such as tankage and meals made from the blood and from the feathers of poultry. Their production is limited by the production of the animals, and much larger increases cannot be expected in the future. Vegetable meals, such as soybean meal and other oilseed meals, are becoming more competitive now that some of the amino acids can be produced synthetically. However, as yet, neither the meat meals nor the vegetable meals are able to provide the UGF that is available in fish.

In short, the demand curve for fish meal follows a series of steps if quantity is represented by percentage of meal in the ration. Up to a certain low level of feeding, it has little competition because it is the only source of UGF. Between this and the next level, it competes with the by-product meat meals and with vegetable meals to which synthetic amino acids have been added. Beyond this level, it competes with general sources of energy, minerals, and vitamins, but only up to the point where it begins to taint the end product.

This stepped demand curve relates only to the individual farmers now using fish meal. For a nation as a whole, the demand curve will probably be smooth because the shift to factory-type poultry production methods and formula feeds is continually bringing in new users of fish meal. There is an interesting indication of this in the recent statistics on the export markets of Peruvian fish meal.[6] Peru exported fish meal to one country in 1951, to seven in 1958, to seventeen in 1959, and to thirty-four in 1962. This could mean that these countries are simply substituting Peruvian meal for other sources of supply, but the size of the increases indicates that a large proportion of demand is made up of new users.

When Peruvian exports started to make a heavy impact on the world market, and during the short-lived depression of world price in 1959–60, Peru and several other countries formed the Fish Meal Exporters' Organization in order to help stabilize world prices. Ninety per cent of world exports of fish meal are ac-

[5] *Commercial Fisheries Review,* Vol. 25 (July, 1963), p. 43.

[6] I. Tilic, *Material estadístico sobre la industria peruana de harina de pescado,* Informe No. 14 (La Punta, Callao, Peru: Instituto de Investigación de los Recursos Marinos, 1963), p. 43.

counted for by the member countries, which include Angola, Iceland, Norway, Peru, and South Africa (including South-West Africa). According to agreements among these countries, the estimated world market is to be divided among them, with Peru's quota set at 60 per cent. However, because the other countries have not been able to fill their quotas in the face of the rapidly rising demands, Peru's share has generally been considerably larger. In 1962, for example, Peru accounted for 75 per cent of total exports of the member countries.

In the face of this, it is unlikely that the exporters' agreement can have much effect in restraining Peru's future expansion. The momentum of the industry is such that even if rigorous efforts were made there would be a long time lag before controls could take effect. The figures in Table 8 give some indication of growth, the forecast for 1963/64 being 50 per cent greater than capacity at the end of 1962.

Table 8. Growth in Peruvian Capacity for Production
of Fish Meal

	Peru's annual capacity for:	
Item	Use of the raw material	Production of fish meal
	(*metric tons*)	(*metric tons*)
Total as of 12/31/61	4,580,000	863,800
Addition through new construction and expansion, 1st half of 1962	896,900	169,200
Total as of 6/30/62	5,475,500	1,033,100
Expansion of existing plants through 12/31/62	1,229,900	232,200
Total as of 12/31/62	6,705,400	1,265,200
Addition from construction of applications being processed in 1963	3,647,600	688,200
Total forecast for 1963/64	10,353,000	1,953,400

Source: Instituto de Investigación de los Recursos Marinos, *La Industria Pesquera de la Anchoveta,* Informe No. 11, La Punta, Callao, Peru, 1963, p. 21.

Such figures as these indicate the impossibility of projecting an accurate estimate of demand into the future. We know that demand has been increasing rapidly. We know that it depends largely upon the production of poultry and swine. We know that there are certain limits beyond which fish meal cannot be fed to livestock without imparting some taint to the meat. But that is about where our knowledge ends. From there on, we are dealing in speculations.

Appendix to Chapter 3—Demand Projection Methods

FOOD USE

Demand projections in Table 9 are based primarily upon the FAO publication, *Agricultural Commodities—Projections for 1970.* This study estimated the income elasticities of demand for all food commodities for a large number of countries, and also projected growth in population and in Gross National Product. From these ingredients, the study derived estimates of percentage increases in demand for the different foods. For most foods, future demand was balanced with estimates of supply. Gaps between these were used as indicators of price changes, and demand estimates were modified accordingly. Such an effort was not made for fish.

Our projections have made use of FAO's estimates of 1957–59 per capita consumption and population and of future increase in demand. Per capita consumption is given in column (A) in Table 9, in terms of edible weight. No estimates were given by FAO for the Sino-Soviet countries and for Burma, South Korea, and Vietnam. The estimates are presented only to one or sometimes two significant figures, which is probably a reflection of their reliability as well as an indication of the relative importance of fish in the diet. The per capita consumption figures for 1957–59 were multiplied by mid-year 1958 population figures to derive total consumption in terms of edible weight. In column (D), we give the estimated increases in total demand for fish as presented in the FAO study, except for the Western Europe total, the E.E.C. countries, and the Sino-Soviet area. FAO's range in projections is based upon high and low assumptions on the growth rate of GNP per capita. Total demand for fish, as shown in column (E), is simply the product of columns (C) and (D) divided by 100. Because of gross rounding errors, the country figures do not add up to the subgroup totals, which we have presented in Table 2 in the text.

In the case of the E.E.C. countries, we have had to make our own projections of total demand. P. Lamartine Yates has assumed

Table 9. Projection of Demand for Food Fish, Edible Weight

Country	1957-59 (A) Fish consumption per capita	1957-59 (B) Population (mid-year 1958)	1957-59 (C) Total fish consumption	1969-71 (D) Index of total demand (1957-59 = 100) Low	High	1969-71 (E) Total demand Low	High
	kg./yr.	*million*	*million kg.*			*million kg.*	
High-Income Countries:							
North America	5	192	960	*129*	*134*	*1,240*	*1,290*
Canada	6	17	100	135	141	140	140
U.S.	5	175	870	128	134	1,100	1,200
Oceania	4	12	48	*130*	*134*	*62*	*65*
Australia	3	10	30	132	136	40	41
New Zealand	7	2	14	127	130	18	18
Western Europe		320	2,370 a	*121* a	*124* a	*2,860* a	*2,950* a
E.E.C.	5	169	850	119 b	121 b	1,000 b	1,000 b
Belgium/Lux.	6	9	54				
France	5	45	230				
W. Germany	7	55	390				
Italy	4	49	200				
Netherlands	5	11	55				
Mediterranean Countries	10	65	650	137	145	890	950
Greece	8	8	64	152	161	97	100
Portugal	20	9	180	125	132	230	240
Spain	11	30	330	137	143	450	470
Yugoslavia	2	18	36	169	195	61	70

See notes at end of table.

Table 9. *(continued)*

Country	1957–59			1969–71			
	(A) Fish consumption per capita	(B) Population (mid-year 1958)	(C) Total fish consumption	(D) Index of total demand		(E) Total demand	
				1957–59 = 100		million kg.	
	kg./yr.	*million*	*million kg.*	Low	High	Low	High
Western Europe (cont.)							
Others	*10*	87	*870*	*112*	*115*	*970*	*1,000*
Austria	3	7	21	126	132	26	28
Denmark	15	5	75	113	116	85	87
Finland	11	4	44	123	127	54	56
Ireland	4	3	12	118	124	14	15
Norway	19	4	76	119	123	90	93
Sweden	18	7	126	110	111	140	140
Switzerland	3	5	15	122	127	18	19
United Kingdom	10	52	520	110	113	570	590
Japan	22	92	2,000	142	148	2,800	3,000
South Africa	7	14	100	140	153	140	150
Argentina and Uruguay	2	23	46	129	133	59	61
Low-Income Countries:							
Latin America [c]	*3*	*173*	*520*	*154*	*161*	*800*	*840*
Brazil, Paraguay	2	64	130	151	158	200	210
Mexico	2	33	66	166	175	110	120
Central America (Excl. Mex.)	3	30	90	151	159	140	140
Others	5	46	230	154	159	350	370
Near East and Africa [d]	*5*	*275*	*1,400*	*156*	*177*	*2,200*	*2,500*
Turkey	1	26	26	162	179	42	47

Other Near East in Asia	2	59	120	164	185	200	220
North Africa (Algeria, Egypt, Libya, Morocco, Tunisia)	6	49	290	159	183	460	530
Other Africa [b]	6	140	840	153	173	1,300	1,500
Asia and Far East [e]	3	736	2,200	154	170	3,400	3,900
Ceylon	6	9	54	149	161	80	87
India	1	417	420	168	200	700	840
Indonesia	5	88	460	142	164	650	750
Pakistan	2	91	180	136	166	240	300
Philippines	15	26	390	157	169	610	660
Taiwan	11	10	110	169	187	190	210
Thailand	9	24	220	159	175	350	390
Sino-Soviet Area							
U.S.S.R.	(6) [b]	207	1,200 [b]	167	200	2,000	2,400
Eastern Europe	(3) [b]	97	300 [b]	133	150	400	450
Mainland China	(3) [b]	669	2,000 [b]	140	160	2,800	3,200

[a] Derived from subgroup estimates.
[b] See text for source of estimates.
[c] Excluding Argentina and Uruguay.
[d] Excluding South Africa.
[e] Excluding Japan. No estimates of per capita fish consumption are available for Burma, South Korea, and Vietnam. Their populations are included in the total population, however.

Source: Columns A, B, and D from *Agricultural Commodities—Projections for 1970* (Rome: FAO, 1962). Column C is product of columns A and B. Column E is product of columns C and D divided by 100. Group totals in columns C and E are *not* derived by summation of individual country figures except for Western Europe. Apparent discrepancies are due to rounding to two significant figures, or sometimes only one, and to the inclusion in the groups of some countries not listed.

49

an income elasticity of demand for fish of 0.1 for *all* of Western Europe.[7] Basing this upon the 1955 quantities consumed, he estimated that by 1970 there will be a 5 per cent increase in per capita consumption and a 13 per cent increase in total demand for fish. Yates's income elasticity is considerably lower than FAO's for each of the countries for which comparisons can be made. In order to match Yates's elasticity of 0.1 for all Western Europe, the E.E.C. countries in FAO's study would have to have an income elasticity of about −0.15.

Hamlisch and Taylor,[8] presenting the results of an unpublished survey by L. M. Goreux of FAO, show the following demand elasticities for certain E.E.C. countries:

Germany, 1950–51, cities of over 5,000 pop.   0.24
Italy, 1953–54, nonfarm pop.   0.18
Netherlands, 1951, all pop. excl. farmers   0.47

These elasticities represent early 1950 incomes and are probably too high for 1957–59 levels. We have assumed that the E.E.C. countries average about 0.2, which is the same as the average given for the "Other" countries of Western Europe. By use of FAO's formula [9] for estimating increase in demand, we have projected an increase in per capita consumption for the E.E.C. countries of 9–11 per cent and an increase in total demand for fish of 19–21 per cent.

Projections for the Sino-Soviet countries are far more speculative. We have had to make rough guesses of both present and future consumption rates. Furthermore, our estimates do not refer to demand but to consumption because of the absence of income information and elasticities. Production in the U.S.S.R. during

[7] P. Lamartine Yates, *Food, Land, and Manpower in Western Europe* (London: Macmillan and Co., Ltd., 1960).

[8] *Op. cit.*

[9] FAO's formula is based upon the semi-logarithmic function

$$y = a + b \log_e x$$

and an elasticity coefficient of $\eta = \dfrac{b}{y}$. The formula is:

$$\frac{y^1}{y} - 1 = 2.3026 \, \eta \log_{10}\frac{x^1}{x}$$

in which x, y, and η refer respectively to per capita income, per capita demand, and elasticity coefficient during the base period, and x^1 and y^1 refer to income and demand at the end of the projection.

1957–59 averaged a little over 2½ million metric tons live weight. Assuming edible weight to be somewhat less than half of live weight, production might be stated in terms of 1,200 million kilograms, edible weight. Although some of this is undoubtedly used for nonfood purposes, there is no adequate evidence of the proportion. We have assumed, therefore, that total production is caught for food. We have also assumed negligible foreign trade. (FAO, *Yearbook of Fishery Statistics, 1958–59,* Vol. X, reports net imports of 105,000 metric tons, product weight.) On these assumptions, present consumption in Russia is about 6 kg. per person. In a similar fashion, consumption rates for Eastern European countries have been estimated at 3 kg., and for Communist China, also at 3 kg. per capita.

Russia's population is expected to increase to about 250 million by 1970. Considerable efforts are being made to increase fish production, as indicated by the increases in number of trawlers and other fishing ships in operation and under construction. Russian catch has been increasing at about the rate of 6 per cent per year, which indicates a growth in per capita consumption of about 4½ per cent per year. If this trend is continued to 1970, the derived per capita consumption would be about 10 kg. and derived increase in "demand" per capita would be about 67 per cent. Total demand would then be about 200 relative to 1957–59 as 100. This seems to be high in comparison with the increases in demand projected for other countries, but may be justified in view of the known increases in intensity of fishing effort. A lower estimate has been derived simply by assuming that the same absolute amount of increase experienced in the past 12 years could be applied to the next 12 years. Total projected catch, on this basis, would increase about two-thirds over 1957–59. These increases, applied to present consumption, mean a range in total "demand" from 2 to 2.4 million metric tons, edible weight. Our high increase is in agreement with the "target" set by the U.S.S.R. for 1965. Russia's latest seven-year plan assumes that catch in that year will be about 4.6 million metric tons, live weight, including whales. The interpolation of our trend gives about 3.9 million metric tons, live weight, excluding whales. Whale catch in 1960 was about 500,000 tons. If this increases to 600,000 tons by 1965, and is added to our estimate of fish catch, the total will be 4.5 million metric tons, which is only 100,000 tons below the "target." Our low estimate, on the other hand, is in keeping with the estimate of Commander M. B. F.

Ranken,[10] who assumes a catch of 4.5 million metric tons by 1975.

For Eastern Europe, the derived per capita consumption rate is similar to that of Austria. Although Poland and East Germany are known to be increasing their fishing efforts at a rapid pace, the other Eastern European countries have no access to marine waters other than the Black Sea. An increase in total output of from a third to a half seems reasonable.

For Mainland China, speculation is replaced by sheer hunch. Output, as shown by FAO statistics, increased tenfold between 1949 and 1959, from 500,000 metric tons, live weight, to 5 million. There is nothing to indicate that an increase of this magnitude has actually occurred. It probably includes underreporting in the early years and inflation of estimates in the later years.[11] The trend, therefore, is felt to be highly unrealistic, and unusable as a basis for estimating future demand. We have simply assumed that total demand will increase at a rate somewhat less than those for other countries of South and Southeast Asia, leading to a 40–60 per cent increase over total consumption in 1957–59. Because China's population is expected to increase at a lesser rate, our estimates imply that growth in per capita consumption will be about the same as those for other South and Southeast Asia countries.

[10] Commander M. B. F. Ranken, "Evolution probable des industries de la pêche en Europe," *La Pêche Maritime* (December, 1960).

[11] According to Choh-ming Li, "Statistics and Planning at the Hsein Level in Communist China," *The China Quarterly,* No. 9 (January–March, 1962), p. 112 ff., statistics on output of mining and manufacturing have been inflated by as much as 200 per cent and average about 60–70 per cent above actual production, beginning in 1958. This inflation results from the inability of the producers to meet the targets set for them and their "buoyant exaggeration" in order to avoid penalties. Although the article makes no reference to fisheries, it is reasonable to expect that similar inflation is made by fishery co-operatives.

The annual percentage increases in catch for consecutive years from 1949 to 1959 are as follows: 85, 22, 30, 10, 21, 10, 5, 18, 30, 24. The large increases in early years probably mean that improved and more comprehensive reporting techniques were being adopted. The large increases in the later years may reflect the practice of inflating production statistics. If we arbitrarily assume that actual catch was 80 per cent of the 1958 figure and 70 per cent of the 1959 figure, then the average catch of 1957–59 would be about 3.2 million metric tons instead of 4 million, and per capita consumption, 2½ kg., edible weight, rather than 3 kg. On the other hand, difficulties in communication may mean that there is still some underreporting in outlying districts, both in marine and inland fishing areas. The net result is unfathomable.

NONFOOD USE

Estimating the future demand for nonfood use of fish products is a task that can only be undertaken with the greatest temerity. Figure 7 (above) shows the growth in world catch of fish for reduction, almost all of which goes into fish meal as a feed for poultry and swine. One of the remarkable aspects of this curve is the rapidity of growth in recent years. Between 1958 and 1962, output rose from 4.3 million metric tons live weight to 11.9 million tons, an increase of over 175 per cent. This is a growth rate of about 29 per cent per year which, if maintained to 1970, would indicate an output of about 90 million tons. Obviously the demand for fish meal will be considerably lower than that; but how much lower is the question.

Where variables are relatively stable, economic analysis of demand elasticities, anticipated price and income changes, etc., can do much to facilitate reasonable and fairly accurate projections of future demand. In 1960 the price of fish meal was temporarily depressed and the market appeared to be saturated. It was felt that a degree of stability in the demand and price structure had been reached. In this context, the papers that were prepared for the 1961 FAO conference on fish meal,[12] projected moderate increases in output and a recovery of prices, although there were some contradictions in estimating the price elasticities of demand. The economic analyses, however, grossly underestimated the changes that actually occurred. It was anticipated that Peruvian production would level off at 600,000–650,000 metric tons of fish meal. In fact, however, this was exceeded by 200,000 tons in 1961 and by 500,000 tons in 1962; at the same time, the world price recovered. The appearance of market stability was considerably misleading.

In the face of these rapidly shifting variables, we do not feel that we can make a satisfactory projection of the future demand for fish meal. We can only anticipate a retardation in the recent rate of growth and provide a rough range within which 1970 demand is likely to fall. Our upper estimate is derived by a rough trend line from 1948. This trend line, showing a growth of about 14 per cent per year, indicates a demand for fish for reduction of about 27 million metric tons in the year 1970. This is more than twice the 1962

[12] *Future Developments in the Production and Utilization of Fish Meal* (Rome: Food and Agriculture Organization of the United Nations, 1961).

output of 11.9 million tons and, while it may be reasonable in view of the phenomenal growth that has occurred in recent years, it appears to be high in terms of absolute amounts. At the other extreme, and giving greater weight to the leveling off of output in Peru in 1963, we might expect an increase of 5 million tons instead of 15 million tons. This would mean a demand of about 17 million tons by 1970. It must be emphasized, however, that the estimate of demand for nonfood fish of between 17 and 27 million metric tons, live weight, is little more than a guess.

As a rough check on this range, we have examined the implications for the proportion of fish meal in the feed rations. The FAO projections indicate that the high-income countries will increase their production of all meat by 32–36 per cent over 1957–59.[13] By subtracting the estimates for beef and veal, the increase in the balance will be about 29–34 per cent. (This includes a relatively small proportion of mutton and lamb as well as poultry and pork, and does not include eggs.) For the low-income countries, the only figures given show an increase in the potential demand for all meat of 62–83 per cent. It is pointed out, however, that consumption is not likely to match the projected demand because of increased prices arising from the limited opportunities for expanding output and inability to increase imports. As a rough guess, production in these countries might increase from 50 to 75 per cent. Since the low-income countries produce about one-third of total meat production, the total world output of poultry and pork in 1970 may therefore be about 35 to 50 per cent greater than in the base period.

This base period is given as 1957–59. By the extrapolation of trends to 1962, this would lead to an increase of poultry and pork production of 23–30 per cent between 1962 and 1970. In order to obtain the 43 per cent increase in demand for fish meal (our lower estimate), the increase in production of pork and poultry would have to be accompanied by a 15 per cent increase in the proportion of fish meal in the feed ration. That is, in the United States, for example, fish meal would have to make up 1.15 per cent of total feed as against the average of one per cent that was used in 1961 [14] (assuming, of course, that U.S. output of pork and poul-

[13] FAO, *Agricultural Commodities—Projections for 1970*, Rome, 1962, p. II–28.

[14] Clarence F. Winchester, "Present and Future Factors that may Influence Fish Meal Demand," *Commercial Fisheries Review*, Vol. 25 (March, 1963), p. 2.

try will increase at the same rate as the world's). In order to reach the 127 per cent increase in demand for fish meal, as represented by our upper estimate, the use of fish meal in the feed ration would have to increase by 75 per cent. In the United States this would mean, on the same basis as above, that fish meal would make up an average of 1.75 per cent of the feed rations for pigs and poultry.

As mentioned in the text above, a 10 per cent feed level for poultry, already in use in some areas, is close to the largest amount that can be fed without tainting the meat. Up to $2\frac{1}{2}$ per cent, the value of the Unidentified Growth Factor is still high. Feeding at levels beyond that has little additional effect in stimulating growth but does provide a concentrated source of amino acids. At about $7\frac{1}{2}$ per cent, additional amino acids derived from fish meal have little additional value for broilers, but the meal will continue to supply other requirements including energy, minerals, and vitamins. Thus, an increase to a level of 1.75 per cent is quite feasible and appears to be a reasonable target for 1970.

Chapter 4

The Productivity of the Seas

A LITTLE more than seven-tenths of the surface of the earth is covered by ocean. Most of these waters lie in areas where temperature and light conditions are favorable for plant growth. However, in spite of the vastness of this area of apparent fertility, the oceans supply but a small fraction of our food and other needs. In this chapter we will discuss the many complex links that make up the chain from the primary productivity of organic material to the consumption of food by human beings. This chain begins with the availability of the necessary mineral elements within the euphotic zone—the upper area of the water where light penetrates sufficiently for photosynthesis to take place. It continues by the transmutation of these elements into minute organisms—phytoplankton—which are consumed by larger organisms—zooplankton. These are the basic food of the marine species that are of present economic importance to man. In some cases, the fish that feed directly on the plankton are those that are sought by man. In other cases, the chain is much longer, leading to predators that prey on other predators.

Elements of Fertility

The mass of living matter (plants and animals) within the oceans has several aspects that are of importance to a discussion of commercial fisheries. First, it depends upon interrelationships between mineral nutrients, sunlight, photosynthesizing organisms, temperature, and other factors. Second, differential fertility leads to concentration of plants and animals in certain areas and diffusion in others. Third, the areas where plants and animals concentrate are not rigidly fixed, but are subject to significant displacement, both between seasons and between years. And finally, it is not only the quantity of the living matter that is significant, but also the quality in terms of species that are of economic importance to man.

In the sea, as on land, animal life is ultimately dependent upon plants. Ocean plants are of two kinds: those that are fixed to the bottom of the ocean and are relatively large in size (the seaweeds and kelps), and those that are free-floating and of microscopic size (the phytoplankton). The seaweeds and kelps are found only in shallow waters where there is sunlight near the bottom. They are of relatively small economic significance, used mainly as fertilizer and as sources of agar and gelling agents and, in some countries, as food. The phytoplankton, however, can grow on the high seas. They are not of economic importance themselves, but they provide the basic food for all marine animal life. Their production and concentration determine the areas of productive fisheries.

Phytoplankton cannot grow without nutrient salts, such as phosphates, nitrates, and others, and sunlight.[1] The depth at which photosynthetic activity can take place depends upon the latitude and the transparency of the water. Generally, transparency is reduced in coastal waters and in higher latitudes. At 60°N (the south tip of Greenland), light conditions permit growth of seaweeds only to a depth of 45 to 60 feet, while in tropic waters such growth can take place down to about 600 feet. These depths represent a vast euphotic zone, within which plant production could take place given the necessary nutrients.

The natural fertilization of floating marine plants, however, is subject to different forces than natural fertilization of plants on land. Organic matter which decays on the land is kept at a level where plant production takes place. However, in sea water, metabolic products and remnants of plants and animals sink towards the bottom so that the ultimate release of mineral sub-

[1] For further detail, see H. U. Sverdrup, "Some Aspects of the Primary Productivity of the Sea," *FAO Fisheries Bulletin*, Vol. 5, No. 6 (November–December, 1952).

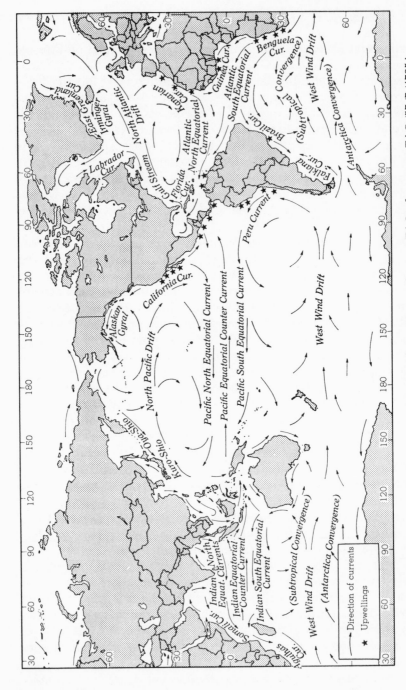

Figure 9. Surface currents of the oceans during northern winter. (*Source:* FAO, document FAO/57/1/4725.)

stances, through decomposition, occurs mostly in depths where photosynthesis cannot take place. Under these conditions, without the possibility of turnover, the upper layers of the ocean would become sterile and plant production could take place only where nutrient salts were washed from the land. In fact, however, plant production is not restricted to estuaries and shallow coastal waters. The relatively rich, deep layers of nutrients are subjected to scouring forces that lead to the replenishment of the euphotic zones and to concentrations of plant life in certain regions of the seas. Wind, winter cooling, and turbulence at the interface of different currents serve to plow the lower level of nutrients and raise them to the surface. The wind, acting by itself, is generally sufficient to mix waters down to 300 feet in depth. In temperate regions, the decomposing matter and nutrients that have settled below the euphotic zone but have not yet reached a depth of 300 feet are returned to the plant-producing surface layer by this action. However, a secondary force related to currents is more powerful. The effect of the earth's rotation is such that the surface layers of water are transported at right angles to the wind—to the right in the northern hemisphere, and to the left in the southern. Where surface water is transported by wind action away from coasts, deep water replaces it, bringing with it the rich nutrients that have settled to the bottom.

For example, during late winter and early spring, the prevailing winds off the coast of California are from the north, thereby inducing westward, off-coast, movement of the surface waters. These are replaced by an upwelling of waters from depths of 600 to 900 feet. The rich plant nutrient salts that are brought up spread out to distances of 50 to 100 miles and permit the development of large plant populations, which, in turn, support large populations of fish.

Significant upwellings are also found in other areas of the world, as shown on the map of world surface currents, Figure 9. One of the most extensive of these is found off the coasts of Chile and Peru, where Peruvian fishermen increased their catch 140-fold between 1948 and 1963, thereby becoming the world's largest producer of fish. Fertile upwellings also take place off the coast of Morocco and the west coast of South Africa. They rarely occur off the eastern coasts of the continents.

The effect of wind currents on water transport is also important along the equator in the Pacific where the prevailing easterlies induce northerly water movements above the equator and southerly water movements below the equator. The divergence of these streams creates an upwelling of the deep nutrients that provide the basis for a commercial tuna fishery.

In the higher latitudes, deep wind plowing has less effect than in the tropic waters, and the principal agent for mixing is winter cooling. As the temperature drops, the surface water becomes denser and heavier than the deeper waters and tends to sink. Where salinity is uniform, as in the areas between Iceland, Greenland, and Labrador, the surface water may sink all the way to the bottom, to a depth of 10,000 to 12,000 feet. The deep water, which rises to replace the surface water is rich in nutrients and, with the coming of spring and increased light, supports heavy plant growth. In the Barents Sea, the waters are shallower and the dead organic matter is only partly decomposed by the time it reaches the bottom. This accumulation of organic matter provides food for large populations of bottom animals and bottom fish, such as the plaice.

The sinking of the waters of the North Atlantic has an important effect on the productivity of Antarctic waters several thousand miles away in the Southern Hemisphere. Within the Atlantic Ocean, the action of the prevailing winds and the character of the coastlines induces a flow of surface waters northward across the equator in amounts that are estimated at about 6 million cubic meters per second or 45,000 cubic miles a year. As these great quantities of surface water flow to the north, they are replaced in the Antarctic regions by the waters from a massive submarine current that originates partly with the sinking waters of the North Atlantic and partly with a deep flow from the bottom of the Straits of Gibraltar. While the deep waters flow far south, they pick up additional nitrates, phosphates, and other matter that have settled from the surface, thus enriching the masses of water that upwell around the Antarctic continent.

Another kind of upwelling is caused by the turbulence that occurs where major ocean currents meet. The warm, northward moving Kuro-Shio meets the cold, southward flowing Oya-Shio off the northern islands of Japan and creates a rich surface water. The high fertility of the Grand Banks results in a similar way from the collision of the Gulf Stream and Labrador Current.

The continental shelves owe their productivity not to upwelling but to the mineral elements and organic materials that are washed off the land. The general configuration of the continental shelf is that of a gentle slope to a depth of 100 fathoms (600 feet), followed by a sharper drop to the ocean floor. There are, however, wide variations within this configuration. On the western coasts of the Americas, south of Alaska, these shelves extend only a few miles out to sea; on the eastern coasts, they may be as wide as 500 miles (see Figure 10). The plants and animals associated with the ocean bottom (the benthic organisms) thrive in the shallow waters of the continental shelves, because the decaying organic matter and the nutrient salts that settle to the bottom are taken up and continuously recycled by the living organisms. Even in the deeper waters of the continental shelves, the coastal currents and eddies create sufficient turbulence to prevent the loss of the nitrates, phosphates, and other elemental materials.

Another zone of concentrated animal life about which very little is known was discovered during the war. Echo sounders, which were designed to locate submarines, recorded the presence of what appeared to be a false bottom. These false bottoms, or "deep scattering layers," have been observed throughout all oceans at depths of 1,000 to 2,500 feet, and are known to rise towards the surface at night. They apparently contain vast quantities of organisms, including abundant numbers of small fish.

In summary, it is clear that the oceans are not homogeneous in terms of living matter. Differential fertility does exist and is generally dependent upon the availability of appropriate plant nutrients and favorable light conditions. These, in turn, are related to the depth and movement of water masses, the underlying topography, conditions of wind and temperature, the effect of the earth's rotation, and proximity to land areas. Figure 11 provides a rough indication of the regional differences in fertility. From this it can be seen that the coastal areas are generally more fertile than those of the mid ocean, although there is a noticeably wide variation in both areas. Estimates of large concentrations of zooplankton which feed on phytoplankton are shown in the northern and southern extremes of both the Atlantic and Pacific, where winter cooling is the effective agent in recirculating plant nutrients. The effect of wind-induced upwellings is quite noticeable in the western coasts of the continents, including the Australian continent. The large concentrations of zooplankton in these areas provide the basis for large fish populations.

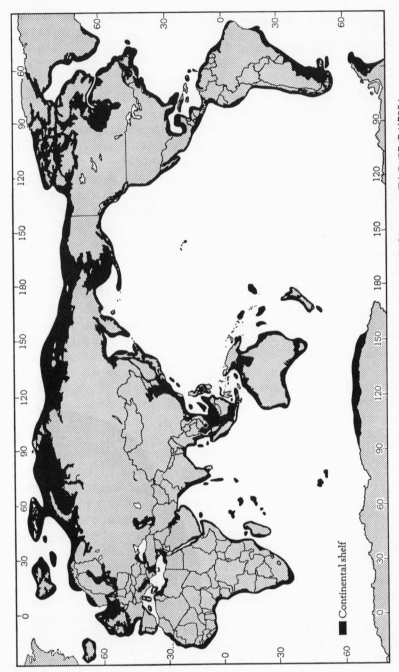

Figure 10. The continental shelves of the world. (*Source:* FAO document FAO/57/7/4725.)

■ Continental shelf

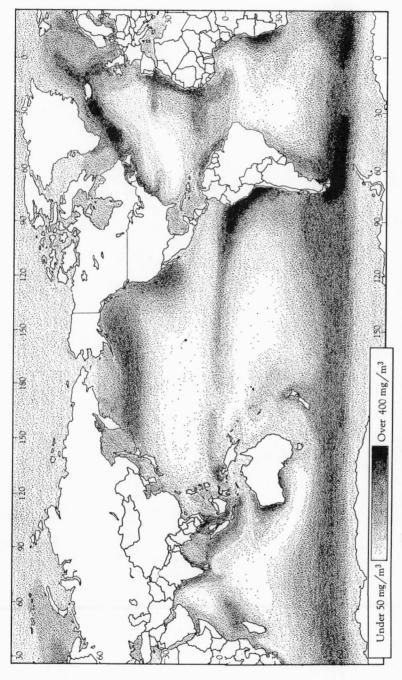

Figure 11. Estimation of standing crop of zooplankton biomass in upper 300 meters (in milligrams per cubic meter). (*Source:* FAO document FAO/57/7/4725.)

Under 50 mg/m³

Over 400 mg/m³

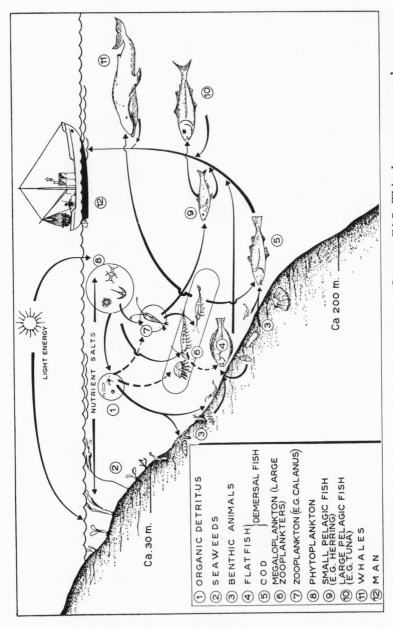

LIGHT ENERGY

NUTRIENT SALTS

Ca. 30 m.

Ca 200 m.

① ORGANIC DETRITUS
② SEAWEEDS
③ BENTHIC ANIMALS
④ FLATFISH ⎫
⑤ COD   ⎬ DEMERSAL FISH
⑥ MEGALOPLANKTON (LARGE ZOOPLANKTERS)
⑦ ZOOPLANKTON (E.G. CALANUS)
⑧ PHYTOPLANKTON
⑨ SMALL PELAGIC FISH (E.G. HERRING)
⑩ LARGE PELAGIC FISH (E.G. TUNA)
⑪ WHALES
⑫ MAN

Figure 12. Food relations in marine ecosystem. (Courtesy FAO. This chart was prepared by Dr. T. Laevastu and appeared in: FAO and WHO, "A Contribution to the UN Scientific Committee on the Effects of Atomic Radiation on the Specific Questions Concerned with the Oceanography and Marine Biology in Respect to the Disposal of Radioactive Waste," FAO/57/7/4725.)

The Food Web

Within the fertile areas of the ocean, there is a tremendous variety of animal life that ranges in size from the microscopic zooplankton to whales. Some of the animals spend their adult life fixed to the bottom of the seas while others range over entire oceans. And each animal has its own particular requirements for temperature, salinity, and food. The interrelationships among these animals, and between them and their environment, are very complex and, as yet, little understood. A schematic illustration of the interrelationships, greatly oversimplified, is shown in Figure 12.

It is shown, for example, that light energy and nutrient salts are necessary for the growth of phytoplankton and that the phytoplankton are a source of food for the zooplankton and the megaloplankton. These, in turn, are consumed by herring which then become a source of food for the larger predatory animals such as tuna. This is commonly described as the "food chain," each successively upward link which is made up of smaller numbers of animals of larger size. But the relationships are not really that neat and simple. Some of the largest animals of the sea, the blue whales, live on some of the smallest. Some fish, as young, consume larger animals than they do as fully grown adults. Some have wide ranges in tastes, consuming both small and large fish of a large number of species. And at different stages in their life cycles, they may be preyed upon or be predators. The term, "food web" is therefore more descriptive of the interrelationships in the marine ecosystem than the term "food chain."

In these relationships it is generally true that the total mass of the smaller plants and animals is greater than that of the larger animals. It takes, for example, "at least ten pounds of plankton to make a pound of whale or of herring." [2]

And it may take ten pounds of herring, more or less, to make a pound of tuna. This is because most of the food that is consumed is devoted to metabolic processes and only a little contributes to the growth of the animal. The feed efficiency (the weight gained relative to the amount of food consumed) varies widely among the animals of the sea and, even for specific animals, may vary widely

[2] Lionel A. Walford, *Living Resources of the Sea* (New York: The Ronald Press Co., 1958), p. 122.

according to the nature of the food, the conditions of the environment, and the age of the animal.

Simply for illustrative purposes, let us assume that there is a "food chain" from phytoplankton to tuna as described above and that the feed efficiencies at each link are 10 per cent. On these assumptions, one pound of tuna would require the consumption of ten pounds of herring, which would require consumption of 100 pounds of zooplankton, which would require consumption of 1,000 pounds of phytoplankton. Thus there would be a ratio of a thousand to one from the base to the top of the "chain." However, it must also be remembered that only a portion of each "link" may be consumed by each higher "link," the remainder dying of causes other than predation. It has been stated, for example, that "in the North Sea about 2 million tons (wet weight) of herring are based on from 50 to 60 million tons (wet weight) of zooplankton annually." [3] This is a ratio of 25 or 30 to 1 between consecutive links, rather than the 10 to 1 assumed above for feed efficiencies. Although there is certainly not enough information to derive such figures for most fishes, if any, at all periods of their life cycle and under all conditions, it is clear that the annual crop of the lower links must be considerable in order to support the higher links or the predatory fishes. For example if the ratio were 25 to 1 at successive links in the above "food chain," an annual production of 15,000 pounds of phytoplankton would support the growth of one pound of tuna; if the ratio were 30 to 1, then 27,000 pounds of plankton would support the growth of one pound of tuna. These figures are not even speculative, they are simply illustrative of the fact that man, by harvesting the larger animals of the sea is taking only a very small proportion of the protein that is produced annually in the form of plankton. It is this process of simultaneous production at many points in the web that has helped to create the popular image of the vastness of the ocean's food resource.

It is true that the "potential productivity" of the oceans is larger than today's harvest. But the idea that all of today's simultaneous growth and reproduction could be harnessed for human use is out of the question.

In the first place it fails to take account of the virtual absence of demand for plankton as a product. Further, it neglects the enormous costs of harvesting plankton in commercial quantities. Thus far—and probably for many decades to come—man finds it more at-

[3] *Ibid.,* p. 124.

tractive and economical to harvest the larger species that, directly or indirectly, have already filtered out the basic organic materials of the ocean.

In the second place, it should be pointed out that not even all of the larger species are utilized by man, and that not all of the areas of high fertility abound in the kinds of fish that are in demand. There are many fish labeled as "trash" fish, particularly by the Western nations, that are avoided by the fishermen or returned to the sea when caught. And the apparent fertility that leads to the growth of large quantities of fish in the "deep scattering layers" is presently useless as far as man's food supply is concerned. Thus the "vast richness" of the oceans is severely circumscribed by the tastes of man.

Finally, the idea of unlimited oceanic fertility results from a confusion between stocks and flows. The entire ecosystem or web that has been described is analogous to a stock of capital goods, working up, in stages, to a flow of raw materials. At each stage, production is taking place. Yet the capacity, or "potential productivity" of the entire process is not the sum of the pounds of goods produced at each stage, but merely the weight of the annual output at the final stage.

In the ecosystem, the stocks at each stage are like machines that take inputs of fish or plankton and produce food for the next stage. Thus, the potential output of the seas is the output of the last stage, which man takes as food. It is true that the system may be wasteful and could produce more food if some of the strands in the web were severed or short-circuited. But it is not true that man could simultaneously harvest the output of all stages steadily. If man found means and taste for using plankton, he would prevent some waste, and for a few years he could harvest the stocks in the web that would no longer be needed. But once these stocks were consumed, he would once again depend on a *flow*—this time of plankton instead of larger fish.

Potential Productivity

The game of estimating the potential productivity of the sea is dependent to a major extent upon the estimator's assumptions about the kinds of species that will make up the future commercial fishery. At one extreme, for example, it is possible to conceive of the ocean as a vast medium for the culture of phytoplankton. If this is considered to be an end product, with appropriate demand and supply characteristics, there is no question that the annual output of protein could be on the order of several billions of tons. At the other extreme, given the demand situation of today, the supply might not be much greater than at present. Herbert Graham and Robert Edwards have summarized several different approaches to the estimation of the potential output of commercial species.[4] Their first approach is based upon estimates of the potentially productive acreage and possible output per acre. The following table presents the results of various efforts to measure the catch per acre in some of the fishing grounds that have been subjected to a long history of intensive fishing effort.

Catch in pounds per acre per year

Location	Demersal	Pelagic	Total
Grand Banks	11.8	0.2	12.0
Nova Scotia	10.8	2.8	13.6
Gulf of Maine	12.7	4.7	17.4
Middle Atlantic	7.7	54.2	61.9
North Sea	10.0	16.6	26.6
Baltic	4.1	3.5	7.8
Barents Sea	15.7	0.8	16.5
Iceland Banks	29.0	5.3	34.3
Adriatic	2.5	2.1	4.6

From this range of estimates, Graham and Edwards have picked 20 pounds per acre as a conservative average for the output per acre of the continental shelves, which cover an area of about 6 billion acres. This leads to a total world production of about 120 billion pounds per year, or 55 million metric tons, which is an increase of about 20 per cent over 1963's catch. It assumes that the catch of pelagic fish, not associated with the continental shelves, will be negligible, and it assumes that the shelves will be uniformly productive in all areas of the world at a fairly low level. When they made their estimates, however, the fishery off the coast of Peru was still relatively small. It is now the largest in the world, producing over 350 pounds of fish per acre.

A second estimate of the potential world harvest of marine fishes

[4] Herbert W. Graham and Robert L. Edwards, "The World Biomass of Marine Fishes," Paper presented at the FAO International Conference on Fish in Nutrition, 1961 (Rome: FAO), mimeographed.

has been based upon knowledge of the primary organic production of the sea and its relation to the production of fish usable by man. The total net production of carbon is estimated to range from 12 to 15 billion tons per year. This is converted to the production of phytoplankton by multiplying by the factor of 37 (the proportion of carbon in the phytoplankton mass), leading to an estimate of about 500 billion tons of phytoplankton. On the assumption that this net production is fully harvested by the herbivores (zooplankton), and that the efficiency of use is 20 per cent, this means an annual production of 100 billion tons of herbivores. Assuming that the primary and secondary carnivores each have a feed efficiency of 10 per cent, then net output of the latter would be on the order of one billion metric tons of bony fishes.

A third approach, based upon the theoretical transfer of energy and the amount lost to production of organisms by being shunted to bottom deposits, leads to a figure of 343 million metric tons of secondary carnivore production annually. Since this includes such marine animals as squids, whales, and sharks, the net production of bony fishes might be two-thirds of that total, or about 230 million metric tons. It is further assumed that only about 50 per cent of this quantity can be harvested without jeopardizing the basic stocks and the ability of the resource to renew itself. Thus potential output by man, on this basis, might be 115 million metric tons. The authors point out, however, that this method and the foregoing one make no allowance for the degree of dispersion or concentration of the commercial species. In conclusion, they state that "it seems reasonable to suggest that although man has not yet fully exploited the marine fish resources it is not so vast as some have been led to believe."

Other estimates of the potential productivity of the oceans were made during the same conference at which the above paper was presented. G. Meseck, for example, in a careful analysis of the developments in each of the continents, felt that a world production of 70 million metric tons might be possible by 1980. On the other hand, certain participants referred to the remarkable growth in Peru's output. They felt that similar developments might occur with such presently little used species as saury and hake and that, as a result, total potential output of marine fish might be five or ten times what it is today.

The wide variations in estimates are due to differences in

assumptions about the kinds of species that will be demanded and also to different, but unexpressed anticipations of the costs of supply. The lower estimates refer to the current patterns of demand and they implicitly assume current techniques and cost structures. The figure of 60–70 million metric tons is thus an estimate of supply. The higher figures, to a greater or lesser extent, relax the constraints of demand and costs, and refer to potential physical output. While we cannot come up with a definitive picture of the future situation, we can, at least, draw two conclusions that are of significance for the future.

First, while the oceans may contain a vast and relatively untapped amount of organic life, the resources that are in demand are limited in number and are not found everywhere. This means that world competition will become more severe and will tend to be concentrated in certain areas of the ocean.

Second, the significant aspect of supply is the specific availability of certain kinds of fish. Where there is a high demand for a particular species, the pressure on the resource tends to lead to increased costs and higher prices. Consumers may then turn to other species in the market, or be willing to accept presently unutilized species of fish. This natural course of events provides a safety valve for the release of pressures on scarce resources. However, while the adjustment is taking place the participants in the industry are faced with many problems. And only foresight and continual co-operation can head off international controversies and facilitate the adjustment process.

Aquiculture

The total supply of fish can be increased by such means as extending fishing effort into little-used but productive areas, fishing more intensively in areas presently used, and creating a market for species for which there is little demand at present. In addition, efforts are being made to find ways of increasing the seas' primary productivity. For example, the U.S. National Academy of Sciences Committee on Oceanography, among others, has proposed that studies be made of the possibility of sinking a nuclear reactor which would warm up the deep ocean waters and create an artificial upwelling that would carry the mineral nutrients from the bottom to the euphotic zones where photosynthesis can take place.

Several other devices have the same purpose. Chains with giant fan blades lowered into the deep Florida current would create a turbulence similar to that of an enormous washing machine. Air pumped through perforated pipes in the bottom of the Gulf of St. Lawrence would raise the nutrients and also help to keep the area free from ice in the winter. The laboratory at the Woods Hole Oceanographic Institution is currently preparing a model of a natural pumping device that is activated by differential temperatures. A plain plastic pipe will be lowered into the cold bottom waters in a region where these deep waters are of relatively low salinity, and the bottom waters will be pumped slowly to the surface by mechanical means. As the waters rise through the pipe, they become warmer and their density decreases. Because of their low salinity, they tend to be more buoyant than surface waters of the same temperature. After the circulation is started, the mechanical pump can be removed, and the natural pumping action will continue through the pipe as long as the temperature and salinity differentials exist. Nutrient-rich bottom water can thus be raised to the surface with little initial effort.

Increases in primary productivity may also result from the application of nutrient salts. The vastness of the oceans and the natural dispersion of elements preclude fertilization on the high seas, but the habitat of estuarine and coastal fish is fertilized indirectly by nitrates and phosphates washed from agricultural land into the rivers and then the bays. Also, direct fertilization is possible within enclosed areas of the ocean. Experiments and practice in fresh water ponds have already indicated the potential increase in productivity from this practice. The Marine Research Foundation, Inc., of Edgartown, Massachusetts, is experimenting with several techniques that could be used to increase the oyster output of the brackish ponds of Martha's Vineyard. Oxygen deficiencies, due to winter and summer stratification of the water, can be relieved by artificial circulation or aeration. At the same time, the chemical nutrients at the bottom will be churned up, permitting the upper layer phytoplankton to make greater use of them. Salinity can be controlled in these ponds, and the direct addition of nitrate and phosphate fertilizers will add to their productivity. In addition to these methods, some of which are already practiced to a limited extent in various countries, attempts have been made to improve productivity by transplanting species into new areas. The Russians, for example, have attempted this for sturgeon and salmon. Such techniques, however, are more directly related to the product than to the primary productivity of organisms.

Aquiculture on the high seas presents some interesting problems for the law of the sea. If a nation invests in a technique such as a nuclear warming device, what right does that nation have to the artificially developed fishery? Do other nations have to abstain from fishing in this area; do they share in the catch, or the revenue from the catch, because they share rights to the common property of the oceans; or is the newly developed fishery up for grabs on a first-come, first-served basis? While it may be several years before the questions become real, it will facilitate the development and application of such techniques if equitable arrangements can be worked out beforehand.

Summary

The popular impression that the oceans are a vast reservoir of fish waiting to be seized and transported to starving peoples is far from reality. Productivity is far from uniform. Some areas are relatively sterile, while others are highly fertile. The coastal waters, within and just outside national boundaries, are highly productive, as are the fishing grounds of the continental shelves and the areas of upwelling in the northern and southern extremes of the oceans and along the western continental coasts. These regions, which are but a fraction of the total ocean area, make the greatest contribution to total production of living organisms. However, a very insignificant proportion of the total production is ultimately used by man.

The estimates of the oceans' future productivity range widely from about twice the present level of output to a billion metric tons, or more. The conservative figure, which is more an estimate of supply than of ultimate productivity, is based upon current average yields of fish for which there is an established demand. It makes no allowance for the development of techniques that would raise maximum sustainable yields, nor for the development of demands for different species. The liberal estimate, on the other hand, is based on physical and chemical rather than economic factors. The limiting factors are the production of carbon and the feed efficiencies of the various levels of animal life up to those of the second-stage carnivores. It is interesting to note under this

theory that ultimate productivity might be 10 billion metric tons
if it referred to first-stage carnivores, and 100 billion tons if it referred to herbivorous zooplankton. Thus it can be seen that the
total potential output of the oceans can be estimated at almost any
level, depending upon the various assumptions about kinds of
product and stages of technology.

Chapter 5

The Fishery Resource

ᖀ. ᖀ.

WHILE the productivity of the ocean is restricted by the lack of uniformly high fertility, the productivity of the fishery resource is even more restricted. It relates to only the very small proportion and very specific kind of total biological production that man harvests—primarily fish, and, to a small extent, marine mammals. Fish, however, is a heterogeneous product, and the demand is not for fish, as such, but for specific kinds of fish and fish products. This diffuse characteristic of heterogeneity applies equally well to the aspects of supply, because man has not a market for "fish" in general. Some commercial fish live on the bottom, others on the surface. Some live close to coasts, some far out. They vary as to size, location, concentration, method of catch, and other factors. Furthermore, they may intermingle during various stages of their life cycle and, generally, being free-swimming, they do not respect artificial boundaries. In some regions, man takes only one kind of fish, in other regions, only another kind of fish, and, thus, a region's "productivity of fish" is largely irrelevant to the actual supply. An examination of four of the methods and problems of classification may help in understanding the heterogeneity of the fishery resource, and indicate some of the difficulties involved in the establishment of international regimes.

The primary classification by the Food and Agriculture Organization of the United Nations is based upon *genetic relationships,* with some modifications. The classification, as presented in the

FAO *Yearbook of Fishery Statistics, 1962,* Vol. XV, is shown in Appendix A. Although the FAO categories are not entirely satisfactory from our point of view, they are the basis for most of the statistics on catch and, therefore, are used in the following chapters.

A broader system of breakdown of fish is based upon the *habitat* of the species. The pelagic fish are those that spend most of their life in the upper layers of the water and feed mainly on plankton or other pelagic fish. Demersal fish are those that spend most of their adult life close to the bottom, or on the bottom substrata, and feed mainly on benthic organisms. During adult life, their movement is generally restricted to continental shelves though they may migrate thousands of miles. The anadromous fish spend part of their life in salt water and migrate periodically for spawning purposes into fresh water. This breakdown, however, has the same difficulties as the one above. The anadromous salmon can be caught on the open seas in the same areas as pelagic species. In some areas, the same gear will take both demersal and pelagic fish.

It would be very useful if fishery resources could be divided up by *regions,* so that unified control could be facilitated. The advantage of a regional approach lies in the fact that as more stocks come to be intensively harvested, the ecological relationships between them become more significant. In a region, for example, the objectives for management of Stock A may conflict with those for Stock B. One species may be in a predator-prey relationship with the other, or they may both compete for the same food source or for similar niches in the habitat. Or it may be that the gear used by the fisherman will take both species indiscriminately. The increasing severity of these conflicts will require co-operative management and research that may be best accomplished under a regional authority. On the other hand, the wide range of some species, and the overlaps of marine ecosystems make the regional approach very difficult.

An instructive attempt at classifying "unit" regional fisheries is shown in Appendix B in the map and accompanying description of areas, resources, gear, fishing nations, and treaty arrangements. This classification was taken from a paper prepared by G. L. Kesteven and S. J. Holt for the International Technical Conference on the Conservation of the Living Resources of the Sea in 1955. It does not reflect some of the significant changes that have been made in following years, such as the entrance of the Russian and Japanese fishing fleets in the Northwest Atlantic and the development of Japanese and other tuna fisheries in the South Atlantic. Nor does it satisfactorily distinguish territorial waters from international waters. This legal distinction is becoming of critical importance as will be seen in Chapters 9 and 10. Pleading conservation objectives or economic need, many nations are extending their limits of exclusive fishing rights. But they are doing so in the almost total absence of knowledge about the fishery resources that lie in these waters. This is a vitally important area for scientific research if future decisions are to be made on a more rational basis.

From an economic point of view, a breakdown of the resource by *gear or size of investment* would be very valuable, but this is complicated by the wide variety of gear used for single species and by the use of variable-purpose vessels and labor. The characteristics of gear, capital, and labor will be described more fully in the following chapter on fishing effort.

It is clear that there is no neat, unique classification of the fishery resource. Besides the estimation of total supply, we are also interested in gauging the location and kinds of conflicts that may emerge from increasing international competition for the resource. In this latter respect, we will tend to focus (a) on the problems of coastal waters, and the extension of exclusive use rights by coastal states; (b) on old and new fishing grounds, where there may be problems of congestion or diminishing economic and physical productivity; and (c) on the pelagic species of the high seas.

Natural Aspects of Fish Populations

Several aspects of fish populations are of direct and immediate concern to the commercial fishing industry and have a bearing on international arrangements for the use of the seas. One of the most important of these is the density of the stock, since this is related to the vulnerability, or the ease of capture, of the species, and therefore to the supply costs. The natural fluctuations of population are also important, both in terms of the change in mortality rates and in terms of change in location or migratory movement of the stock. A third element of significance is the ecological relationships among different species. These will be described below before turning to the additional factor of mortality—the fisherman.

In recent years, the scientific knowledge of fish populations has been greatly advanced, but the difficulties of understanding animal movements in an opaque and fluid medium are tremendous. It is not surprising, therefore, that so much still remains unknown about fish and their environment and ecology. Because of this paucity of scientific knowledge, international arrangements and agreements must be flexible. They must be made to facilitate rather than to impede change.

DENSITY OF STOCKS

In general, the commercial fisherman is primarily interested in locating high concentrations of the stock that he is fishing, because the higher the density of the stock, the lower the effort and cost of capturing it. Density varies widely. At one extreme are the anadromous species that spawn in fresh water and that congregate seasonally in narrow straits or streams. Harvesting of such species is relatively simple and can be accomplished by placing a net across their migratory path. Salmon are particularly vulnerable to this form of capture, and shad, some herring, and many other species can also be taken easily in this manner. The seasonal congregation of fur seals on the breeding islands in the North Pacific is another example of high-density occurrence that facilitates harvest.

Other species of fish move in tight cohesive schools and can be captured by encircling gear. In some cases, the schooling fish are sought as food by other fish and serve as a concentrating force for a desired predator stock.

At the other extreme, some of the pelagic species, such as swordfish, occur in relatively diffuse patterns and over wide territories. Such fish must be valuable and large in bulk to justify a commercial fishery.

There is, therefore, a wide range in the natural patterns of concentrations of fish stocks. This occurs both between species and, for given species, at different places and different times.

POPULATION FLUCTUATIONS

Of considerable importance to the commercial fisherman is the natural fluctuation in size or location of the population. Mortality rates are not constant over time but vary widely in response to changes in the environment. A reduction in oxygen, or a change in the salinity or temperature can be particularly destructive at times when spawning takes place and the young have little resistance to change. In some cases the result of changes in the environment may not be mortality of the fish but a shift in the pattern of migration so that the stocks are difficult to find or are outside the range of the traditional fishing techniques. These and many other factors can affect fish catches and lead to abundance in one year and scarcity in the next, or even to long-term cyclical fluctuations. Such changes not only create considerable risk for the industry but also provide major complications for the job of management.

For the scientist, the challenge is one of understanding and predicting the changes that occur and, perhaps in the future, of controlling the changes. For the social scientist, the task is one of understanding the effects of these changes on the structure of the industry, from the harvesting stage through those of processing and distribution, and of devising systems that can adapt with the least cost to changes in the availability of the resource.

ECOLOGY

There are frequently close interrelationships among fish species occupying the same or overlapping regions. In some cases, one species may prey upon another, while in other cases, the different species may compete for the same food source. These interrelationships are of particular importance where fishermen focus most of their efforts on one or at most a few species. European and American fishermen have become adept at taking the species for which there is a high demand and leaving those for which the demand is low, the so-called trash fish. If this process of selection is efficient enough, it may be that the trash fish will replace the highly valued species in the ecosystem. Off the coast of California, intensive fishing for the Pacific sardines in the 1930's was at least a partial reason for the reduction in the population and the replacement in the same biological niche by anchovies. Unfortunately, there is very little scientific information about interrelationships among species. Lionel Walford points out that research is under pressure to focus on the commercially important species, thus ignoring the "many commercially worthless but biologically enormously effective predators and competitors." [1]

The interrelationships among species provide some of the more intractable problems of international agreements and arrange-

[1] Lionel A. Walford, *Living Resources of the Sea* (New York: The Ronald Press, 1958), p. 49.

ments. As more species come to be used and demanded and as more nations engage in fishing on the same grounds or in the same regions, the problems of agreement on regulations become more intricate and complicated. The fishermen of each nation bring with them a different set of incentives and costs. The wage-price structure of one nation may lead its fishermen to concentrate their efforts on one stock, while fishermen from other nations may desire a different stock and one that may be competitive or a predator or prey of the other. Even where the stocks may not be ecologically related, the harvesting techniques may interfere with each other. Indeed, the interference of gear has already become the subject of controversy on certain grounds. Such forms of congestion and competition will become more severe in the future. Conservation and management agreements must pay increasing attention to the external effects of the chosen measures and must become more regional and comprehensive in scope and less oriented towards specific species. This is discussed in more detail in Chapters 11 and 13 when we turn to present and future patterns of agreements, but it is useful to point out here that an international agreement that would take account of ecological relationships would pose many difficult analytical problems for the economists as well as the fishery scientists.

We have emphasized previously the economist's choice of the maximization of net economic revenue as the chief criterion for international arrangements. But in cases where the fishermen from different nations are fishing for ecologically related species, it becomes difficult to define a maximum net economic revenue for the region's fisheries. In some ways this is a familiar problem in cases where multiple use of a common resource base is attempted. But in other ways the problem is unique, because instead of dealing with a single uniform wage-price structure, it involves a variety of wage-price structures. Different prices, or values, may be placed upon the same commodity, and different costs applied to the same input. These differences may not be difficult to reconcile where the economies involved are similar, but they may be almost insuperable where such diverse economies as the Soviet, the Japanese, and those of the West may be focusing their efforts on the same species or on different but related species in the same region.

One of the early tasks for economic research should be a series of theoretical analyses of different situations, in order to develop guidelines for rational arrangements for the development of regional fisheries. This provides the basis for one of the research ideas suggested in the final chapter.

Extinction, Depletion, and Controls

We have pointed out above some of the natural conditions affecting fish stocks. We now turn to the effects of human predation, discussing first the negative aspects of extinction and depletion, and then the positive objective of achieving appropriate yields.

It was formerly believed that the living resources of the sea flowed from a cornucopia; that they were inexhaustible and could not be extinguished, no matter how heavily used. Even today, while most people recognize the finiteness of these resources, it is popular to speak of the vast and bountiful ocean as the source of tremendous quantities of food and materials. And yet, the increasingly frequent reports of conflict and congestion on fishing grounds seem to belie these popular beliefs.

These beliefs and the differences are important because they color the decisions that are being made on the law of the seas and on the management of its resources. We know, of course, that the resources are not infinitely available, but there is room for argument as to how vast or how scarce the resources are. Those who believe in the seas' great wealth tend to see no need for management and conservation programs. They believe that the resources are so vast that they can be shared by all to the detriment of none and that this is one reason why nothing need or should restrain the widest inclusive use of the oceans.[2] On the other hand, there are many who are so concerned about the apparent or real depletion of the fisheries off their coasts that, in their anxiety, they propose the extension of exclusive fishing rights in order to prevent the "foreigners" from harvesting the scarce supplies. Fears of depletion also frequently lead to the advocacy of "conservation" measures which, in effect, keep out the new and efficient producers and preserve the fishery for the "ins."

To be sure, not all those who fear depletion advocate such measures. There are more moderate ways of preventing depletion. But it is generally true that the first cries and the greatest pressures

[2] See Myres S. McDougal and William T. Burke, *The Public Order of the Oceans* (New Haven: Yale University Press, 1962), pp. vii–viii.

are for the appropriation of exclusive rights to the resource.

Our position lies somewhere in between. We cannot accept the view of the "cornucopians" that the resources are so vast that all can share without loss or increased cost, because we observe inefficiency, congestion, and conflict in the use of these resources. Furthermore, while we feel that total world demand can probably be met without difficulty, over the next decade at least, we anticipate that there will be problems within regions and between nations and that these problems will become increasingly severe.

EXTINCTION AND DEPLETION

As pointed out in Chapter 2, there is a tendency for a fish stock to become stabilized and for rates of mortality (including fishing by man) to come in balance with rates of reproduction. Under these equilibrium conditions, there is a sustainable yield from the fishery. The sustainable yields are low at *both* low and high rates of fishing. With low levels of fishing effort, the population is high and equilibrium is maintained by high natural mortality rates. Where high levels of effort are maintained, the yield is also low because the population has been reduced and recruits to the population are low. In between, at some level of effort there is a maximum yield that can be maintained over time. This is illustrated in Figure 1 of Chapter 2.

Depletion is a relative and imprecise term and one that is frequently invoked to support arguments for controls on a fishery. In some cases, depletion may be claimed because there is a decrease in the catch *per unit of effort*. Actually, this may simply reflect a large increase in the total number of fishermen and a sharing of the total catch by more producers. In other cases, fishermen may claim that a stock is depleted because there are decreases in the *total catch,* but sometimes such decreases are due to heavy natural mortalities or to shifts in migratory paths or seasons. Generally, however, it refers to a combination of *low total yield and low population levels*. This occurs after a more or less prolonged period during which rates of catch (combined with natural mortality) have been greater than the rates of recruitment to the stock. Both yield and population level are important. The economist is concerned with the yield because it is the source of revenue, and with the population because its density determines the cost of catching fish. The size of population may also affect the size and yield of neighboring, interdependent stocks.

Depletion, in the sense of applying effort beyond the point
where the maximum sustainable yield is attained, is the typical
consequence of unrestrained use of common property resources.
This is not true of fisheries where supply costs are high and/or
demand is low (the shark fishery for example). For most exploited
fisheries, however, the supply costs and demand are such that depletion has taken effect, and that higher sustainable yields could
be attained with less application of fishing effort.

To understand how a fishery becomes exploited to the point of
depletion, it is necessary to relax the assumptions of equilibrium
that we have used above and to point out the dynamic factors that
change the conditions of the fishery over time. Simple supply and
demand curves can be used to illustrate the economic forces that
are at work (see Figure 13). With a newly developing fishery, the
supply curve will be relatively far to the right, assuming, for the
moment, that its position is chiefly explainable by the density of

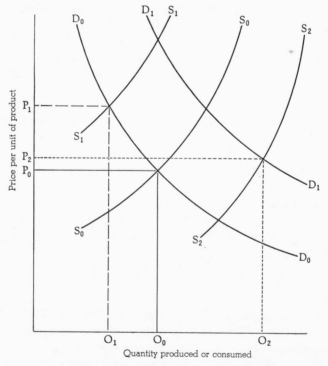

Figure 13. Effect of changing density, technology, and demand on output levels.

the population of the species. As output levels increase, they eventually begin to have an effect upon the density of the population, making it more difficult and more costly to catch the fish. The supply curve then shifts upward and to the left—from S_0S_0 to S_1S_1. With the demand curve at D_0D_0, the output level will drop to O_1 from O_0, and the new "equilibrium" price will be at P_1. This process continues until the quantity produced (annual yield) is small enough to allow the population to remain constant. This typical movement is the basis for the belief that is held by some that a species cannot be extinguished. That is, the density of the stock has decreased; the cost of catching the fish has increased; this, in turn, leads to a higher price to the consumers; and with the high price, consumption decreases, thereby relieving the pressure on the stock.

This simple relationship, however, neglects two important changes that are generally occurring and that affect both the supply and demand curves. First, the position of the supply curve is set not by density alone, but also by the costs of all factors of production. Technological innovation can operate to shift the supply curve downwards and to the right, to a position S_2S_2, for example, thereby reducing price levels and inducing increased consumption and output levels. At the same time, the demand for the product can increase, in response to increases in population, in income levels, to changing tastes, etc. As this occurs, the demand curve will shift outwards and upwards, perhaps to a position D_1D_1 where output will be at point O_2. In other words, the developing technology and the higher demand can make it economical to fish lower densities of the stock.

This path of exploitation, which is usual for a fishery, resembles in many respects the path of exploitation of a nonrenewable resource.[3] The reproductive capacity, which represents the renewing element, becomes diminished with the decrease in population. And while the stock can be renewed if the use of the fishery is restrained, there is no incentive on the part of the individual pro-

[3] A further point of resemblance is that the decreased density of the stock is much the same as the decreased grade of mineral ores. With higher incentives and improved technology, the mineral producer can "catch" the same amount of metal from much larger bodies of raw material. Examples are the shift to taconites and to low-grade copper mines. However, while there appear to be extremely low densities to which the mineral producer can turn (the minerals in sea water, for example) the limit of a fish stock is not so distant.

ducers to restrain their use. Thus reproductive capacity can conceivably be reduced to zero if a demand increases along with technological capability. A zero reproductive capacity may not be represented only by the last male and female. Decreased population, for example, also increases vulnerability of the stock to disease and natural predators. This is particularly true of schooling fish. Therefore it may be that the threshold for survival [4] of a species may be made up of a relatively large number of individuals. In short, the truism that a stock can never be extinguished because it costs too much to catch the remaining individuals, is of doubtful validity.

CONTROLS

The possibility of extinction, however, may be academic because man generally responds to decreases in catch per unit of effort by adopting measures designed to prevent the further depletion of the stock. Some of these measures strive to protect the reproductive potential by establishing nursery areas in which fishing is prohibited or by preventing the taking of fish that have not reached the age of reproduction. Generally speaking, however, the stated objective of the measures is to regulate catching so as to achieve the maximum physical yield that can be maintained indefinitely. Whatever regulatory regime is selected, it means an initial reduction in the level of catch in order to permit the stock to replenish itself.

The amount of catch is a function of the number of fish in the population, the effectiveness of the gear that is used, and the amount of effort that is applied. Controls are established either on gear or on effort.[5] Examples of the former are the prohibition of salmon traps and regulations on the size of mesh in the nets. Controls on effort take the form of either a quota on the catch or a limitation on the length of the season.

Effort, which is the product of the number of fishermen (or vessels) and the amount of time worked, is conventionally expressed in terms of "fisherman-days" or, with more refinement, "standard vessel-days." Where seasonal limits are established, the amount of time worked is subjected to control, but no limits are

[4] See S. V. Ciriacy-Wantrup, *Resource Conservation—Economics and Policies* (Berkeley and Los Angeles: University of California Press, 1952) on "irreversibility" and a "safe minimum standard," chapter 18.

[5] See R. Hamlisch, ed., *The Economic Effects of Fishery Regulations* (Rome: FAO, 1962).

placed on the number of fishermen or vessels. Quota controls, by reducing permissible catch, imply a reduction in effort but nothing is said about which component of effort is to be reduced. The likely response of the industry, as illustrated by the Pacific halibut agreement mentioned in Chapter 2, is to reduce the season while maintaining the number of vessels and men. From an economic point of view, it is preferable to limit the number of producers rather than the length of the season. But this form of regulation, for various reasons, has never been instituted in international agreements.[6]

One other form of control has recently been proposed. Under this system, which is based upon the theory of eumetric yield, as developed by R. J. H. Beverton and S. J. Holt,[7] the amount of effort is permitted to increase. Depletion is prevented by increasing the size of mesh that is used in the nets so that only the larger and older fish are taken and the younger and smaller ones escape. Although natural mortality will reduce the number of individuals in successively older year classes, there is assumed to be a net gain in *total pounds* because of rapid growth rates of the individuals. There may, for example, be fewer six-year-old fish than five-year-old fish in the population (assuming stable birth rates), but the total weight of all six-year-olds will be greater than the total weight of all five-year olds. If, by increasing the mesh size, the five-year-olds are permitted to escape and only six-year-old and older fish are harvested, the yield, in terms of pounds of fish that can be sustained indefinitely, may be higher. For example, if a certain fishery makes use of a net with a mesh size that takes five-year-old and older fish, the maximum *number of pounds* of fish that can be caught each year over an indefinite period may be at the point where *20 per cent* of all individuals five years and older are taken. But if the mesh size is enlarged to permit the five-year-olds to escape, then the maximum sustainable number of pounds caught may be *larger* and, at the same time, permit the taking of *30 per cent* of the individuals that are six years and older.

The significance of this theory is that increased intensity of fish-

[6] The Fur Seal Treaty may be considered an exception, although the controls were not specifically established to reduce the number of producers. This treaty vested exclusive use rights in the hands of the nations that owned the breeding grounds of the seals—Russia and the United States—and these nations have managed the fishery as if they were sole owners, although profits have been split with the Canadians and the Japanese.

[7] See R. J. H. Beverton and S. J. Holt, "The Theory of Fishing," in *Sea Fisheries,* ed. M. Graham (London: Edward Arnold, Ltd., 1956).

ing effort does not necessarily mean reduction in the sustainable yield. This theory, however, applies to only a few species of fish. It may be inapplicable because of different patterns of behavior and different growth rates, or it may be irrelevant because there is a specific demand for smaller size fish. Furthermore, in actual practice, it may be difficult to achieve the required changes in nets or to anticipate the intensity of effort.

While this eumetric form of control, unlike the others that have actually been adopted, makes specific allowance for changes in effort, it nevertheless fails to satisfy the economists' desire for economic efficiency. Because entry is still free, there will still be excessive use of vessels and men and low returns per unit of input. Total costs and revenues will tend to become equal and economic rent will be dissipated. Only if effort is restricted by limiting the number of producers can the economic efficiency be improved.

Summary

There appear to be two views of the fishery resource that are currently prevalent. One is the long-range view that ignores the economic elements of supply and demand and looks upon the ocean as a vast reservoir of undifferentiated protein material. Those who hold this view tend to bemoan the size of the present catch and advocate large investments in research to facilitate greater output from this "underutilized" resource. Because they see great potential output that can be shared by all, they do not regard the problems of competition and international conflict as being of very great significance for the future.

The other view, and the one we share, is that the fishery resource is not undifferentiated but is a heterogeneous resource varying widely in size, in location and depth, in density of population, and ease of capture. No single species is inexhaustible nor is it free from the possibility of depletion. The economic forces that dictate the intensity of fishing effort are concentrated on single species or groups of species, and it is here that competition induces conflict and international tension.

Chapter 6

The Fishing Process

స. స.

THE steps that lie between fish in the water and fish products in the home are basically the same today as they were in the days of the earliest fishermen. Fish must still be located, caught, transported, and processed. The search is still of prime importance. Hooks and nets are still used for catching, and the industry is still dependent upon surface vessels and boats.

However, even though the basic steps remain, many refinements have taken place. Diesel engines, power blocks, nylon nets, and refrigeration are only a few of the many innovations that have led to significant increases in catching power and in the preservation and distribution of fish. In the last fifteen or twenty years, the pace of technological development has increased rapidly, spurred on by the technical knowledge gained during the Second World War, and supported by governmental research. Some of these innovations, while reducing the cost of catching fish from a given population, also tend to reduce the size of the population and to lead to depletion of stocks that are already fully exploited. Other innovations extend the range of fishing effort so that local fishermen find themselves more and more in competition with those from far-distant nations. Such changes tend to aggravate the conflicts and difficulties that are presently being experienced in the exploitation of marine fisheries.

In the following pages, the basic elements of the fishing process are discussed in more detail, with special emphasis given to the trends that are apparent. These trends, together with some possibilities of new technological innovations, indicate that there will be a greater and more pressing need for the development of regimes and arrangements that will facilitate a rational utilization of international fisheries.

Locating the Fish

The surface of the sea reveals little of the depth or environment of the fish. They must be sought blindly, or attracted, and they must be in sufficient concentrations to permit efficient use of gear.

There are two aspects to this search. The first is the location of the general areas of potential productivity, and the second is the specific location of the fish. As to the former, the coastal waters of the world's continents hold relatively few secrets, since they have been subjected to local fishing efforts for centuries. Most of the world's major fishing grounds are equally well known. Those of the North Atlantic and North Pacific waters have long since been discovered as a result of the explorations of early commercial fishermen. The fishing grounds of the Southern Hemisphere, while relatively untouched commercially, have been located by scientific studies. Much less is known, however, about the location and distribution of the high seas pelagic fisheries, and considerable efforts are being invested by national governments in the search for these species. On the whole, it is unlikely that any new areas of high potential fertility will be discovered.

But this is only one aspect of the search. Of more significance to the commercial fishermen is the ability to surround a school or locate a stock of fish with reasonable exactitude. The differences in behavior among species leads to different requirements in this respect. Anadromous species can be easily located during their seasonal runs. For some pelagic species there are various clues that facilitate finding. The feeding of flocks of gulls on small fish indicates the presence of large carnivorous species. Whales and swordfish give evidence of their presence by surfacing. For most demersal species, however, few clues are available, and they are located by trial and error. Since the war, the development of various techniques have refined some aspects of the search. Echo sounders, which were developed to locate submarines, have been found very useful in finding schools of fish, as well as in depicting the topography of the ocean floor. The readings of the shadows on the screen can sometimes identify the species as well as its depth, location, and density. Light airplanes are now in use along the coastal waters of the United States. The pilots are able to spot the schools by watching for surface activity or by noticing deeper shades of color in the water. Their reports are passed by radio to the catching vessels. More traditionally, fishermen find schools by simply observing the activities of other vessels within their view.

As an alternative to searching for the fish, there is the technique of attracting the fish to a specific location. Bait placed in traps is the usual method for catching crabs and lobsters. Both demersal and pelagic fish are frequently caught by baited hooks that are attached to long lines. Bait can also be used without hooks in order to draw fish into a certain area, where they may be caught by net or bare hook. Newer techniques for attracting fish, which are described more fully below, include the use of jack lights and the construction of artificial reefs. These serve to concentrate, as well as attract the fish, and they achieve the same purpose as the primitive technique of driving fish into fixed traps and nets.

Catching the Fish

There is considerable variety in the kinds of gear that are used to take the fish. Some forms are designed for a particular species, such as harpoons for whales and traps for salmon; others, such as otter trawls and gill nets, are used to catch a large number of different species. Certain kinds of gear can be used at varying depths, others only at the surface or at the bottom. Some forms are stationary and others mobile. An indication of the variety can be found in the classification of gear in the United States (see p. 90). A few of the more important forms are briefly described below.

Purse seines are an encircling type of gear that is mainly used to concentrate schools of pelagic fish. In the United States this device accounted for more than half of the total domestic catch in 1959. It is used both for menhaden, caught for industrial purposes by relatively small vessels operating in coastal waters, and for tuna, caught by large (180-foot) tuna clippers in waters far beyond territorial seas. The net, the top of which is floating on the surface, is drawn around the school of fish. When the circle is completed, the bottom is drawn together, or pursed, and the diameter of the circle

Commercial Fishing Gear in the United States ª

Encircling or Encompassing: Seines (haul, stop, purse); lampara; bag nets, trawls (beam, otter).

Entrapment: Weirs, pound and trap nets, hoop nets, fyke nets, pots and traps, slat traps.

Entanglement: Gill nets (anchor, drift, semi-drift, runaround, stake, bar nets, rip rap nets), trammel nets.

Lines: Hand, troll, long or set with hooks, trot with baits, snag.

Scooping: Dip nets, lift nets, reef nets, push nets, cast nets, wheels.

Impaling or Wounding: Harpoons, spears.

Shellfish: Scrapes, dredges, tongs and oyster grabs, rakes, hoes and forks, shovels, picks, crowfoot bars.

Miscellaneous: Frog grabs; brush traps; hooks (sponge, other); diving outfits; by hand.

ª *Source:* William H. Dumont and G. T. Sundstrom, *Commercial Fishing Gear of the United States,* Fish and Wildlife Circular 109 (Washington: U.S. Fish and Wildlife Service, 1961).

is decreased. The fish are concentrated in a tight body, and hoisted up in scoop nets. The use of these purse seines for tuna was started in the 1920's, but the recent development of light, strong nylon cord and power blocks has led to a much wider use by the industry.

Trawls also account for a large percentage of world total catch. They made up about a third of Japanese marine catch in 1960 and about two-thirds of the West German catch, and are the chief gear used in the North Sea. They are bag- or funnel-shaped nets, which are drawn across the ocean bottom and used for catching demersal species of fish. The fish are concentrated in the cod-end—the bag at the end of the trawl. This is usually raised on board the vessel over the side and opened to release the catch. The cod-end can vary in mesh size in order to permit the escapement of fish below a certain size. A recent development is the use of stern trawlers which permit the net to be hauled directly up an open ramp at the stern of the vessel, thereby facilitating handling, and allowing also for a direct drag from the stern. Some trawls are capable of taking as many as 25,000 pounds of fish in a single tow. Cod, haddock, ocean perch, scallops, and shrimp are some of the many kinds of fish taken by trawlers.

Lines range from those that are used by hand or dropped or trolled over the side of the vessel to those that extend for several hundred feet and are set to anchors or floats. Salmon and tuna are frequently taken by hand lines. In the latter case, the vessel may troll a baited line until a strike indicates the presence of a school. Chum (small live fish) are then released to attract and concentrate the school, which feeds with frenzied activity. The fish strike readily at unbaited barbless hooks which are attached to short lines and to stout poles. The fishermen simply heave the fish on board. Tuna and other fish are also taken by long-lines to which are attached a series of baited hooks on short lines. For halibut, the lines (frequently of stainless steel wire and up to 1,200 feet in length) are usually anchored to the bottom. Lines do not permit as much control over the size of fish taken as do some nets.

Gill nets can be fished at the surface or at the bottom and are used for a wide variety of species. The fish are trapped in these nets somewhere behind their heads. They cannot go forward because of the size of their bodies. And they are kept from going backwards by their scales, spines, or gill covers.

Traps are usually fixed to the bottom, although in shallow water they can extend from the bottom to the surface and, in some cases, are floated from the surface. They usually have funnel entrances which make entrance easy and escape difficult. Trap nets are used for anadromous species at the mouths of spawning streams—a practice that is currently illegal in some parts of the United States. They are also placed in shallow coastal waters at the end of a header which crosses migratory paths and may extend a mile off the shore. Pots, usually of wooden or wire mesh construction and baited, are used for crustaceans, eels, and other species closely associated with the bottom.

Dredges, scrapes, rakes, and *tongs* are designed to collect the sedentary shellfish that live in or on the bottom of shallow waters. These can be drawn from moving boats, or operated from stationary boats or even by fishermen wading in the water. Modern refinements include hydraulic and suction dredges.

Harpoons have long been used by the whaling industry for the taking of individual animals. They are also used to capture swordfish and other fish in areas where reefs impede the use of nets or traps.

This brief account cannot give full recognition to the immense variety of devices used to take fish, nor does it provide much indication of the differences in technique between primitive and developed fisheries. There are no statistics by which the relative importance of these devices can be measured on a world basis, although statistics are available for certain countries. Table 10 shows catch by gear in the United States in 1959.

Table 10. U.S. Catch by Gear, 1959

Gear	Quantity [a] (Mil. lb.)	Value ($Mil.)	Quantity as % of total	Value as % of total
Purse seines	2,622	52.3	51	15
Otter trawls	1,182	104.6	23	30
Lines	383	56.3	7	16
Gill nets	190	25.9	4	7
Pots and traps	168	28.0	3	8
Dredges	109	37.6	2	11
All other	468	41.4	9	12
Totals	5,122	346.1	100	100

[a] Live weight.

Source: U.S. Bureau of Commercial Fisheries, *Fisheries Statistics of the United States, 1959* (Washington: U.S. Government Printing Office, 1961).

The six forms of gear listed in the table above accounted for 90 per cent of the quantity and 87 per cent of the value of total U.S. catch. Purse seines and otter trawls, which do not include other kinds of seines and trawls, alone accounted for almost three-fourths of the volume. The relative importance of purse seines is high in terms of quantity and low in terms of value because most of the purse seine catch is menhaden with a low unit value. The reverse situation holds for pots, traps, and dredges, which take shellfish of high unit value.

In Japan, of the marine fisheries catch in 1960, 29 per cent could be identified as obtained by otter and other trawls, 16 per cent by purse seines, and 13 per cent by line. These three forms of gear are probably at least as important for each of the major producing countries except Mainland China and India, which obtain large amounts of fish from inland waters.

Transporting and Processing Fish

The rapid deterioration of fish means that fishing vessels are either restricted to voyages of short duration or must process their catch on board.

Although most of the world's fish are still caught within coastal waters, a growing proportion are coming from fishing grounds and areas that lie many days' distance from home ports. These distant water fisheries have required considerable changes in the size and kinds of vessels. Catching vessels are not only getting larger and more powerful, but they are also being accompanied by factory and mother ships that provide processing facilities and services on the fishing grounds. Some indications of the size and power of fishing vessels can be shown by a few statistics. In Japan, between 1948 and 1960, the *number* of fishing craft dropped by 15 per cent, but total *tonnage* rose 43 per cent and total *horsepower* by 92 per cent. In Russia, between 1948 and 1956 (the latest year for which figures are available), the total number of *all craft* increased by 36 per cent, but the total number of *powered craft* and their *horsepower* both increased by 300 per cent.

The European and North American countries have not experienced such dramatic changes, partially because their vessels were already relatively large and high powered before the war. Total United States tonnage rose 30 per cent between 1948 and 1959. The number of Norwegian vessels over 70 feet in length increased 60 per cent, while those under 70 feet showed a slight decline between 1938 and 1960. Over the same period, the tonnage of first-class vessels in England and Wales rose by a little over a half.

These increases generally refer to large, steel-hulled vessels that are capable of spending several weeks or more at sea. Most of them are purse seiners or trawlers and some are equipped with devices for freezing or processing their catch immediately. They are competing for herring and tuna, and for the demersal species on the major fishing grounds.

In the lower-income countries, the shifts have been mostly toward the use of power rather than toward the use of larger craft. Many of these countries are making strong efforts to substitute small motors for hand and wind power. In Peru, the number of motorboats increased five and a half times between 1948 and 1960. During the same period, powered craft in the Philippines rose almost four times while non-powered craft increased only 80 per cent. The shift toward larger vessels in the Philippines is indicated by the fact that total tonnage increased more than six times. Pakistan had one powered trawler in 1953 and 87 by 1960. The number of other powered boats jumped from 23 to 257. Ceylon, which had no powered craft at all in 1958, had 726 in 1960, accounting for 4 per cent of total fishing craft. In Thailand, powered craft made up 5 per cent of the total in 1948 and 71 per cent of the total in 1959.

For the most part, these changes indicate more intensive use of the fish supplies of the coastal waters of these countries. Peruvian efforts, for example, are almost entirely focused on the anchovetas close to their shores. Although some of the increases may be due to rehabilitation of the war-damaged fishing industries, the major proportion represents a bona fide increase and one that has been stimulated largely by the efforts of the Food and Agriculture Organization of the United Nations and other foreign aid organizations.

Most of the major fishing nations, besides increasing the power and size of their ocean-going vessels, are also turning toward the other methods for overcoming the problems of distance and perishability. The first fishermen who traveled long distances were those who worked the Newfoundland coasts in the early 1500's. From that time until the development of refrigeration devices following the First World War, fishermen depended mostly upon salt to preserve their catch. Freezing on vessels on the high seas became of importance following the Second World War and has been of rapidly growing significance in recent years. Freezer trawlers and freezing tanks on tuna boats are becoming commonplace for distant-water fishermen.

Further developments along these lines have led to the recent introduction of factory ships that are equipped to reduce fish to fish meal and oil as well as to clean, fillet, freeze, and package fish for human consumption. A factory ship may catch fish itself or operate with catcher vessels. It may serve a whole fleet that remains on the grounds throughout the season, as does the *M/S Vitus Bering*, one of four fish carriers and motherships recently built in Danish shipyards for the Russian industry. This vessel has a dead weight of about 2,600 tons, is almost 300 feet long, and is reputed to have a loaded speed of 14 knots. It carries a crew and a factory staff of 102 men. It is equipped with a controllable pitch propeller, which gives increased efficiency at towing as well as running speeds, and it also carries a small propeller attached to the rudder, thus permitting it to maneuver, even when making no headway. The catch, mostly cod, can be loaded either directly from the catching vessels, or from trawl bags which the catching vessels have filled with fish and left floating in the sea. The trawl bags, a new development, may be marked with buoys or with radar reflectors to facilitate their finding. The catch is sorted on deck, with irregular fish going directly into a raw product bunker to be automatically processed into fish meal, and the rest of the fish being cleaned and beheaded and automatically frozen and packaged.

Another technique for facilitating the handling and processing of fish is the establishment of bases close to fishing grounds. These bases serve the fishing vessels and process their catch. They are of particular importance to the Japanese who have extended their fishing operations many thousands of miles away from their homeland. Japan has established bases in the South Pacific (Fiji Islands, New Caledonia, etc.), in Malaysia, Burma, and Ceylon, on the coasts of Africa, and South America, and in the Caribbean (see Figure 23 in Chapter 7). Typically, these bases involve joint investment in processing plants by Japan and the host country and include the use of Japanese vessels and crews. The products, mostly frozen or canned tuna but also including bottomfish, shrimp, and some other species, are generally shipped directly to the importing country.

Two trends of considerable significance for future economic and political arrangements are worthy of some emphasis. The first of these is the increasing utilization and development of fleet operations, largely by the Russians and the Japanese. The different steps of the fishing process are being separated so that some vessels are used primarily for catching, some primarily for processing, and some for transporting the processed commodities back to port and returning with fuel and materials for the fleet. In some cases, there are vessels whose primary function is to provide salvage and engineering services, hospital facilities, and even entertainment for the fishermen. With such support, the fleet can remain on the grounds throughout the season, while other distant-water vessels, operating by themselves, must spend a large part of their time traveling back and forth from port to ground. In addition, fleets of vessels under unified control achieve certain economies of scale in the processes of locating and catching the fish. Acting in concert, the vessels of the fleet can "sweep" large areas with either fish-finding devices or with nets.

The second significant trend is the world-wide extension of effort. This is partly facilitated by fleet-type operations, although it is also accomplished by the use of large vessels equipped for both catching and processing. One result of distant-water operations and of self-sufficient fishing fleets is to make coastal fishermen fully, and sometimes painfully, aware that waters they have traditionally considered to be their own are, in fact, the common property of the world community.

Fish Cultivation

The mobility of fish makes their cultivation extremely difficult and, for certain species, perhaps impossible. For example, it is difficult to conceive of management and control of the tuna's environment and habitat which may extend over several thousand square miles. However, other fish, less widely traveled, are more amenable to cultural practices, and certain attempts along these lines have been made for centuries.

Molluscs are the most sedentary of water animals. Most species of molluscs are either fixed firmly to the bottom of the oceans or capable of only limited movement. The culture of oysters began at least 2,000 years ago when Sergius Orata established artificial oyster beds in the Lucrine Lake on the Italian coast. The techniques developed in those days are still practiced. In France, brackish ponds are created by dyking, and baby oysters are collected and grown on roofing tile and other materials. In Japan, cultch (the material to which baby oysters attach themselves) is suspended from rafts which are placed in favorable environments. In the United States, in the waters of Long Island Sound, the beds are cleaned and planted with cultch, attempts are made to control predators, and seed oysters are transplanted from breeding grounds to growing bars or storage beds. This practice is made possible not only by the sedentary nature of oysters but also by the ability to obtain exclusive use rights to the beds.

Anadromous fish also lend themselves to a form of cultivation during that part of their life cycle which takes them into fresh water. Part of this has been through the construction of fish ladders to overcome the obstacles to upstream migration caused by dams. More significantly, attempts have been made to raise salmon fry in the artificial environment of hatcheries and to establish runs from streams free of obstructions.

Besides the cultivation of species that are sedentary or anadromous there is the widespread practice of fish culture in small, enclosed bodies of water, both fresh and brackish. In certain countries, such as Israel, India, Indonesia, and Thailand, the production of freshwater fish from artificial ponds and rice paddies represents a significant proportion of total fish catch. In some areas, the techniques for raising the fish, usually carp, are quite refined. The artificial ponds may be in series, in order to make full use of fertility in outflows. Drainage of a pond is followed by the introduction of a small amount of water which permits rapid growth of vegetation and zooplankton. After a few days the pond is filled and fish fry are introduced. Fertilization of the water and feeding of the fish increase the rate of growth. When the fish are of marketable size, the pond is drained and the fish are harvested and the cycle started anew. In Southeastern Asia and Japan, the output of fish is combined with the output of rice in the irrigated paddies. And in some areas, fish are harvested from oxidation ponds, which are a final stage in some water treatment systems. Within the United States and some of the European countries, trout are also raised in artificial ponds, but the requirements of trout are much more severe than those of carp and the costs are commensurately high. They are raised either for the luxury food market or for release into sports fishing waters.

Undoubtedly there are opportunities for increasing the protein output in low-income countries by the cultivation of fresh and brackish ponds. The degree to which these opportunities are taken up depends upon the structure of the demand for protein in this form and upon the costs involved in producing it.

New Developments in the Fishing Process

One of the major difficulties in estimating the future supply of fish lies in the rapidity with which technological innovations are being developed and adopted. These innovations can have significant effects upon the costs involved in the fishing process as well as upon the size of the population and the yield. Some of the techniques that are just beginning to be used and some that have been suggested for use in the future are described below.

LOCATING TECHNIQUES

The international competition for fish is matched in intensity by the international efforts to gain knowledge about the oceans. The U.S. National Academy of Sciences Committee on Oceanography, in reference to its research recommendations, has stated that *"action on a scale appreciably less than that recommended will jeopardize the position of oceanography in the United States relative to the position of the science in other major nations, thereby accentuating serious military and political dangers, and placing the nation at a disadvantage in the future use of the resources of the sea."* [1]

The dangers of submarine warfare together with the desire to appropriate as great a share as possible of ocean resources explain the recent mobilization of research efforts in oceanography. Most of the emphasis has been given to the problems of submarine warfare, but the resultant research also carries benefits for commercial fishermen. The studies on topography and on ocean and wind currents and temperatures help to provide basic knowledge about the environment of fish. Some of the tools and techniques developed for these studies can also be used for direct research on marine biology and ecology, just as the echo sounders perfected in the Second World War for locating submarines are now extensively used for locating fish. Oceanographic research vessels are being used to study salinities, plankton, and other ecological factors as well as currents and the physiography of the ocean bottom. The U.S. Atomic Energy Commission, in analyzing the effects of the dumping of radioactive wastes in the oceans, is making significant contributions to the knowledge of deep-water currents, stratifications of layers of different salinities, temperature differences, etc. The American Geographical Society has undertaken the preparation of a mammoth Serial Atlas of the Marine Environment for the whole North Atlantic from the equator to the north pole and from the ocean bottom to the surface. This may facilitate forecasting the presence and migratory paths of plankton, and therefore, of fish associated with the plankton. Some of the recently developed equipment used in these studies include surface and deep-water buoys that automatically make continuous measurements and report these to surface vessels by radio when the information is requested; deep-water, manned vessels such as the *Aluminaut* which travel at depths of 15,000 feet and which are equipped with sonar, underwater television, and robot hands; sea sleds that can be

---

[1] National Academy of Sciences—National Research Council, *Oceanography 1960 to 1970*, A Report by the Committee on Oceanography, Volume 1, "Introduction and Summary of Recommendations," Washington, D.C., 1959, p. 2. (Italics in original.)

towed behind vessels at different depths and which will carry television cameras; and many others. The advances in the basic knowledge of the seas will undoubtedly be of value to future fishermen in their search for the general location of productive areas.

Technological developments are also occurring in the search for the specific locations of schools of fish, or good fishing grounds. Echo sounders are being perfected so that they can cover wider areas in a horizontal field as well as reach greater depths. The Russians are reportedly using helicopters which drag waterproof sonar devices beneath the surface.[2] Radio direction finders and Loran devices permit great precision in fixing the location of fishing vessels and facilitate the navigational aspects of the search even in overcast or foggy weather.

ATTRACTING TECHNIQUES

Some of the more significant developments are occurring in the field of attracting fish. The use of light, practiced by primitive cultures, is being brought up to date by the Russians in the Caspian Sea, where it is reported that over 170,000 tons of kilka (a small schooling anchovy-like fish) were caught in 1959 by the light-pump technique.[3]

Looking further into the future, there appear to be possibilities of attracting fish by the use of electric currents, or by sounds, scents, and even, perhaps, tastes. Experiments with electric currents have indicated that certain species of fish respond by turning in the direction of the current and swimming towards the anode where, presumably, they can be gathered by suction pumps. However, the area of influence is small and requires considerable electric power, particularly in salt water which has a lower conductivity than fresh.

2 Our discussion of new developments is partially based upon *Conquest of the Sea,* by Cord Christian Troebst (New York: Harper and Row, 1962). See also Hawthorne Daniel and Francis Minot, *The Inexhaustible Sea* (New York: Collier Books, 1961) and Lionel Walford, *Living Resources of the Sea* (New York: The Ronald Press Co., 1958).

3 See J. L. Kask, "Russia: Advanced Ocean Fishing Country," *Fishing News International,* Vol. 1, No. 3 (London: Arthur J. Heighway Publications Ltd., April, 1962), pp. 9–15. Kask describes the methods of a modern fishing refrigeration vessel. After the fish have been located with a sonic depth finder, electric lights and a hose that is attached to an electric pump on deck are lowered. Fish are attracted by the light to the funnel of the hose and then pumped up into a hopper on deck. Under good conditions it is claimed that 3 tons per hour can be taken in this way.

The homing instinct of salmon, which leads them through thousands of miles of salt and fresh water to their spawning grounds far upstream, is under study. Experiments indicate that the salmon are able to distinguish, through taste and scent, extremely small variations in the chemical content of the water. If this could be understood and controlled, the migrating patterns could be managed. It is also known that fish emit sounds and that different sounds may have different meanings. Here, too, there are possibilities for management, although certainly not in the near future.

Artificial habitats are also used to attract fish. This method has been used with some success in U.S. sports fisheries. Old automobile bodies, linked together by chains, have been dumped in shallow waters off the Gulf Coast. By providing shelter and protection from predators, they attract large concentrations of fish. Jacques-Yves Cousteau has designed concrete apartment buildings to facilitate his studies of fish ecology. These shelters are to be located off the coast of Monaco in depths of 100 to 400 feet. Different floors will be equipped for different species, the buildings will be connected by illuminated "roads" to attract the fish, and chemical nutrients will be provided to increase food supply.

CATCHING TECHNIQUES

The use of suction pumps to haul fish on board will probably be restricted to relatively small fish that can be concentrated into small areas. Larger fish such as tuna are being caught by German fishermen with a hook that contains an electrode. Another electrode is placed a short distance away. When the fish is hooked, the electricity is turned on and passes through the body of the tuna when his struggles result in contact with both electrodes. A similar method, requiring a 200-volt alternating current, has been tried in whaling. With this device a whale may be killed, inflated (to prevent sinking), and tied up to the whale catcher within ten minutes.

One of the problems in mid-depth trawling has been the difficulty of knowing the exact location of the net opening relative to the concentration of fish. Depth indicators attached to the net and read in conjunction with echo soundings of the school help to overcome this problem. Underwater television cameras which were developed to observe the behavior of fish within the net are now also being used experimentally to see the precise location of the school of fish. A further refinement, reportedly in the planning stage in Russia, would substitute a pair of midget submarines for the trawler and thereby provide more direct operation and control of the net.

In vessel technology, the most important trends are toward powered vessels, better shaped and more seaworthy hulls, better protection for crews, more storage capacity for catch, and better unloading facilities. Special purpose craft that divide up the elements of the fishing process are also being developed.

CULTIVATION TECHNIQUES

Some of the new or potential developments for cultivating the sea have been described in the chapter on the sea's productivity. These are chiefly concerned with devices for enriching the nutrient salt content of the euphotic zone. Other approaches involve the enclosure of ocean areas and the transplantation or genetic development of species.

Natural brackish ponds provide a ready base for experiments in aquiculture. The possibility of fertilization of such areas for oyster growth has already been mentioned. Another experiment is now taking place in sea-water ponds along the Australian east coast, where shrimp are being successfully bred and raised to maturity. The output has thus far been restricted because of the inability to provide sufficient quantities of zooplankton for the adult stages of the shrimp. The returns, however, have been sufficient to indicate the great potential for protein output.

An extension of this idea lies in the proposals for artificial enclosure of sea areas. A curtain of air bubbles is known to impede the movement of certain species of fish. Electrical currents may also be used to provide a wall through which fish will not pass. The "fencing" of fish opens the way for animal husbandry.

Transplantation of species has been practiced for many years, particularly in the sports fishery of the United States. As far back as 1880, shad were introduced to the North American Pacific coast, and catches reached over a million pounds a year. Flounders have been introduced into English waters, and the Russians are now trying to establish Pacific salmon in their Barents Sea streams. Interesting experiments are also being carried on in the hybridization and selective breeding of fish. The Japanese over several centuries have had spectacular success in developing extreme modifications of the goldfish. The selective breeding experiments on trout in the United States have also proved successful. Rainbow trout are reaching a weight of 3 to 5 pounds at the end of one year and 7 to 14 pounds at the end of two years. They are far more prolific than their forebears, capable of producing 25,000 eggs at the end of four years as against the 1,000 eggs of the original stock. Similar experiments are being initiated for salmon, and application to other commercial species may be reasonably expected in the future.

These cultural techniques raise very interesting and significant questions about the international agreements and legal arrangements for the use of the seas, especially where the investment is made by a single nation in a resource that reaches harvestable stage on the high seas. The principle of abstention, which is discussed in more detail later, was developed for a similar situation. As applied to the Pacific salmon industry, the Japanese have agreed to abstain from catching salmon on the high seas in the eastern Pacific Ocean on the basis that Canada and the United States are investing in the management of, and fully exploiting, the salmon that spawn in the streams of Northwest America. The treaty under which this principle was established is now being renegotiated. It remains to be seen whether this principle will become an accepted part of international law, and whether, in view of other difficulties, it is a desirable approach. What is clear, however, is that the present system of the law of the sea does not readily accommodate extensive cultivation techniques.

Conclusion

The recent rate of growth of technological innovation is impressive. With the exception of steam power and otter trawls, the fishing industry was much the same at the turn of the century as it had been for hundreds of years. Until the Second World War, the introduction of new techniques was steady but slow. Since then, however, ocean fisheries have been undergoing a technological revolution. Devices and techniques are being developed and adopted at a rapid rate. Most of them are devoted to increasing the efficiency of locating and catching the fish and to extending the range and season of operations. In the absence of techniques to increase the resource base, and in the face of growing demand, the stocks of fish are being subjected to pressures never before experienced except in small local areas.

The rate of growth in innovation, however, is far from uniform throughout the world. It varies considerably between low- and high-income countries, among major fishing nations, and even within nations. In the low-income countries that are dependent upon coastal waters the adoption of established techniques can have significant effects upon their industries. The problems they face are not those of developing new devices but of adopting and adapting old ones. They face considerable difficulties in revising marketing institutions, in the construction of transportation facilities, and in adopting handling and processing techniques, as well as in developing their efficiency in locating and catching fish.

The problems facing the major fishing nations, however, are quite different. The developments in the fishing process, together with the growing demand, are leading to increasing competition for the fishery resources owned in common by the world. Technological innovations that tend to reduce the cost of catching fish place greater strain upon the resource. The consequent depletion, or threat of depletion, evokes demands for international management agreements. At the same time, the world-wide extension of fishing effort leads to direct, and sometimes painful, confrontation between fishermen of different nations.

Chapter 7

Supply: Fishing Effort

IN this chapter we continue our account of the supply potential of world fisheries by turning from the fertility of the waters to the fishing effort being made by the various nations. The total world catch of fish in 1938 was about 21 million metric tons, live weight. In 1948, before full recovery of fishing effort from wartime immobilization, it was under 20 million. Since then, output has increased steadily and rapidly, reaching about 46 million tons in 1963. The distribution among nations has shifted considerably during this period. Peru is now the leader, having increased its output 140 times since 1948. Japan is now in second place. The United States, formerly second, became third in 1957 and dropped to fifth in 1960. Russia has remained in fourth place but has increased its proportion of the total take. The United Kingdom, the fourth largest producer before the war, has experienced both absolute and relative declines and is now eleventh. These shifts and many others may be explained by different rates of introducing technological innovations and of mobilizing increased fishing effort. The trends and background information on these nations provide indications of the future supply situation and of the problems that may emerge from the competition for the common property fishery resources.

Trends in Output

The following series of charts indicates some of the main patterns and trends that are developing among the nine nations that had the highest catches in 1955–59. Annual output is shown in Figures 14–16, and percentage changes in Figure 17. Peru's rate of growth has been fantastic, averaging about 40 per cent per year. Mainland China's reported output in 1959 showed a considerable increase, but, as pointed out in the Appendix to Chapter 3, the figures are questionable. Russia and Japan show growth rates close to those of the world average while the output estimates of other important nations show only moderate changes.

The nine countries listed in Table 11 accounted for almost two-thirds of total world output in 1963.

Table 11. Fish Catch by Nine Countries, 1955–59 and 1963

	1955–59 Catch		1963 Catch	
Country	Mil. metric tons, lv. wt.	As % of total	Mil. metric tons, lv. wt.	As % of total
World	31.4	100	46.4	100
Japan	5.29	16.8	6.70	14.4
Mainland China	3.47	11.1	5.02 [a]	10.8
United States	2.83	9.0	2.71	5.8
U.S.S.R.	2.60	8.3	3.98	8.6
Norway	1.77	5.6	1.39	3.0
United Kingdom	1.03	3.3	0.95	2.0
Canada	1.03	3.3	1.19	2.6
India	0.99	3.2	1.05	2.3
Peru	0.82	2.6	6.90	14.9

[a] 1959 figure, assumed to be the same for 1963.
Source: FAO, *Yearbook of Fishery Statistics, 1963, Vol. XVI*, Rome, 1964.

Figures 18–20 show the relative importance within separate nations of various groups of species for 1938 (where data are available), and for 1948 and 1962. (For the kinds of fish included in each group, see Appendix A, which shows the classification system used by FAO through 1962. Since a new system is carried in the 1963 FAO Yearbook, it is difficult to use the 1963 data to show trends because of inconsistencies with breakdowns in previous

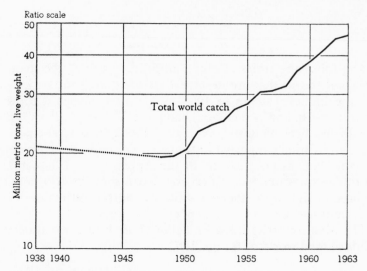

Figure 14. Total world catch of fish, 1938, 1948–63. (*Source:* FAO, *Yearbook of Fishery Statistics, 1963,* Vol. XVI, Rome, 1964, Table A-1.)

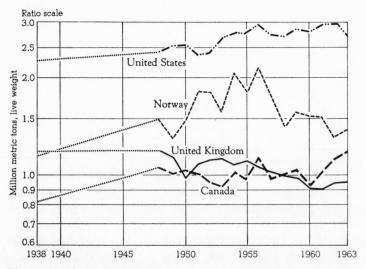

Figure 15. Annual catch of fish by the United States, Norway, United Kingdom, and Canada, 1938, 1948–63.

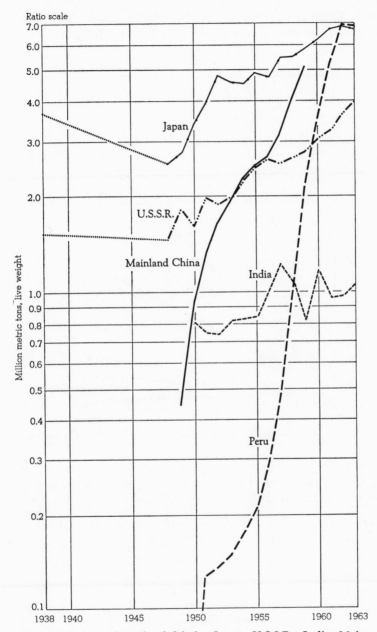

Figure 16. Annual catch of fish by Japan, U.S.S.R., India, Mainland China, and Peru, 1938–63.

years.) These charts (Figures 18–20) provide indications of several
important elements in the patterns of fish supply.

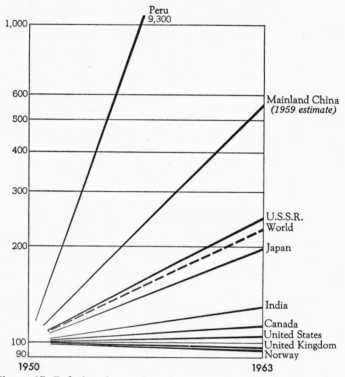

Figure 17. Relative change in volume of catch from 1950 to 1963
(1950 = 100).

The differences between diversity and specialization are re-
vealed by the amount of total catch by weight, represented by two
groups of species. This is summarized below:

                    Relative importance of top two
                        groups of species, 1962

Peru	Herrings, 97%; Tunas, 2%;	99%
Norway	Herrings, 43%; Cods, 41%;	84%
U.K.	Cods, 70%; Herrings, 11%;	81%
Canada	Cods, 39%; Herrings, 28%;	67%
U.S.	Herrings, 40%; Molluscs, 21%;	61%
U.S.S.R.	Herrings, 35%; Cods, 24%;	59%
India	Fresh, 34%; Herrings, 24%;	58%
Japan	Mullets, 23%; Molluscs, 17%	40%

At the two extremes are Japan and Peru. For the former, each of eight groups of species makes up 6 per cent or more of total national catch, and only one makes up more than 20 per cent. The most important single species, the jack mackerel, accounted for only 8 per cent of total landings. In Peru, the single herring spe-

TOTAL WORLD CATCH

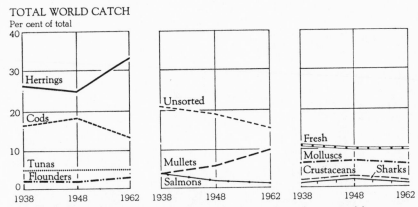

Figure 18. Change in pattern of catch by groups of species; quantities as percentage of total, 1938, 1948, and 1962.

cies, anchoveta, made up 97 per cent of the total take. Among the remaining countries, specialization is more apparent in the nations of West Europe and North America than in Russia or India. Over a third of the catch in Norway, the United Kingdom, and the United States is devoted to a single species. These differences in specialization partially reflect the different patterns of demand and partially the differences in the local availability of species. The two are, of course, interdependent.

During the period covered by the charts, in which total output dropped slightly between 1938 and 1948 and then more than doubled, there were only relatively minor changes in the composition of catch for the world as a whole, with two major exceptions. Herrings, the most important group of species, rose in relative importance; cods, the second most important group, dropped. Both groups increased in absolute terms. However, the major proportion of the increase in herrings was due to Peruvian output of anchoveta, used mainly for fish meal.

In all other groups, the changes were minor. The decline in "unsorted and unidentified (and unspecified)" fishes was matched by the rise in the "mullets, jacks and sea-basses"; the sum of both remained at 25 per cent of total world catch. It is probable that

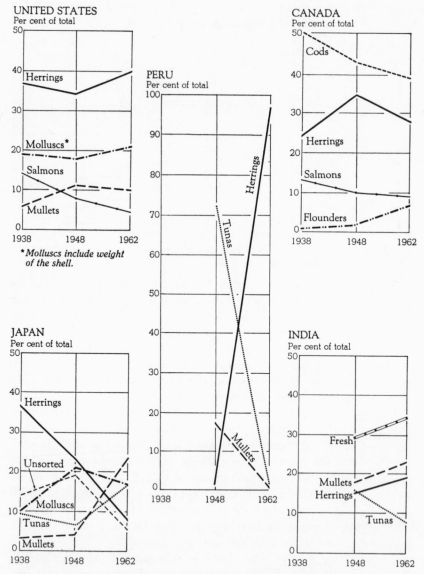

Figure 19. Change in pattern of catch by groups of species; quantities as percentage of total, Peru, Japan, India, Canada, and United States, 1938, 1948, and 1962.

better identification and reporting has led to the placing of a large proportion of the former into the latter category, which is a diverse collection of miscellaneous teleosteans. The remaining groups changed no more than one percentage point in relative importance, except for salmon which fell by three points.

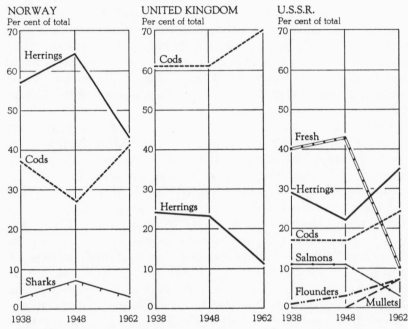

Figure 20. Change in pattern of catch by groups of species; quantities as percentage of total, Norway, United Kingdom, U.S.S.R., 1938, 1948, and 1962.

In contrast to the world as a whole, the composition within individual nations has shifted considerably. Some of these shifts are readily explainable. The relative and absolute decline in catch of the salmon group generally reflects the fixed or declining availability and the great vulnerability of these species, which are mostly anadromous. The shifts in the Soviet Union, which are generally upward except for the salmon group and the freshwater fishes, is a manifestation of Russia's mobilization of marine fishing effort. In Peru, both the mullet and the tuna groups have increased fourfold in absolute terms since 1948, but these increases are dwarfed by the very rapid development of the abundant anchoveta fishery that lies close to its shores.

The supplies of herring from the North Sea, the chief source for the United Kingdom and Norway, have fallen off sharply in the last few years. The reasons for the decline are not fully understood. Some believe that there is a natural cyclical fluctuation of population with troughs every thirty years or so. Others feel that conditions (climatic or food) are leading to different migratory patterns so that the seasonal herring concentrations are occurring beyond the usual range of fishing vessels. And finally, there is some belief that the decline is due to overfishing. The Russians have been able to increase their herring catch by moving further afield and fishing in the Northwest Atlantic and in the Pacific. These areas have also provided good sources for Canada and the United States.

Unfortunately, there are few statistics showing the shifts from domestic waters to the high seas and distant waters. In Japan, the portion of total catch from the high seas rose from 1 to 12 per cent between 1953 and 1962, and in Norway the catch from distant waters increased from 11 to 15 per cent of the total between 1948 and 1960. Despite the shifts, by far the greatest proportion of Japanese and Norwegian catch is still in local waters. The expansion to distant waters is undoubtedly greater for Russia than for Japan and Norway. On the other hand, for most other nations it is probably far less. In the United States, for example, less than 10 per cent of total catch comes from the high seas off foreign coasts.

The chief fishery not included in the above accounting is that of whales. The total catch for all whales has been increasing (Figure 21) but at a much lesser rate than for all fish. The kill by major nations has shown dramatic changes (Figure 22). Japan and the Soviet Union now take well over half the total, whereas before the war they took only about 15 per cent. Norway, the United Kingdom, and South Africa have shown not only relative but absolute declines as well.

The blue whales of the Antarctic, the largest animals in the sea, provide a significant illustration of a depleted resource. In the 1937/38 season there were over 15,000 blue whales killed, about 27 per cent of the total whale take. In 1947/48 the number killed had dropped by half and the 1962/63 kill was less than 10 per cent of what it was before the war. Since 1948, there has been an international commission on Antarctic whaling, covering not only the blue whales but other species found in the same area (the fin, humpbacked, sei, and sperm whales). The commission established

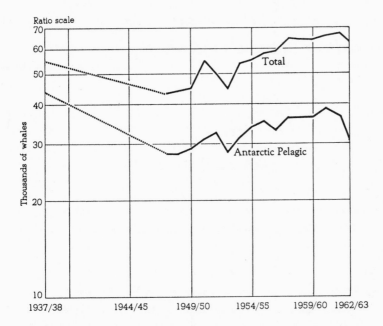

Figure 21. Catch of whales, world total and Antarctic pelagic, 1937/38, 1947/48 to 1962/63.

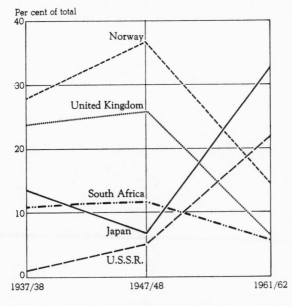

Figure 22. Catch of whales by Norway, United Kingdom, South Africa, Japan, and the U.S.S.R. as percentage of world total, 1937/38, 1947/48, and 1961/62.

quotas on the total permissible kill and the whaling nations agreed to divide up the quotas among themselves. The agreements broke down in the 1960/61 and 1961/62 seasons, and in recent years the quotas that have been agreed upon have been greater than the yields that could be sustained. The annual kill, though below the quotas, has still been large enough to further diminish the stock.

Currently, the only nations sending fleets to the Antarctic are Japan, the Soviet Union, and Norway. The fleets of the United Kingdom and the Netherlands, along with their quotas, have recently been sold to Japanese firms.

To summarize, certain clear trends can be identified that have significance for future international arrangements for the use of marine fisheries. One is the upward trend in output for all fisheries, which is at the rate of about 6 per cent per year, but drops to less than 5 per cent per year without the Peruvian catch. However, of more significance for international fisheries, are the changes that are taking place in the fisheries of Japan and Russia. Catches in both these countries are increasing at the rate of 6 per cent per year, while catches in the leading fishing nations other than Peru and Mainland China range from declines to increases of no more than 2 per cent per year.[1] In addition, almost all of the increase in catch by the Japanese and Russians is probably coming from international waters far from their home shores.

Fisheries in National Economies

There are wide variations in the degree to which different nations are dependent upon their fisheries industries. At one extreme is Iceland, whose economy is more closely associated with fish than that of any other nation. Its per capita consumption of fish is extremely high, a high percentage of its labor force is devoted to fishing and fish processing, and fish and fish products make up more than 90 per cent of all exports. At the other extreme are the nations where fishing makes no significant contribution, although, in some cases, this situation is likely to change. The growth in output in both Peru and South Africa may set examples for other South American and African nations and fishing may be-

[1] Of the nations not included in our listing, several show rapid growth rates to positions of significance. These include South Africa, Spain, and Indonesia, each of which caught more than 900,000 tons of fish in 1963.

come important for nations that have few other known resource opportunities. Such nations are particularly jealous of the resources that lie close to their shores and are, therefore, generally anxious to extend their territorial boundaries and establish exclusive use rights.

It is difficult to measure the importance of fishery industries to different national economies not only because of the economic imprecision of the concept "importance," but also because of the absence of statistical information. However, some rough and commonly-quoted indicators are available for seven of the nine most important fishing nations but not for Russia and Mainland China. These measures are shown in Table 12.

Table 12. Importance of Fishery Industry in National Economies

(per cent)

Country	Per cent of total protein intake derived from fish, 1954–56	1959 value of fish exports as per cent of all exports	1959 value of catch as per cent of national income
Norway	19	19	2.9
Peru	n.a.	14	n.a.
Japan	72	6	2.8
United Kingdom	9	a	0.3
India	9	1	n.a.
Canada	6	3	0.4
United States	4	a	0.1

ª Negligible.

There is not much that emerges clearly from this picture except that fisheries are rarely an "important" national industry today and that Norway, Peru, and Japan are considerably more dependent upon their fishery industries than are the four other nations listed. As a rough guess, it is probable that the Soviet Union lies somewhere in between these two groups.

Among these nations, Japan, Norway, and Canada exported almost half of the *value* of total world exports of fish and fish products in 1959. (Peru's fish meal exports, which are high in volume, are relatively low in value.) The United States and the United Kingdom, in the same year, imported almost half of the value of all world imports, as shown in Table 13.

Table 13. Value of National Trade as Percentage of World Trade
in Fish Products, Eight Countries, 1959

(per cent)

Country	Exports	Imports
Japan	18.3	0.2
Canada	13.5	1.3
Norway	13.5	1.1
Peru	4.0	a
United States	3.5	27.4
U.S.S.R.	3.2	2.6
U.K.	1.8	17.0
India	1.2	0.5
Total, eight countries	60.0	50.1

ª Negligible.

In recent years some significant changes have occurred in foreign trade, as shown in Table 14.

Table 14. Foreign Trade (Exports or Imports) in Fishery Products,
Selected Countries, 1948, 1953, and 1959

Country	1948	1953	1959	1959
	(1,000 metric tons, product weight)			*(1953 = 100)*
United States imports	291	482	647	134
United Kingdom imports	429	370	491	133
Norway exports	461	422	558	132
Japan exports	11	146	436	300
Peru exports	6	32	353	1,100
Canada exports	228	267	290	109

The United States is still the world's largest importer of fishery products. In 1948, imports in terms of weight were small in proportion to total supply, accounting for about 20 per cent. This was due both to large domestic catches and to small exports from Europe which was still suffering postwar difficulties. In the next four years, however, the domestic catch declined and European exports rose, so that imports made up about 35 per cent of total U.S. supply in 1951. During the 1950's there were some fluctuations between 30 and 40 per cent but a general continuation of the upward trend. Since 1960 the increase has been marked, imports being 58 per cent of U.S. supply in 1963.

The Peruvian and Japanese exports are growing very rapidly. Those of the former nation are made up almost entirely of fish meals and oils, although frozen and canned tuna are of some significance. Exports from Japan are mostly products with a high unit value. Salmon and tuna each account for about a third of the total value of all fishery exports. The remaining third includes whale oils, crabmeat, and a wide variety of miscellaneous commodities.

Although Norwegian exports were higher in 1959 than in 1953, the latter year was a relatively bad one for Norway. Exports in 1954 amounted to about 600,000 metric tons and fluctuated between 550,000 and 640,000 in the intervening years.

The Canadian trade situation has been similar to Norway's. Neither of these countries has been maintaining its relative position in the world trade in fishery products.

Fishing Vessels and Facilities

The preceding general observations on the economic characteristics of the fishing industry and its resource, and about the importance of the fishing industry to various nations, must now be supplemented by some more specific discussion of the nations' inputs into the fishing effort. We begin with vessels, which are the basic unit of the harvesting process, and then turn to the fishing labor force, attempting in both cases to show the role of governments in influencing the size and form of these inputs.

In spite of the continuing growth in catch, the actual number of vessels on the seas has not increased markedly. This statement is difficult to substantiate, because the statistics on the number, kind, tonnage, power, etc., of craft devoted to fishing are very poor for most of the leading countries and virtually nonexistent for India and Mainland China. Some general trends, however, are evident. Only in Russia and Peru has there been any increase in the *number* of fishing craft. For most countries there appear to be increases in the tonnage, power, and size of vessels, reflecting the increased emphasis of distant-water effort, more hours on the grounds, shorter delivery periods, and greater ability to handle rough weather.

Japan. This change in the nature of the fleet is nowhere seen better than in Japan. Prior to the Second World War, the pressures of population had already led to a vigorous expansion of the pelagic fishery. Unlike most other fishing nations at the time, large monopolies were formed which both divided up the domestic market and reduced competition on fishing grounds. These companies received heavy construction subsidies from the government as well as concessions for fishing in distant waters and protection of rights in domestic waters. Following the war, during which the industry suffered heavy losses of equipment, the government's role became even more pronounced. The National Fisheries Agency, established in 1948, has conducted an active program of financial aid, research and development of technological innovations and new resource areas, and of fostering the growth of export markets.

The National Fisheries Agency of Japan has also had a considerable impact on the amount of fishing effort and investment.[2] Practically all Japan's important offshore and distant water fisheries are under a licensing system that controls the activities of the fishery by limiting the number of licenses issued, the size of vessels used, area of fishing, method, species, period of fishing, etc. The controls, which have developed over many years, are primarily for the purpose of reducing costly competition between large firms. Other stated purposes include the conservation of the resource and the prevention of international disputes.

The limitation on entry has not been entirely successful in improving economic efficiency, largely because the Japanese system permits the fishermen to fully appropriate the rewards from participating in a controlled fishery. The profits that are produced may, therefore, provide sufficient incentive to the fishermen to circumvent or overturn the controls. Some of the difficulties are presented below.

In the case of a newly developing fishery that holds promise for long-term yields, fishing companies may anticipate the future application by the Fisheries Agency of controls on the number of producers. They may, consequently, be anxious to have clearly established interests in the fishery before the controls are instituted so that they will be among those having rights to the stock. This, in turn, may lead to overinvestment sooner than would have been the case in the absence of entry limitations.

As is pointed out above, the profits that accompany a limited

---

[2] For an interesting account of the National Fisheries Agency, see Hiroshi Kasahara, "Japanese Fisheries and Fishery Regulations" in California Museum of Science and Industry, *California and the World Ocean*, 1964.

entry fishery may induce the excluded fishermen to apply political
pressures to overcome the restrictions and open the fishery to
broader use. This places a heavy burden upon the Agency. But
even in cases where the Agency is successful in combating such
pressures, the licensed participants may be tempted to increase
their intensity of fishing through technological innovation or
changes in the pattern of fishing.

Where there is already overinvestment in a fishery and no controls on entry, some companies may choose to remain as participants even though the profits may be low or negligible. The
fishermen may anticipate the establishment of controls by the
Japanese Fisheries Agency and may be afraid to lose rights that
may become valuable. Or they may remain because they expect
governmental inducements to compensate them for leaving the
fishery.

In addition, there are difficult problems in the distribution of
the licenses to companies, particularly in the distant-water fisheries
that require very large investments in fishing fleets.

The Japanese experience indicates some of the difficulties involved in using an entry-limitation system to improve economic
efficiency. But the nature of the difficulties also reflects the economic value of limiting entry since, in each case, it is this value
that provides the incentive for the expansion of fishery rights—an
expansion which, unfortunately, leads to a dissipation of the
profit. The political problems are indeed great, but they are not
insurmountable. A stronger central control or a reduction in the
incentive to acquire rights may help to overcome the difficulties.

Since the war, the statistics for Japan are quite good. In 1947,
there were about 430,000 fishing craft. This increased to 480,000
in 1950 and then dropped to 404,000 in 1962. While the total
number of all craft declined by 6 per cent from 1947 to 1962, the
number of *powered* craft doubled, rising from 20 per cent of the
total to 47 per cent. At the same time, the total *tonnage* increased
90 per cent to reach 1.8 million gross register tons by 1962 and,
power (mostly diesel) increased 180 per cent.

About 16 per cent of the tonnage is devoted to tuna longline
fishing and skipjack pole and line fishing. The tonnage in this distant-water group has almost tripled since 1947. Japan's program
not only includes increases in the size and power of its fishing fleet,
but also includes the establishment of foreign bases throughout
the world. (See Figure 23.) For each mark on the map, Japanese

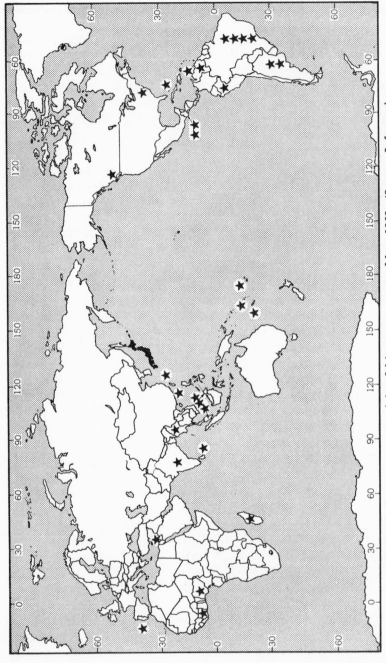

Figure 23. Japanese overseas joint fishing ventures as of late 1963. (*Source:* Information provided by the Japanese National Fisheries Agency through A. Futagoishi, First Secretary of the Embassy of Japan to the United States, January 23, 1964.)

companies have invested in the development of fishery facilities. In a typical arrangement, the Japanese firm puts up about half of the required capital and the host country the other half. The firm provides technical guidance, usually including the masters of the vessels, and conducts a training program for the fishermen of the host country. The base usually includes a processing plant for freezing the products, and it frequently serves as the origin for exports to other countries. Most of the Pacific bases are devoted to tuna, while those in the Atlantic are more diversified, covering tuna, whaling, trawling, and the production of fish meal and fish sausage. With the entry of the Japanese into the Northwest Atlantic fishing grounds, it is likely that more bases will be established in the North Atlantic in order to service the fleets. The developments in the Indian Ocean are still largely exploratory.

Peru. The increase in the number and size of Peru's fishing vessels has been as dramatic in its own way as the expansion in catch. In 1953, there were 50 vessels over 35 feet in length,[3] and more than half of these were between 35 and 40 feet. By 1962, only nine years later, there were more than a thousand vessels over 35 feet, and about half of them were between 65 and 70 feet in length.

U.S.S.R. The Soviet Union fishing industry is rapidly turning away from domestic waters that are believed to be overexploited, and is probably taking 80 per cent of its catch from the open oceans.[4] This shift to distant waters, evident in the North Atlantic and North Pacific, is accompanied by a major construction and purchase program of large and well-equipped vessels. Commander Bernard M. Kassell[5] estimated in 1961 that the Soviet fleet had about 100,000 fishing craft, 23,000 of which were steam or diesel powered and of modern design. The Russians have announced that 14,000 new units will be added during the current seven-year plan. These will include 68 factory ships with freezers, 47 refrigerator ships for transporting catches from grounds to ports, and 26 floating canneries for crabs, as well as the many trawlers and seiners involved in the catching.

[3] I. Tilic, *Información estadística sobre embarcaciones utilizados en la pesca industrial en el Perú 1953–1962,* Informe No. 8 (La Punta, Callao, Peru: Instituto de Investigación de los Recursos Marinos, 1963), pp. 9–10.

[4] Bernard M. Kassell, "The Fishing Fleet of the Soviet Union," *United States Naval Institute Proceedings,* Vol. 87, No. 11 (November, 1961). See also: U.S. Senate, Committee on Commerce, "The Postwar Expansion of Russia's Fishing Industry" (Washington: U.S. Government Printing Office, January 23, 1964).

[5] *Op. cit.*

Following the war, Russia procured many vessels from the ship-yards of European nations. Between 1956 and 1960, Finland built 15 trawlers of the 800-horsepower size and 38 medium trawlers of the 300–400 h.p. class. England constructed for Russia 20 trawlers specially equipped for operating in Arctic waters. West Germany also built about 20 trawlers and factory ships. Poland is providing Russia with 15 herring trawler tenders of 11,450 gross register tons, each of which can carry 9,300 tons of cargo and is equipped with helicopter landing facilities. Denmark has already delivered 21 refrigerator vessels, two of which are of the class of the M/S *Vitus Bering,* described above (p. 94). Shipyards in Japan, the Netherlands, and Sweden are also under contract to provide fish-ing vessels for the U.S.S.R. In addition, Russia's own shipyards are rapidly building fishing vessels. The yard in Nikolayev, for exam-ple, is scheduled to build 30 stern trawlers of 3,170 gross register tons, and these are to be equipped with the latest fish-finding and navigational devices. Other shipyards are also contributing to the total investment in modern, efficient vessels. Although there is no readily available data on the total construction and purchase pro-gram, it is evident that the rate and amount of investment are greater than for any of the other leading fishing nations.

Behind the rapid expansion lies the belief that the returns to capital and labor in fisheries far exceed those in animal hus-bandry. In a paper presented to the 22nd Congress of the Commu-nist Party of the Soviet Union, S. V. Mikhaïlov [6] stated that the production of one head of beef requires 20 man-days, while the production of an equivalent amount of protein from fish would take only 5 man-days.[7] To produce a million calories would take 15–20 man-days by fishing and 56 man-days by beef farming. In terms of capital investment, Mikhaïlov stated that an annual out-put of 100 kilograms live-weight of beef requires a capital invest-ment of 2,000–2,500 rubles, while that for fish, only 1,500–1,700 rubles. Production costs for the same amount of beef are stated to

[6] S. V. Mikhaïlov, "On the Comparative Efficiency of Production of Some Products of the Land and Sea," *Okeanologiiā,* Vol. 2, No. 3, 1962, pp. 385–92; translated by W. G. Van Campen, U.S. Bureau of Commercial Fisheries, Hon-olulu, Hawaii, 1962.

[7] This refers to fishing industries in the Northern and Far Eastern waters and implies a catch rate of 164 pounds, live weight, per man-day or about 13–14 man-days per metric ton. In the report of the U.S. Senate, Committee on Commerce, *op. cit.,* it is stated that 70 man-days is the average required per ton of fish.

be 600 rubles and those for fish, 200 rubles. "Thus according to all economic indices (except the labor expenditure per unit of oil extraction), superiority is on the side of the fishing industry. . . . The relatively high efficiency of capital investment in fisheries gives us an obligation to use all means to develop the resource base by seeking new fishing areas and new species to exploit, by improving commercial fish-culture in interior waters, and by broad measures for the artificial propagation of commercial species." [8] While there may be some questions about the calculations and assumptions that underlie the conclusions, these are not as important as the extent to which the conclusions guide the policies of the Soviet Union, and the extent to which these policies, in turn, affect the exploitation of the commonly owned fisheries of the world.

United States. The contrast between the fisheries of the Soviet Union and those of the United States is sharp, but it must be remembered that the differences in motivation, capital and labor costs, and structure of enterprise are so great that comparisons are not really meaningful. The centrally directed government enterprise of the U.S.S.R. is strongly motivated by the difficulty of providing other sources of animal protein. In the United States, the free competition, limited governmental support, and high construction and labor costs have resulted in quite different forms of operation, and a considerable portion of supply comes from imports. The U.S. vessels are neither as large nor as modern as those of the Soviet Union. In 1962, for example, there were only twenty-six U.S. fishing vessels over 500 gross tons, and these averaged only about 1,000 tons apiece. Twenty-two of these were built before 1946 and four since then.[9] Though there has been a slight trend upwards in size of vessel, less than 3 per cent of all fishing vessels in the United States are over 100 gross tons. There are, of course, wide regional differences, with New England and the Chesapeake Bay fisheries generally having the oldest vessels. On the Pacific Coast there are several relatively new, large tuna vessels which are well equipped with freezing tanks, nylon purse seines, and modern power blocks. A few new vessels are also being constructed for the shrimp and menhaden fisheries off the Gulf and Atlantic coasts.

[8] Mikhaĭlov, *op. cit.*, pp. 10 and 12.
[9] U.S. Treasury Department, Bureau of Customs, *Merchant Marine Statistics, 1963* (Washington: U.S. Government Printing Office, 1963).

The U.S. government has been less directly involved (through loans, subsidies, and other programs) in the fishing enterprise than have the governments of most other countries, and it has spent its greatest effort in research and education. A loan program started in 1956 for financing fishing operations and for repair of vessels and gear had loaned less than $16 million through 1963. In 1960, a subsidy not to exceed one-third of the cost of new construction of fishing vessels was established for certain fisheries. This subsidy program (recently expanded) is designed to help overcome the high construction costs in the United States which the fishermen cannot avoid because of the law that requires all vessels to be produced domestically. At the end of 1963, $500,000 had been awarded under this program.

Norway. In Norway, where fisheries are of social and political as well as economic importance, the government has adopted a direct supporting role. The National Fishery Bank has encouraged and aided the modernization of the fishing fleets by mortgage loans which, in some cases, cover as much as 95 per cent of construction costs. The government has also sponsored "professional associations" to determine and stabilize prices and to provide some centralized control over the export trade.

This new approach to fish marketing is believed to be quite effective, but the raw statistics do not reveal that much over-all modernization of the Norwegian fleet has resulted from subsidizing vessel construction. In 1960, the average age for decked motor vessels was about 26 years for the wooden boats and 31 years for the steel.

The total number of fishing craft in Norway has changed but little since the prewar period, although there have been two marked shifts in composition. As in other leading countries, the number of large vessels has been increasing. Those of 70 feet or more increased from about 580 before the war to 870 in 1962. At the same time, open motorboats which are used in Norway's inshore fisheries rose from about 11,000 to almost 28,000, over 40 per cent of which have been built since the war. Since the total number of open boats (motorized and nonmotorized) has actually declined, this trend represents a marked shift to the use of power.

Canada. The Canadian fleet is largely coastal as is indicated by the fact that only about a third of the Atlantic catch and almost none of the Pacific catch is deep-sea. The Atlantic inshore fishery is usually conducted within 15 miles of land by individual fishermen in small rowboats, sailboats, or motorboats. The offshore Atlantic fleet, which has had a long and important history, has been undergoing considerable changes. The large deep-sea trawlers of the Atlantic (200 to 400 gross registered tons) increased in number from 14 in 1948–49 to 49 in 1958–59. The deep-sea fleet may continue to show increases as a result of a federal subsidy program that became effective in 1961. Under this program, the federal government provides up to 35–40 per cent of the construction cost of vessels of 100 gross tons or more, and up to 50 per cent of the cost of steel trawlers of more than 75 feet that are built as replacements for outmoded trawlers.[10]

Since 1947 the smaller deep-sea draggers and longliners (under 65 gross tons) of the Atlantic fleet have been under a subsidy program that was set up to aid small boat fishermen to modernize their efforts. By June 1961, 486 vessels had been built at a cost to the federal government of about $3 million.[11] In addition, provincial governments have provided loans at low interest rates and the Province of Newfoundland has also contributed construction grants. Careful analysis of this program has shown that some classes, or sizes, of vessels are far more profitable than others. One study has concluded that with the subsidy, only four of the sixteen classes surveyed, representing about half of the vessels in the program, "could pay off their debt from earnings in a period less than the vessel's useful life." [12] The more profitable classes, those from 45 to 65 feet in length, have received increased subsidy since 1961, the rate rising from $165 to $250 a gross ton for vessels built in the Atlantic provinces.

United Kingdom. The industry has had considerable help from the government through the Herring Industry Board and the White Fish Authority, which provide grants and loans for the purchase of new vessels, for the reconditioning of old vessels, and toward the costs of new gear, equipment, and processing plants. The Authority, between 1951 and 1960, made grants and loans of almost $100 million. Assistance is also provided through a direct subsidy

[10] John Proskie, *Operations of Modern Fishing Craft, Atlantic Seaboard, 1960* (Ottawa: Economics Service, Department of Fisheries of Canada, 1962).

[11] Of the 486 vessels, 40 have been lost at sea; 23 through fire, 8 because of navigation errors, 4 from icing and foundering, and 5 lost in foul weather and rough seas. The entire crews were lost in five of the accidents. *Ibid.*, p. iii.

[12] Edward Lynch, Richard Doherty, and George Draheim, *The Groundfish Industries of New England and Canada,* U.S. Fish and Wildlife Service, Circular 121, Washington, 1961, p. 21.

on fish. This was originally paid only to the owners of near- and middle-water vessels, but recently, the owners of distant-water vessels were included in the program. Payments, amounting to about $7 million per year in the late 1950's are gradually being phased out. There has been a general decline in the number of fishing craft and not much change in tonnage, indicating a slight shift to larger vessels. The distant-water trawler fleet is the most modern in that about half of the vessels have been constructed since the war. Prior to the grants and loan program, the near- and middle-water trawlers were largely coal-burning vessels averaging 40 years in age, but now most of the fleet has been modernized to the point where about 90 per cent of the fleet's catch is from vessels built in the last ten years.[13]

Summary. There appears to be a sharp distinction between the construction programs of Japan and Russia and those of the other leading fishing nations. The first two are building up extensive and modern deep-sea fleets capable of fishing in all oceans of the world and even on grounds that are close to foreign nations. The United States, Norway, Canada, the United Kingdom, and Peru are still focusing the major part of their effort on coastal fisheries although most are making some exploratory trips into new deep-sea and distant waters. Generally, these offshore efforts are more financially successful than the inshore fisheries and therefore more attractive for private investment and more likely to be expanded. On the other hand, the greatest employment is associated with the inshore fisheries and these, being distressed, tend to attract more government aid.

This discussion has focused on the physical aspects and has emphasized the modernization and expansion of the Japanese and Russian fleets and their increased ability to take fish. However, not all such expansion is to the economic benefit of a nation, since the costs of additional or renovated equipment may well outweigh the additional economic returns. Indeed, it is generally true that the capital investment in most North American and Western European fisheries is already excessive. The few exceptions to this occur where fisheries are being developed or new techniques applied. In both cases, the exceptions are frequently short-lived, since the new profits attract additional effort which leads once more to excessive capitalization, depletion of the resource, and to the disappearance

[13] Letter from Austen Laing, Director General, The British Trawlers Federation, Ltd., May, 1963.

of profit and economic rent. When the fisheries become stabilized (i.e., the total catch no longer increases), the catch per ton of vessel diminishes. Between 1948 and 1958, for example, the catch per ton of vessel in ten Western European countries dropped by 14 per cent.[14] This was the result of an increase in catch of only 18 per cent and an increase in tonnage of 38 per cent. While these changes cannot be readily translated into monetary terms, it appears most unlikely that the subsequent return to capital warranted the increase in total investment, both public and private.

An indication of the relationships between different amounts of effort (days fished) and physical and economic returns for a stable fishery is shown in Table 15. The data are based upon estimates of fishing effort and yields in the haddock industry on the Georges Bank for 1931–48, and they make certain assumptions about mesh regulations, costs, prices, and average effort. During the period 1931–48, the average annual number of days fished was 7,306, which was taken to be "100 per cent effort level." Under the assumptions given, the illustration shows that the physical return, in terms of total landings, varied only slightly by changing the number of days fished from half "normal" to twice "normal." As a consequence, the average catch per boat (unit of effort) drops very rapidly. The highest net profit per boat occurs, as might be expected, at the lowest level of effort. For the fleet as a whole, the maximum total net profit would occur at about the point where 22 vessels were used instead of the average of 44 that fished during 1931–48. This figure would be further reduced, of course, if cost-saving or catch-increasing technological innovations were introduced.

The government programs tend to focus on those fisheries where employment is greatest. In North America and Western Europe, these are the inshore and near- and middle-water fisheries, the ones that have been exploited for centuries and are least likely to expand. Public programs and private assistance from buyers and packers that aid the construction of new vessels and the modernization of the fleet encourage the greater use of a resource that cannot be significantly expanded and, consequently, lead to a greater sharing of the return by more economic units and a decline in the catch per unit of effort.

In international waters, a temporary advantage may be gained

[14] Organisation for European Economic Co-operation, *Fishery Policies* (Paris: OEEC, September, 1960).

Table 15. Revenue-Expense Relationships Per Boat as Fishing Effort Changes
(based upon estimates of fishing effort and yields in the haddock industry, Georges Bank, 1931–48)

I Effort level (per cent)	II Effort in days fished	III Number of boats	IV Fleet landings (millions of pounds)	V Annual Yield per boat (millions of pounds)	VI Total revenue per boat [a]	VII Trip expenses per boat [b] (65.35 per cent of gross revenue)	VIII Contribution to overhead	IX Average overhead [c]	X Profit (or loss) per boat
25	1,827	11	73.6	6.69	$568,650	$371,613	$197,037	$65,000	$132,037
50	3,653	22	103.8	4.72	401,200	262,184	139,016	65,000	74,016
75	5,480	33	115.5	3.50	297,500	194,416	103,084	65,000	38,084
100	7,306	44	120.7	2.74	232,900	152,200	80,700	65,000	15,700
125	9,133	55	122.0	2.22	188,700	123,315	65,385	65,000	385
150	10,959	64	121.7	1.90	161,500	105,540	55,960	65,000	(9,040)
175	12,786	74	120.8	1.63	138,550	90,542	48,008	65,000	(16,992)
200	14,612	81	119.4	1.47	124,950	81,655	43,295	65,000	(21,705)

a At 8½ cents per pound.

b Source of trip expense rates and daily crew expenses are Settlement Sheets of Atlantic Fishermen's Union, 1956–57. Trip expenses also include captain's bonus, usually 10 per cent of owner's gross share. Trip expenses are 65.35 per cent of gross revenue: 3.75 per cent is joint expenses; 57.75 per cent is gross crew share; 3.85 per cent is captain's bonus.

c Based on data submitted by vessel owners to the United States Tariff Commission in 1956 and Boston College in 1958.

Source: Edward Lynch, Richard Doherty, and George Draheim, *The Groundfish Industries of New England and Canada*, U.S. Fish and Wildlife Circular 121, Washington, 1961, Table III-12, based upon physical estimates "from unpublished manuscript of Clyde C. Taylor, Fishery Research Biologist, Woods Hole Laboratory, United States Fish and Wildlife Service, Woods Hole, Mass."

by the fishermen whose nation gives them the greatest support and permits them to adopt technological innovations most rapidly. If total catch then declines, as is likely, social and political pressures are built up to conserve the resource by regulating the take. Where total quota controls are put in force, the fishermen are encouraged to increase their investment in power and capacity, since each fisherman wants to get the greatest share of the quota for himself. Where, on the other hand, gear restrictions develop, the most efficient producers are penalized and more effort is required in order to obtain the same catch.[15] The most efficient use of capital can only be achieved by regulations that restrict the number of economic units that can participate in a fishery although, as pointed out later, this would raise difficulties, such as that of finding alternative employment for the displaced fisherman.

On the whole, government support has not been part of a well-planned general program of fisheries expansion and development. Indeed, most government policies seem to reflect a mixture of motives: creating or assisting employment, and aiding the shipbuilding industry, stranded communities, and ineffective firms. Why is this so? Various reasons for this generous attitude have been advanced. Once again, we are brought back, not to the inherent opportunities of world fishing, but to the industry's inherent weaknesses. It has been mentioned before that there is a great deal of risk and uncertainty involved in the fisheries industries. There are severe natural fluctuations in the availability of the resources: the Alaska herring catch, for example, varied during four consecutive years (1948–51) from 171 million pounds to 35 million to 168 million to 88 million. There is also high risk in fishing operations due to the vagaries of weather which can prevent or impede fishing activity as well as damage or totally destroy equipment. Though prices also fluctuate, income levels are generally low for several reasons, one of which is that high prices usually quickly lead to increased numbers of fishermen and dissipation of profit. Furthermore, in most nations, the fishing industry is made up of many small individual units which are unable to spread their risks among fisheries.

Fishing, always a chancy operation, has seldom appeared to be an attractive investment for commercial banking houses. When

[15] Gear restrictions are a popular solution since they tend to preserve the status quo and discourage newcomers. At the same time, most governments are doing considerable research on methods for increasing gear efficiency.

private capital does come in, it is usually in response to the sudden discovery and rapid development of a new fishery resource or technique. As a result, in most nations where fishing is important (as a source of food, income, or outlet for labor), government has assumed a supporting or protecting role. The roles, however, vary considerably, with the centrally-planned efforts of the Soviet Union at one extreme, and the slight government support in the United States at the other extreme.

Fisheries Employment

The labor devoted to the fishing industry—another factor of considerable importance in the determination of the degree of fishing effort—is difficult to evaluate, both because of the inadequacy of the statistics and because the kind of labor employed ranges widely from the part-time coastal fishermen in rowboats to the skilled crews of factory vessels. Yet information on fisheries employment is critical, not only because of the economist's desire to evaluate economic efficiency, but also because the protection of employment is frequently stated as a national goal.

In the following pages, we discuss some of the available measures of employment in the major fishing nations, and then turn to some of the characteristics of fisheries labor and to the questions of efficiency.

The task of measuring the labor force is beset by many problems. Most serious is the large proportion of seasonal and/or part-time employment in many fisheries which means that the concept of "employment" on the familiar annual basis does not apply. The state of Maryland provides an illustration of the difficulties of interpreting employment statistics. The requirements for licensing in this state facilitate enumeration. However, the licensees may range from high school students whose only effort in fisheries is in tonging for oysters on occasional Saturdays and holidays to full-time fishermen who engage in a variety of fisheries according to the season. Under these conditions, it is difficult to derive meaningful measures of labor productivity.

Aside from the problem of interpretation, there are real difficulties in estimating the number of people engaged in fishing. This is largely because most inshore and coastal fishermen live in small towns and villages scattered along the coastline, rather than in easily enumerated centers of population. There are, consequently, only a few countries for which estimates are readily available. These are shown in the following table, with some breakdown on differing bases of "employment." [16]

Table 16. Number of Fishermen, Four Countries,
1938, 1948, and 1958

(thousands)

Country	1938	1948	1958
Norway, full and part time	110	98	76
Full-time equivalent	72	65	52
United Kingdom, full and part time	47	47	27
Full-time equivalent	43	42	25
Canada, full and part time	97	94	79
U.S., full and part time	130	161	135
Full-time equivalent	85	104	92

Estimates of the fishing labor force of the other major fishing nations are difficult to obtain. Japan's fishermen may number about a million, based on rough calculations from Table 17. For the U.S.S.R., a report prepared for the U.S. Senate Committee on Commerce quotes a Russian source stating that "the labor force in the fishing industry . . . now stands at approximately 500,000 persons, of whom one-third are employed aboard ship." [17] For Peru, based upon the number of vessels and an assumed average size of crew, there may be on the order of 7,000 fishermen. On the basis of these rough estimates and others, it is apparent that fishing takes a larger percentage of the working force in Norway than in any of the other leading nations: something more than 5 per cent. In Japan, fishermen may make up 2–3 per cent of their labor force; in Canada about 1–2 per cent; in Russia, probably slightly less than 1 per cent; and in the United States and the United Kingdom, less than 0.3 per cent.

In the United Kingdom, Norway, and Canada, there is evidence

[16] OEEC, *op. cit.*

[17] U.S. Senate, Committee on Commerce, *op. cit.*, p. 18. The report also states that "about 70 man-days are spent to produce a ton of fish." With a catch of 3.6 million tons in 1962, this would mean 250 million man-days, which implies a far larger labor force than that quoted above. The estimate of productivity, however, is probably incorrect.

that the number of fishermen is declining, both in absolute and relative terms. In the United States, the decline in the number of fishermen was interrupted shortly after the war by a sharp increase. Entry was attractive because the U.S. fleet was in better shape than the war-damaged fleets of Western Europe and the stocks of fish were high because of the respite in fishing effort during the war years. The number of U.S. fishermen has since resumed its decline and will probably decline more rapidly in the future. With a few exceptions the industry is neither attracting nor holding many recruits to the labor force.

The Peruvian fishing force is undoubtedly rising, although no figures are readily available. It is hard to say whether the Soviet fishermen are increasing or decreasing in number. The Russian effort is being mobilized mostly in the direction of the distant-water and capital-intensive fishing, which requires relatively less labor per unit of catch than their former inland sea and coastal industries. In Japan, the relationship between labor and capital costs is such that the increase in effort is probably accompanied by an increase in the number of fishermen.

In describing employment in fisheries, two characteristics are particularly important. One of these is that the fishermen of many countries are traditionally rewarded on a share system similar in many respects to share-cropping in traditional agriculture. This system, in which pay fluctuates in relationship to the return, serves to mitigate some of the effects of the large risks borne by vessel owners. Since large returns are accompanied by high rewards, it also apparently appeals to fishermen, who may be more willing to gamble on their income than non-fishermen. However, in certain fisheries where labor's share is high and relatively unchangeable, the system may impede technological innovation because new equipment costs must be carried by the owners, yet the increased returns are shared by the fishermen. But because the arrangements are so different throughout the world, and renegotiation of shares is frequently possible, it is dangerous to summarize the general effect.

A second characteristic lies in the heterogeneity of fisheries employment, already touched upon above. The range from local and part-time coastal efforts to skilled, full-time high seas labor is shown in Table 17, below, with respect to Japanese fishery operations. At one extreme is the small family enterprise which is usually located in small villages scattered along the coast and which operates in the shallow inshore waters. By far the greatest number of Japanese fishermen are engaged in this kind of fishing. However, their productivity is relatively low, and they must supplement their earnings by farming or working at other jobs. At the other extreme is the "industrial" fishery, made up of a small number of large operations. This group includes several very large corporate enterprises, with diversified operations in the whale, tuna, salmon, and other fisheries, and with large fishing fleets manned by hired crews. Although no other nation has such a diversity of operations, some, particularly those of North America and Western Europe, show similar distinctions between "family" and "industrial" fisheries.

In these western countries, as in Japan, the largest number of fishermen work in local and coastal operations. In the United Kingdom, less than 25 per cent of the fishermen are involved in distant-water fisheries. In the United States, more than two-thirds are fishing from the shore or from craft of less than 5 net tons. Such operations, concentrating on resources that have been fished for centuries, are generally marked by an inefficient use of labor as well as capital.

The calculation in Table 15 for the haddock fishery on the Georges Bank indicates that labor, as well as capital, is not utilized as economically as it would be under systems that limit the number of fishermen. In addition to the absence of ownership of the resource, there are other reasons for the general overapplication of labor in the stable or declining fisheries of North America and Western Europe. Most fishermen have, or believe they have, few alternative opportunities for employment. Living, as many of them do, in isolated villages along the sea coast, it is difficult for them to find or to learn other jobs. Furthermore, the isolation is frequently accompanied by lower educational opportunities and this, too, impedes mobility into other industries. Thus, a decline in catch per unit of effort, for whatever reason, is only sluggishly adjusted by the transfer of labor to other forms of employment. However, these conditions are less true now than they were formerly. The advances in the facilities of communication and transportation are leading to increased mobility of the labor force, evidence of which lies in both the declining and fluctuating numbers of fishermen in the countries of North America and Western Europe. Although these declines are in the direction of a more rational use of labor, fully rational use is unlikely to be attained so

Table 17. Salient Characteristics of the Three Groups of Fishery Operations in Japan

	GROUP 1 Small family operations		GROUP 2 Fishing households of small scale				GROUP 3 Fishery enterprises of larger scale	
			(Type A)		(Type B)			
Scale of operation and number of units	(1) Non-powered boats	116,205	(5) Powered boats 3–5 tons	8,108	(8) Beach seines	4,288	(10) Powered boats 30–100 tons	2,810
	(2) Powered boats under 3 tons	62,234	(6) Powered boats 5–10 tons	6,815	(9) Fixed nets of large type	2,166	(11) Powered boats over 100 tons	934
	(3) Fixed nets of small type	8,418	(7) Powered boats 10–30 tons	6,166				
	(4) Shallow-sea fish culture	33,603						
	Total	220,460	Total	21,089	Total	6,454	Total	3,744
Organization of operation	97% of the total is operated by individuals, the rest on joint account.		75–85% by individuals, rest mostly on joint account.		50–60% by individuals, the rest mostly on joint account.		50% by individuals 50% on joint account and by companies. In case of boats over 100 tons, 34% by companies.	

No. of fishermen per unit	33% . . . one person; 66% . . . 2–5 persons. On the average, 2–5 persons.	33% . . . 2–5 persons; 40% . . . 6–29 persons. On the average, 6–9 persons for boats under 10 tons; 15 persons for 10–30 ton boats.	65% . . . 6–29 persons; 21% . . . 30–99 persons. On the average, 20–25 persons.	10–29 persons for 30–100 ton boats; 30–99 persons for boats over 100 tons. On the average, 30–70 persons.
Composition of labor force	80–90% . . . family labor only; the rest . . . family labor and employed labor.	Less than 30% . . . family labor only; more than 70% . . . family labor and employed labor.	100% . . . family and employed labor.	100% . . . employed labor in enterprises of larger type.
Major types of fisheries	Nets of small type (gill nets, lift nets, surrounding nets, fixed nets), angling and long-lining of various types, gathering of shellfish and sea-weeds, shallow-sea fish culture.	Drag nets of small type, lift nets, surrounding nets, gill nets, angling and long-lining of various types.	Beach seines, fixed nets of large type.	Medium trawler fisheries west of 130° E, drag nets of medium type, large surrounding nets, stick-held dip-nets, salmon gill nets, skipjack and tuna long-lining.

Source: Fisheries Division, Food and Agriculture Organization of the United Nations, *Report of the Technical Meeting on Costs and Earnings of Fishing Enterprises,* London, September, 1958, Table 9.

long as the resources are held in common and there are no restrictions on entry.

The conditions of labor supply in the distant-water fisheries are quite different from those in the coastal fisheries. In the latter, the labor costs represent a high proportion of total costs, but in the former they are relatively small because of the size and refinement of the capital equipment. The supply of labor in the high seas fisheries generally comes from the larger ports and cities, where other opportunities for employment exist and where labor's wage is more in line with the wages of other industries. Furthermore, high-seas fisheries generally require long absences from home, and involve conditions of discomfort and danger, so that the men tend to make more careful calculations of their alternatives elsewhere. In general, therefore, deep sea labor is neither immobile nor isolated from the general labor market. Consequently, one of the factors leading to overemployment is relatively diminished in importance. On the high seas, therefore, it is the free-entry aspect of common property that must be held responsible for the excessive use of labor and capital, not the lack of alternative jobs for fishermen or of alternative outlets for saving.

Summary

Turning from the economic conditions common to all fisheries, to the explanation of differences between national fisheries, we find that the standard generalizations of economics apply much better. All western nations at least have the same common-property situations in their territorial waters and the same right of access to the high seas. Hence, as we would expect, the size of their fishing industry depends upon the cost of labor and the cost of capital relative to the extent of the resource and the value of the catch.

As in all such international industry comparisons it is difficult to make evaluations of comparative advantage. In the fishery, the capital goods (particularly nets, but also some vessels and other equipment) are internationally traded and so have a known cost. Labor, as has been shown above, is difficult to cost because its alternative employments are vague and depend upon the efficiency of the labor market. As for the value of the product, fresh fish are frequently protected by a tariff, so that demand is based chiefly on local influences including supply, taste, and income. Preserved, frozen, and canned fish are more often imported and have an international value. Similar statements could be made for most industries and their inputs.

It is in the "extent of the resource" on the high seas that we find an unusual situation. The coastal waters are usually territorial seas, and are fished only by the local industry. But the high seas fisheries are open to all. On a given fishing ground the intensity of exploitation depends in part on the distribution of the nationality of the vessels. Vessels operating close to each other but from different nations will differ in the labor-capital mix they use; the species and sizes they take; and the time they spend at sea. But these vessels are also competing with each other, so that the intensity of effort by each nation's fleet also depends on the number of vessels from other nations. Consequently, it is extremely difficult to predict how much each nation will participate in a given high seas fishery, even in static conditions. And when techniques, labor costs, tastes, and incomes are changing at different rates, in each country, the outcome cannot be guessed.

One suggestion is that on the high seas, the increasing use of large capital-intensive fleets is tending to equalize the cost of fishing among the great nations. The smaller the relative use of labor, the less important are differing labor costs. And if the capital goods are internationally traded, the uniformity of costs is increased. If this is true, it may be possible to predict the distribution of fishing effort among countries solely on the basis of differing valuations of fish. But this is sheer speculation—research on the matter has scarcely been begun.

Chapter 8

Meeting Future Demand

रें. रें.

IF the supply of fish continues to grow at the 1947–63 rate of 6 per cent per year—and there is no sign of slackening—it will reach 70 million metric tons by 1970. This suggests that there will be little difficulty in meeting the 1970 demand which we have estimated at between 57 million and 72 million metric tons. But dealing with all fish on a world basis is misleading. It is like trying to balance the total world output of food with the total world demand, ignoring some countries' surpluses and others' deficiencies, or the abundance of some foods and painful scarcity of others. We have stressed the heterogeneity of products that fall within the term, "fish," ranging from industrial commodities to luxury foods on the demand side and from sedentary shellfish to pelagic whales on the supply side. We have also pointed out the extreme differences among nations in the amount and kind of effort that is applied. It is in these aspects, examined in the following pages, that the problems and conflicts are likely to emerge.

Sources of Supply

Freshwater Supplies

Most freshwater fisheries lie within national boundaries and, therefore, are of interest to us only to the extent to which their development will relieve pressures upon marine fisheries. As pointed out earlier, there are great potentials for increasing supplies from this source. Although the technical aspects can be much improved, enough is known at present to permit the production of large quantities of protein per acre from artificial ponds, rice paddies, and irrigation systems. The major impediments to such production are economic and institutional. While the costs of production are apparently low, the costs of processing, distribution, and marketing are relatively high. These, and the prevailing inflexible marketing institutions, will probably dictate a slow rate of growth of freshwater fisheries in the low-income countries of Asia and Africa.

COASTAL FISHERIES SUPPLIES

The greatest output of fish comes from the relatively narrow band of seas around the coasts of the continents and islands of the world. This band does not carry any sharp demarcation nor does it carry any very helpful relationship to the legal definition of the territorial seas. In a few cases, a distinction between coastal fisheries and the major fishing grounds referred to below is meaningless, but in most cases, the distinction exists and is useful in pointing up the different kinds of problems that are emerging.

The coastal fisheries of nations whose fisheries have long been an important industry are already fully utilized: large increases of catch of species that are presently demanded are not possible. There are two types of "full utilization." In Japan, at one extreme all kinds of fish are taken from inshore waters and, while there are fluctuations in the component species, the total volume of supply is relatively fixed. In North America and Western Europe, on the other hand, the demand is species-oriented so that a large proportion of the fish of marketable size is either avoided or returned to the waters. Consequently, slight shifts in kind of demand could lead to some increases in the total supply of fish from these waters.

This situation is quite different along the coasts of the countries where fishing has not been an historically important occupation. The example of Peru is a dramatic (and extreme) case of development of a previously neglected coastal fishery. Although no other nation is known to have neglected resources of such great abundance, many do have significant stocks of relatively untouched fish, particularly the nations of the west coast of Africa, where some notable catch increases have already occurred. (Morocco's output is four times greater than it was before the war,

Angola's output is ten times greater, and the catch in South Africa and Southwest Africa is up seventeen times.) There are also known large stocks of fish off the coasts of Chile, Argentina, and Brazil. In most of these nations output is restricted by processing and marketing costs and institutions rather than by limitations of stock.

Since the war, a number of nations where coastal fisheries are of predominant importance have attempted to prevent foreign vessels from using their resources by extending the width of their territorial seas. Iceland has been one of the foremost advocates of a 12-mile limit of exclusive fishing rights. Peru, Chile, and Ecuador have claimed rights out to 200 miles from their shores; these claims, though not recognized in international law, still serve to hamper some of the activities of "foreign" tuna vessels.

A story in the *New York Times* a short while ago gave some indication of the pattern of conflict that is likely to become more frequent along productive fishing coasts. It also indicated the problems of congestion and the pressures for extending exclusive use rights.

A critical stage has been reached in the battle for herring in the Strait of Dover and sixty French fishing boats have pulled into Boulogne-sur-Mer in protest.

Three small French warships have taken up patrol posts on the herring fishing banks to protect French interests. But at the moment there is nothing that they can do as 400 fishing ships, for the most part Russian, East German, and Polish, crowd the banks off Calais.

The banks are only eight miles long and two miles wide, and the French fishermen describe the congested situation there as hazardous. Rules of navigation are not being observed, they say, and modern equipment, which searches the depths to locate the schools of herring, increases the risk, because fishing smacks by scores converge on an area when the fish are detected.

As a result, the owners of the French ships, after a general parley, have sent out an order by radio for the entire French fishing fleet to get back to port.

The catch, they feel, is not worth the risk of damage to the ships and equipment entailed in keeping at sea. By their action the owners also hope to induce the French Government to extend the country's territorial waters from three to 12 miles.

At stake, the French fishing owners say, are not only the jobs of the fishermen, but also all the jobs of the workers engaged in processing the herring, canning and salting the catch in towns of the Channel coast.[1]

It should be pointed out that such assertions are equally prevalent along the coast of the United States and other major fishing nations. Such reactions are to be expected where local fishermen are faced by severe competition from highly efficient foreign vessels in waters that the local fishermen have long had to themselves. But competition for fish is only part of the problem. Equally important is the fact that competition frequently becomes so severe that it leads to congestion of vessels, which increases the costs of operation. Where this occurs, it is a manifestation of excessive use of capital and labor resources.

MAJOR FISHING GROUNDS SUPPLIES

The output of the traditional species of most of the fishing grounds of historic importance has become relatively stable. In the North Atlantic Ocean, the major grounds are those off the Northwestern European coast and those off the Northeastern American coast. Within the waters of the former region, which include the North Sea, the Norwegian Sea, the Barents Sea, and the Iceland grounds, the catch has been chiefly herring and whitefish (cods, haddocks, hakes, etc.). There appears to be little opportunity for increasing the catch of the whitefish. Indeed, fishing nations in this area have already signed a convention designed to prevent further depletion of stocks.[2] Even for the herring fishery in these waters, there now appears to be some question as to whether or not catches can be maintained.

The important grounds off the North American coast range from the Georges Bank, off New England, to the Grand Banks, lying to the east and south of Newfoundland. The fact that these waters have been brought under the protection of the International Commission for the Northwest Atlantic Fisheries indicates a lack of opportunity for materially increasing the size of catch. Maximum sustained yield has already been reached in the had-

[1] Robert Alden, "French Call Off Herring Battle," *New York Times,* November 25, 1962.
[2] The Convention for the Regulation of the Meshes of Fishing Nets and Size Limits of Fish was signed in 1946 and came into force in 1954 when ratified by all signatories. The measures, however, were felt to be inadequate and a new agreement, the North-East Atlantic Fisheries Convention, was signed in 1959. See Chapter 11, below.

dock fishery of the Georges Bank. The demersal species on the banks of the Gulf of St. Lawrence, the Nova Scotia Banks, and the Grand Banks, are also in the process of stabilization, even though they are being subjected to increasing effort. The Japanese have recently started fishing in these waters. The appearance of Russian fleets has increased rapidly in this area, although their primary catch is not the cods and haddocks, but herring and redfish for which some increases may be expected. These additional vessels add to the congestion, and the Soviet herring drift nets, which are sometimes lost, also impede trawling operations.

Although the fishing grounds of the North Pacific—the Gulf of Alaska, Bristol Bay, and the Bering Sea—have not been as intensively fished as those of the North Atlantic, certain of the major species involved have already been subjected to strict conservation programs designed to prevent further depletion and to build up stocks. In fact, the first major international fisheries agreement dealt with the fur seals of the North Pacific, which were already close to extinction at the turn of the century. These have been carefully managed for more than half a century; stocks were built up and yields increased until the maximum sustainable yield was reached. Major increases in the catch of the Pacific salmon and halibut, the other two species controlled, are also unlikely. The whole kill fluctuates but is unlikely to become a major fishery. There are, however, other fish in these waters that may be taken in considerably greater numbers in the future. The Japanese have promoted a very active king crab fishery, and both they and the Russians are developing a trawl fishery for flounder, rockfish, hake, and other groundfish. The Alaskan shrimp industry of the United States is also undergoing rapid development.

In these waters, where increases in the total supply of all fish may be expected in spite of the relatively fixed production of seals, salmon, halibut, and whales, there are growing problems arising from the complex interrelationships among the fish and among the fishing operations. There is a predator-prey relationship between fur seals and salmon, both of which are the subject of conservation measures. Halibut, which are strictly controlled by Canada and the United States, are sometimes taken in Japanese and Russian trawling operations for flounder, hake, and other groundfish. The same vessels may economically participate in several fisheries, according to the seasons. These relationships complicate the job of establishing international agreements.

In the western Pacific, the major fishing grounds of the Yellow Sea and East China Sea have been intensively fished for centuries. Although few statistics are available, it is unlikely that these areas can produce much more than at present. Furthermore, because the industries already make little differentiation as to species, no new stocks are available to be exploited.

In the Southern Hemisphere, however, there are several productive fishing grounds that have considerable opportunities for exploitation. Until recently these have been outside the range of the major fishing nations, but the increasing trend toward distant-water operations and self-contained fishing fleets using factory ships or foreign bases is making their commercial development possible. In addition, the neighboring southern nations are beginning to participate. The extent of the supplies in these areas is not fully known and much research and exploration needs to be undertaken. The Antarctic region and the extensive continental shelf off the coast of Argentina may be particularly rewarding to future efforts. For example, it has been estimated that the Argentinian grounds could produce more than 3 million tons and those of Brazil, over 1 million per year.[3]

Supplies of Certain Species

Demand, particularly in North America and Western Europe, is concentrated on certain species of fish rather than on fish as a whole. Although the future characteristics of supply are difficult to pin down because of the absence of research, some general conclusions can be drawn from the available evidence.

The *herrings*, including menhaden and anchovies, appear to be widely abundant, although shortages may appear in certain local areas. Some of these shortages are temporary, caused by shifts in migration patterns or "natural" cycles in population levels. Others, however, such as those in the Skagerrak-Kattegat and East Anglian waters, may be permanent, owing to very intensive fishing efforts in the past. On the other hand, the abundance of herrings off the Peruvian coast and the possible development of herring fisheries

[3] G. Meseck, "Importance of Fisheries Production and Utilization in the Food Economy," Paper No. R/1.3 presented at FAO International Conference on Fish in Nutrition, September, 1961.

in many other areas of the world, indicates that supply is unlikely to fall short of growing world-wide demand for many years to come.

The *cods* (haddocks, pollacks, hakes, etc.) are in a different situation. Most of these groundfish presently come from areas that have been intensively fished for a long time, and it is unlikely that increases in catch of the higher-unit-value species will be significant. Two changes may occur. Supplies from the North Pacific may be developed to supplement those of the North Atlantic and, at the same time, there may be slight shifts in demand to some of the lower-unit-value and less-utilized species such as hake. Similar situations and changes may face the *flatfishes* (halibut, flounder, sole, etc.), although the potential increase in the North Pacific seems to be greater for this group (except halibut) than for the cods.

Catches of the *salmons* are steady or declining in almost all nations. (The one major exception is Norway where there has been a rapid increase in the take of capelin, which is used for fish meal.) The declines are due not only to overfishing but also to obstruction or pollution of the freshwater streams to which the spawning fish migrate. The reintroduction of salmon into some of the Atlantic streams has been attempted both in North America and Europe, but with little effect thus far. It is likely that the future demand for salmon can be met only at higher costs.

The future prospect for the *tunas* is quite uncertain. These fish are truly pelagic, ranging across entire oceans. As a result, very little is known about the size of stocks, migratory patterns, and growth rates or about the intermixture of subspecies. There are some indications that increased pressures upon the eastern Pacific yellowfin tunas will deplete the stocks and, on the basis of this evidence, control measures are being instituted through the Inter-American Tropical Tuna Commission. On the whole, however, sizable increases in the catch of all tuna can reasonably be expected for the next several years.

For *shrimp* and similar species the outlook is good. There are abundant supplies in the tropical and temperate waters of the oceans, particularly along shallow coasts where primitive fishing techniques have made little impact upon the supplies that are available. Great increases in catch can be expected with relatively small improvements in techniques, as is indicated by the large gains that have already occurred in the low-income countries of

Asia, South America, and Africa. Between 1948 and 1958, for example, total African output rose from 1 to 8.2 million pounds while that of South America rose from 1.9 to 38.6 million pounds. In short, there is no reason to anticipate a stringent world supply problem for many years to come.

The supply situation for *whales* is not so favorable. The pelagic whaling operations of the Antarctic, now the chief remaining source of supply, have been "regulated" for many years, except for a few seasons when international agreement could not be reached. But many people believe that the current harvest of this source is also too high to be maintained, so that some reduction of kill will be necessary in order to obtain a sustained yield in the future.

National Situations

The changing supply conditions described above will have quite different effects upon the participating nations. *Japan's* output has been increasing at about the rate of 6 per cent per year, which, if continued to 1970, would mean an output of about 10 million metric tons. This is probably a high estimate of Japan's future supply. G. Meseck, of the West German Department of Fisheries, reports that Japan intends to produce about 7.4 million tons by 1970.[4] This estimate appears to be too low. Japan's *demand* for food fish is expected to be 42–48 per cent greater than that of 1957–59. If the pattern of exports and food and nonfood demand remains the same, then supply would have to be on the order of 8.0–8.3 million metric tons, an increase of 19–24 per cent over the 1963 catch of 6.7 million tons. However, the pattern of use is not likely to remain the same, and the relative increase in export requirements is likely to continue. Thus, total demand may be on the order of 9–10 million tons at present relative prices. In view of past performances and the continuing extension of fishing activity, it appears likely that Japanese supply will reach this figure.

The situation for *Mainland China* is almost impossible to anticipate. One is tempted, because of the extremely large population, to estimate an extremely large demand for supply of fish. Evidently the Chinese themselves are thinking in these terms and would like to reach a target of 10 million tons by 1980, according

[4] *Ibid.*

to Dr. Meseck's report.[5] If there is any truth in their reported output figures, this target would appear to be quite reasonable, since an extension of the past trend leads to a figure of about 20 million tons by 1970. However, their output statistics are highly questionable and apparently include under-reporting in the earlier years and some inflation of estimates in the later years. Their catch in 1957–59 is probably closer to 3 million than to the reported 4 million tons. An increase in demand of between 40 and 60 per cent would indicate a total demand of about 5 million tons by 1970. A supply of this amount may be obtainable. It would apparently come largely from production in inland waters.

For *Peru* the future situation is also difficult to anticipate—not because of the absence of statistics, however, but because of the phenomenal growth rate that has occurred since the Second World War. Catch increased from 31,000 tons in 1947 to over 6.9 million tons in 1963. If this growth trend were continued to 1970 it would indicate the astonishing figure of over 100 million metric tons, which is more than twice current catch for the world as a whole. However, recent figures indicate a retardation in the rate of growth. The 1963 catch showed a slight decrease from that of 1962, whereas the annual increase in the previous year had been about 30 per cent and in the year before that, about 50 per cent. This lack of increase was apparently "because a fishermen's strike paralyzed the industry during 40 days in the best fishing season and due to the difficult financial situation afterwards faced by the fishmeal producers." [6] Some recovery is evident by the fact that fish meal production in the first ten months of 1964 was 32 per cent greater than for the same period in 1963.

Total world demand for such nonfood fish for 1970 was placed in Chapter 3, rather arbitrarily, between 17 and 27 million tons. If the rest of the world provided from 7 to 12 million tons, then Peru's share would range from 10 to 15 million. This would indicate a very marked retardation in growth rate; down to between 5 and 11 per cent per year as against the previous rate of more than 30 per cent per year. However, in absolute terms, the increase is very large, from almost 3.5 to 8.5 million more tons of fish. There is no way of knowing whether or not the resource can support catches up to as much as 15 million tons per year. On the face of it,

[5] *Op. cit.*
[6] Manuel Elguerra, "A Policy for Marine Resources: Peru's Experience," in California Museum of Science and Industry, *California and the World Ocean,* 1964.

the forecast seems to be far too optimistic. However, it has been pointed out that the guano-producing birds, whose immense numbers have lived off the anchovy for years, probably take as many fish as does the fish meal industry. The total take by both birds and fishermen has been estimated at 14 million metric tons per year.[7] This gives some indication of the fantastic quantities of fish in this area. It also indicates that if Peru chose to cut down the bird population, it might be able to increase the take by fishermen. The desirability of this step would depend upon the ecological ramifications as well as upon the relative values of the guano and fish meal industries.

Russia's demand for fish is increasing more rapidly than that of most other nations and may be expected to be between one and two-thirds and twice as much as it was in 1957–59. This indicates a total demand between 4.5 and 5.5 million metric tons, live weight (excluding whales) by 1970. The reported target for 1965, of about 4 million tons, was already achieved in 1963. At this rate, their supply may be at the upper limit, or perhaps even above, our estimate of demand. Russia's supplies will come increasingly from distant-water fisheries. They may be expected to increase their shares of the catch on historic fishing grounds, and they will probably exploit new areas in the Central and South Atlantic Oceans —areas that are already being explored by their vessels.

In the *United States,* although the increases in demand for food fish may be moderate (between 28 and 34 per cent higher than in 1957–59), total 1970 supply will depend more and more upon imports. Total supply of food fish in 1957–59 was about 3 million tons, of which about 40 per cent was imported. Total demand in 1970 for food fish will run about 4 million metric tons, live weight, of which about 2 million may be domestically produced and 2 million imported. In value terms, the percentage is likely to be higher because the growth in imported commodities will be made up largely of the high-unit-value items such as tuna, shrimp, and groundfish fillets.

For nonfood fishes, the total supply in 1957–59 was about 1.5 million metric tons, live weight. In 1963 supply had increased by an additional million tons. This was made up of a fourfold increase in imports together with a slight decline in domestic production. No estimate has been made, but it is clear the U.S. demand for nonfood fish products will continue to grow. A twofold increase between 1963 and 1970, which would match the increase

[7] *Ibid.*

of the previous seven years would probably mean an even greater reliance upon foreign imports than at present.

In 1963, *Norway's* catch of winter herring was about 2–3 per cent of its catch in 1956. The reasons for the decline are not fully known. In part it may be due to changing migratory patterns which bring the herring later in the season and farther north than usual. In part it may be the result of some natural fluctuations in population. It is argued that this is a part of a long oceanic cycle, and that a return to a major winter herring fishery cannot be expected for another 25–30 years.[8] And, finally, there is some belief that the decline is due to overfishing. But whatever the cause, this is a matter of critical importance to the Norwegian fishing industry. Although other herrings are being caught in increasing quantities, the winter herring has long been a staple of the industry— making up about a third of the catch of all fish in 1953–57. Further difficulties are being experienced because of an inability to increase the catch of the cods, whose stocks are believed to be diminishing. In view of these problems, the government is encouraging the exploration and development of new fisheries. However, it is unlikely that Norway will be able to maintain its present share in the world export market.

Of the nine major fishing nations, the *United Kingdom* is expected to have the smallest increase in demand for food fish between now and 1970: only 10–13 per cent over 1957–59. The trend in domestic catch has actually been downward, dropping from 1.2 million tons in the late 1940's to about 950,000 tons in 1963. Besides the decreasing stocks of fish in the traditional British fishing waters, the United Kingdom is facing the loss of about 9,000 square miles of water that is now fished by its vessels. This is due to the proposed and actual extension of territorial seas by the Danish, Faroese, Norwegian, and Icelandic governments. The losses of catch, because of the closures of waters to British fleets have been estimated to "range between 20 per cent and 35 per cent of the total annual catch from distant waters in recent years (10 per cent to 18 per cent of total landings of white fish from all waters), plus nearly 50 per cent of the middle water catch (roughly 3 per cent of total white fish landings). . . . The advantage [to the United Kingdom] of an extension of its own fishery limits to twelve miles would be negligible by comparison, al-

---

[8] "Norwegian Fisheries," *Market News Leaflet 56*, Branch of Market News, U.S. Bureau of Commercial Fisheries, August, 1962.

though it would no doubt benefit the inshore fisheries to some extent." [9] It is not anticipated that these losses can be made up by shifting to other grounds that are within the range of the present fleet. Certain increases in total landings might result from increased effort on certain underexploited species such as redfish. However, redfish "is not popular with British crews, for its sharp spines make it disagreeable to handle; and the owners of distant water vessels show little interest in it, pointing to its low price on the British market, and informing [the Committee] that it took twenty years to bring it into favour with German consumers." [10] On the whole, therefore, the total domestic catch is not likely to be greater than the recent average of about a million tons, and total supply will depend more and more upon imports.

For *Canada,* estimates of future potential supplies, made by Dr. W. E. Ricker,[11] are summarized below:

Canada: Potential Landings in 1980
Relative to Actual Landings, 1951–55

Zero change to
15% decrease .... Atlantic Clams, Atlantic Halibut.

Zero change to
10% increase .... Atlantic Lobster, Redfish, Lake Trout, Pacific Clams, Chinook Salmon.

10–25% increase .... Haddock, Cod, Coho Salmon, Pacific Halibut.

25–50% increase .... Mackerel, Lake Whitefish, Chum Salmon, Herring, Atlantic Flounder.

Over 50% increase .... Pacific Soles, Pink and Sockeye Salmon, Oysters, Scallops.

These estimates average to about a 30–40 per cent increase in landings for all fish by 1980. They are based primarily upon physical supply characteristics and maximum sustainable yields, with

[9] *Report of the Committee of Inquiry into the Fishing Industry* (London: H.M.S.O., January, 1961), p. 27.
[10] *Ibid.*
[11] W. E. Ricker, "Productive Capacity of Canadian Fisheries—An Outline," in *Resources for Tomorrow,* Vol. 2 (Ottawa: Queen's Printer, 1961).

some estimates of the Canadian share of international fisheries.
The relatively high projections for pink and sockeye salmon
assume a high degree of management practices on the major producing streams.

Our projections of Canadian demand for food fish indicate a
35–41 per cent increase over consumption levels of 1957–59 by
1970. If this is extended to 1980, total demand may be about 80
per cent higher than 1957–59. The total supply picture is thus not
very encouraging and indicates that Canada, like Norway, will
probably decline in its relative contribution to total world
exports.

India's output, as reported by FAO, shows a slight rising trend,
although this is obscured by large fluctuations. Future demand
estimates, however, are well beyond the reach of the trend, because they anticipate an increase of 68–100 per cent, or a total demand of up to 2 million metric tons. On the other hand, there
appears to be considerable disagreement about the accuracy of the
catch statistics. The U.S. Foreign Agricultural Service estimated
India's 1958 catch on the order of 2.5 million tons; the FAO figure
is 1 million. In the face of these discrepancies, little can be said
about the future supply and demand situation.

Outlook for Supply

Three kinds of changes predominate in our view of the future
changes in the location of effort, in the kinds of fish caught, and in
the relative importance of the producing nations. In terms of location of effort, one major change is the shift away from the Northern Hemisphere. This area, which produced 82 per cent of total
catch before the war, produced only 59 per cent in 1963. The shift
is largely due to the increased Peruvian catch. The coastal waters
of the northern Atlantic nations will be contributing a diminishing
share of total catch, as will the major fishing grounds of historic importance (the Grand Banks, the North Sea, Georges Bank, etc.).
New coastal waters will be gradually developed and exploited, particularly those of the southern Atlantic. Efforts may be started on
some of the relatively untouched fishing grounds of the Southern
Hemisphere, but, because of lack of knowledge, it is difficult to anticipate the extent of supplies in these areas. Pelagic fishing on the
high seas will probably become increasingly important through-

out the world. In short, the major increase in future supplies will come from waters that are relatively far removed from the coasts of the traditional fishing nations.

The future situation for the different kinds of fish is more complex, primarily because of the wide differences in demand among the major consuming nations. Though world supplies of herring are abundant there is a rapidly growing demand for herring products, and it is not clear whether output will be able to continue to meet the demand at present prices.

The world supplies of some of the high-unit-value fish, such as shrimp and tuna, appear to be adequate in terms of world demand, although there may be some shifts between particular species. But the outlook for others, such as salmon and perhaps halibut, is such that prices may show considerable increases. Within the cod group, some of the more highly preferred species are in relatively short supply. Although new processing techniques and new forms of utilization are permitting substitution of some of the less preferred species, the total supply may not be able to satisfy increased demand in North America and Western Europe at the current price levels.

The stocks of freshwater fish are relatively small but, unlike most marine species, supplies can be considerably increased under conditions of cultivation and management. However, unfavorable economic and institutional characteristics will continue to impede rapid development of these fisheries in most countries during the next decade.

The major changes in the relative importance of the producing nations are already under way and can be expected to continue through 1970. The most significant shift is the diminishing relative importance of the countries of North America and Western Europe. This shift is related to the diminishing significance of the supplies in their coastal and nearby waters and also to their unwillingness or inability to expend a great deal of effort in locating and developing new and distant grounds.

The Source of Conflict

In looking forward to the next several years, we do not see dramatic shortages of fishery resources, nor do we anticipate the sudden outbreak of hostilities between fishing nations. The course we are following in exploiting the common wealth of the seas is more gradual—and more insidious. It will gradually worsen along three lines: through depletion of stocks, through decreased returns per unit of effort, and through increasing numbers of local conflicts. If present arrangements and procedures for solving these problems are continued, there may be temporary relief but no lasting cure.

Continued, localized depletion is inevitable. We have pointed out that demand and effort are focused primarily on a few species within relatively small areas of the ocean. Increasing effort, and increasing pressures upon the supplies, will occur along coastal waters and on the major fishing grounds of the North Atlantic and North Pacific. We cannot expect immediate relief from the development of new fishing grounds or the utilization of different kinds of fish, for not until a fishery has already become depleted do the costs generally become high enough to induce movement away from the resource to new grounds or other species.

Depletion brings with it the stimulus to establish controls on use. If properly chosen and executed, these controls can serve to rehabilitate the stock and put the fishery on a sustained yield basis. But that is all they can do. It is becoming more and more clear that the forms of control adopted in the past do nothing to overcome the loss of income per unit of effort. The inherent economic inefficiency of the exploitation of common property resources can only be prevented by controlling the numbers of producers—by, in a sense, assigning property rights to the resource.

Conflict emerges because the great wealth in sea fisheries tempts nations to appropriate the fisheries by extending national rights farther out to sea. The local fishermen who suddenly find themselves in competition with foreign vessels for relatively fixed supplies are understandably angry at these threats to their source of income. Although such fisheries may be beyond their national waters, the local fishermen have come to believe that the fish are "theirs." Controls on use that are designed to maximize sustainable yields will do nothing to ameliorate these conflicts because the resource that is conserved is still unowned.

The economic forces that stimulate attempts to appropriate fisheries are the same forces that will determine the viability of international regimes and arrangements. In the next several chapters we discuss international law and agreements; the concept of the "freedom of the seas," its basis and its consequences; and the necessity for including economic criteria in future decisions.

Chapter 9

The Role of International Law

≋. ≋.

INTERNATIONAL law is better understood and better worked out in its application to the use of the seas than in its application to many other international problems. This is not surprising, for it has been hammered out over the centuries by many nations in the process of balancing the claims of certain states against their acceptability to other nations in the light of their own over-all national interests and their sense of right and wrong. Lawyers, courts, and scholars have needed to consider not only the problems of wars, blockades, and navies, but also the continuing peacetime interests of individual fishermen and merchant ships.

This hammering-out process has produced the present set of rules or doctrines, which reflect the technical conditions and the interests of the dominant states in a situation which is being rapidly altered. These rules are sometimes invoked thoughtlessly, without recalling the particular problems to which they were once the peaceful, efficient, or ethically attractive solution. In later chapters we suggest that the rules or principles are no longer applicable; that the time has come for the community of nations to reconsider its joint and several aims and methods for the use of the sea. Here, though, we examine the background, and discuss, first, the basic doctrine of the freedom of the seas and how it has been modified over the years; and, second, the claims that have been made by various states to complete or limited sovereignty or jurisdiction over the seas; and, third, the mass of "statute-law" that has grown up in the form of treaties between states, compromising the absolute freedom implied by the first element and the complete sovereignty of the second.

The Freedom of the Seas

In the early middle ages, doctrines dealing with the rights of men to the seas were advanced and occasionally enforced, but they were largely of regional application, reflecting the power of dominant cities or states. In fact, it could be maintained that men believed, or acted as though they believed, in the freedom of the seas.

But the fifteenth and sixteenth centuries brought many claims of exclusive jurisdiction and these were maintained with varying degrees of enthusiasm and success. Best known today is the division of the newly discovered parts of the Atlantic, the Pacific, and the Indian oceans between Spain and Portugal by Pope Alexander VI in 1493. In addition, the Scandinavian kingdoms asserted similar rights over the Baltic and the adjacent Atlantic; Britain claimed the "British Seas"; and all were perhaps inspired by the earlier claims of Venice and Genoa to the Adriatic and the Ligurian Seas.

These attempts to gain exclusive control of the seas were challenged in the seventeenth century, particularly by Holland's enterprises in the Indian Ocean. In defense of these enterprises, and in refutation of the Spanish and Portuguese claims to the high seas and to a right to exclude foreigners from them, Hugo Grotius published in 1608 his *Mare liberum*. This was some seventeen years before the publication of his *De jure belli ac pacis,* which became one of the main foundations of international law. Although directed primarily to justifying the warlike defense of its trade by the Dutch East India Company against attempts at arrest by Portuguese vessels, his argument was sufficiently general in form to cover other uses of the high seas, especially fishing.[1] It did not depend on the study of theological sources or canon law, but on the newer "natural law" approach. This system led him to use "reason" in his search for a high seas regime that would be comformable with the rational nature of man in his attempt to use his environment.

[1] T. W. Fulton, *The Sovereignty of the Sea* (Edinburgh: Blackwood and Sons, 1911), pp. 344–46.

In dealing with the high seas, Grotius eclectically drew upon a variety of sources and arguments. Most important, however, is his logical argument that property itself cannot exist on the oceans because the usual conditions for the holding of property rights do not apply. These conditions he took to be two: first, the power of occupation, which may be interpreted as the power of a navy to hold a body of water,[2] but may more generally be interpreted as the ability to enclose and appropriate a body of water; and, second, the exhaustibility of the resource.[3] Land is both appropriable and exhaustible, therefore it can and should become property. The seas are inappropriable and inexhaustible, therefore they are not property and may be used inoffensively by everybody. This argument, so curiously anticipatory of the many political-economy arguments of the nineteenth century, is based on conditions that have changed considerably in recent decades. The idea of exhaustibility is now recognized to require economic as well as physical definition; nothing was said about conflicting uses or about congestion, which indicates exhaustion of the space required for fishing; and the impossibility of occupation is now open to serious question.

"Freedom of the seas" was far from achieving wide acceptance in Grotius' own day. Britain, soon to become the main naval power, rejected both Grotius' doctrine and one advanced earlier by Queen Elizabeth that the "use of the sea and the air is common to all." [4] In 1635 John Selden published his *Mare clausum,* asserting that the "sea, by the law of nations, is not common to all men, but capable of private dominion or property as well as the land" and, "that the King of Great Britain is lord of the Seas flowing about, as an inseparable and perpetual appendant of the British Empire." [5] (These seas were claimed by Selden to include all of what is now called the North Sea and much of the Bay of Biscay, as well as a good part of the Atlantic west of the British Isles.) [6] Indeed, it was not until the nineteenth century that Britain discontinued her claims to sovereignty, although at least a century earlier

---

[2] L. Oppenheim, *International Law,* H. Lauterpacht, ed. (8th ed.; London: Longmans, Green and Co., 1955), Vol. 1, p. 593.

[3] See Ralph Van Doman Magoffin (trans.), *Grotius on the Freedom of the Seas* (New York: Oxford University Press, 1916), where the translation makes no mention of the "naval" occupation as used by Lauterpacht.

[4] Cited in Fulton, *op. cit.,* p. 107.

[5] Cited in Magoffin, *op. cit.,* "Introduction."

[6] See Fulton, *op. cit.,* frontispiece.

she had conceded, with most other states, a freedom of navigation. The intervening century, being one of almost unremitting naval warfare, permitted only uncertain and hesitant progress toward a general acceptance of complete freedom of the seas—the doctrine which essentially holds today.

Territorial Seas

As states continued to assert a variety of claims over their coastal waters, it was not long before a "territorial sea" became a formal claim to an extended sovereignty of the state and a geographic limit to the freedom of the seas. Sometimes the claims were for wider internal waters, or a broader band between the actual shore and the base line from which the three-mile or other territorial sea is measured; sometimes they were for special fishing zones. But until recently, the width of the territorial sea has been the question that has epitomized the others.

When this width was considered at a conference called by the League of Nations in 1930, it was found that more countries favored three miles than any other distance from the coast,[7] but a surprisingly large number of other widths were claimed, ranging from the four-mile tradition prevalent among the Baltic nations through the six-mile tradition of some Mediterranean states and former Spanish possessions to the twelve-mile claim of Russia. At the 1958 Geneva Conference on the Law of the Sea, only 23 of the 86 nations represented expressly claimed a three-mile territorial sea.[8]

The different widths have their sources in wars or disputes in which the actual width of the territorial sea already claimed was put to some sort of test. Many countries were forced to reduce their extensive claims to what are now high seas to narrower belts over which they could exercise a more complete jurisdiction. The Scandinavian states, for example, reduced their sweeping claims to the Baltic and Northern Seas to a marginal belt of territorial waters one sea league in width—the Scandinavian league being roughly four nautical miles, while most of Europe uses a three-mile league. The first reduction was made by Norway in 1743.

[7] See report on this conference in *American Journal of International Law,* Vol. 24 (Supp.) (1930), p. 27.

[8] *Law of the Sea,* UN Doc. No. A/Conf.13/C1/L.11/Rev.1, Corr. 2.

The suggestion that the width of the coastal belt should be determined by the range of cannon shot is usually attributed to the Dutch jurist Bynkershoek who, in 1703, coupled the extent of the dominion of the land with the limit of the power of land-based arms. This notion evidently depended upon his view of earlier practice in Mediterranean waters where the problem was one of delimiting a width within which shipping could be said to be in neutral waters. The cannon-shot rule caught the imagination of many subsequent authorities, so that throughout the eighteenth century many claims and proposals for a clearly-defined territorial sea were accompanied by discussion of the actual range of cannon.

It was not until the late eighteenth century that the cannon-shot and sea league traditions were brought together. In 1782 the Italian writer, Galiani, following an earlier suggestion of France, approximated the cannon-shot length to three nautical miles; and this approach was confirmed by an American definition of its neutral waters to three miles in 1793 on the understanding that cannon range was usually stated at one sea league. This width was also accepted by Britain and France.[9]

In the nineteenth century, the three-mile limit was confirmed both by practice and treaty. It was used to define the Canadian coastal fisheries in the convention of 1818 between Great Britain and the United States, the first of a long series of fisheries and customs treaties (culminating in the Bering Sea Arbitration of 1893 and the subsequent treaty on fur seals) that took three miles as a basis. Some countries never accepted three miles, but few followed a significantly different practice until after the First World War. Both for coastal fisheries and other purposes, three miles was found to be a convenient distance, enclosing most activities closely related to the activities on land, and capable of regular protection, surveillance, and enforcement.

[9] See H. S. K. Kent, "The Historical Origins of the Three-Mile Limit," *American Journal of International Law*, Vol. 48 (1954), pp. 537–53. Kent asserts that the three-mile limit emerged as a compromise between the cannon-shot rule of Holland and the Mediterranean countries and the four nautical miles claimed by the Scandinavian countries. He writes in answer to the thesis advanced by W. L. Walker, "Territorial Waters: The Cannon Shot Rule," *British Year Book of International Law*, Vol. 22 (1945), pp. 210–31, that it was ". . . not altogether improbable that the two rules [the three mile limit and the cannon-shot rule] never had any real historical connection. . . ." See also the brief general discussion in *The Territorial Sea*, Reference Division, U.K. Central Office of Information, January, 1960, p. 2.

Treaties before 1945

Treaties dealing with high seas fisheries are for the most part concerned with one of three problems: congestion, conservation, or fishing rights.

The treaties dealing with congestion are an attempt to resolve conflicts in fisheries where more than one type of vessel or gear is used or where for some other reason there is interference between vessels of different flags. Here the aim has been to do for the fisheries what has also been done for merchant ships and men-of-war: to set up rules and provide for their enforcement. An outstanding example is provided by a series of treaties between Britain and her neighbors governing the registration and visit and search of vessels in the North Sea, beginning with the Convention of 1882.[10] It is noteworthy that such treaties do not attempt to deal with the management of the fishery. Indeed, the fish stock is still treated as though it were inexhaustible. Rather, the conflicts arise because of the crowding of vessels and gear.

A second group of treaties deals with what is now called the "conservation" of marine stocks. One of the most significant was the set of agreements and regulations relating to the seal fisheries of the North Pacific, arising out of the Bering Sea fur seal controversy between Great Britain and the United States and the Bering Sea Fur Seal Arbitration of 1893. The search for a more viable method of regulation culminated in the multilateral convention of 1911 to which Russia and Japan were also parties.[11] Under this convention, Russia and the United States are managers of the resource and operate as agents for the parties of the convention. Fur seals may not now be taken on the high seas, where capture is inefficient, but only on the islands where they breed. The United States and Russia invest only as much effort as is required to take the maximum sustainable yield from the herds on their respective islands. The returns are then split with the other signatory nations

[10] For a list of treaties with similar provisions, see A. P. Daggett, "The Regulation of Maritime Fisheries by Treaty," *American Journal of International Law*, Vol. 28 (1934), p. 712, fn. 128.

[11] See L. L. Leonard, *International Regulation of Fisheries* (Washington: Carnegie Endowment for International Peace, Division of International Law, 1944), pp. 55–95.

which are, in a sense, being paid to give up their right to take seals in international waters. This system has the economic merit of producing the permissible yield at the lowest cost and of preventing wasteful competition.

This kind of arrangement, however, is unique. There is no other fisheries treaty that grants full rights of exploitation to a single authority. Instead, the many conservation treaties permit the participants to invest as much effort as they please, subject only to such controls as the size of the mesh, the length of the season, the protection of nursery areas, etc. Most of these treaties call for research activities as well as regulatory devices. A few, such as the International Council for the Exploration of the Sea, established in 1902, deal only with research.

The third group of treaties may be called "fishing rights" treaties for they give a country the right to fish in circumstances where it would otherwise be barred. For example, in the Treaty of 1763 (Peace of Paris), France was given rights to fish in the Gulf of St. Lawrence. Britain has a series of treaties with Denmark, beginning in 1901, concerning the coast of Iceland and the Faroe Islands. The Treaty of 1925 between Mexico and the United States set forth fishing rights in the Gulf of Mexico. Still another type of agreement is less concerned with rights to fish than with rights to use harbors and to obtain bait on the neighboring coast. The North Pacific Treaty signed in 1952, and a Japanese agreement with Russia in 1956 are in a sense modern versions of the "fishing rights" treaty, since Japan agreed not to fish certain stocks. Like many recent treaties, however, the North Pacific Treaty is a blend and is directed toward conservation as well as fishing rights.

Prior to 1945, fisheries were the chief ocean resource noticed in cases in international law or in treaties. Rights over the continental shelf, minerals in it, and shellfish on it were rarely mentioned, presumably because rarely used. Some mineral workings extended under the sea from Cornwall; and Britain claimed jurisdiction over pearl fisheries on the bed of the sea extending well beyond Australian and Ceylon coasts. The first international agreement on minerals is the Anglo-Venezuelan Treaty of 1942, where the two countries agree on a line separating their submarine oil deposits, without otherwise affecting the status of the open sea in the Gulf of Paria, lying above ("superjacent to") them. Concern about the continental shelf did not really commence till 1945, though it was noticed as early as 1923 that neither of Grotius' two conditions for the freedom of the seas was applicable.[12] In the preparation for the 1930 Hague Conference on the Codification of the Law of the Sea, the existence of the continental shelf as a biological entity was noticed; but its geological significance emerged later.

Developments since 1945

By 1945, then, the legal position concerning the use of the oceans was fairly clear. The principle of the freedom of the sea for fishing was well established, subject only to a territorial sea under national jurisdiction, the limits of which defined residually the extent of the high seas. The width of the territorial seas differed from one country to another (as did the position of the base line from which this width was measured), but it was usually three miles. Inside this line national fishing regulations were possible; outside it, the states could only claim to regulate the conduct of their own nationals. The legal position of the continental shelf and the "sedentary" shellfish on it was untested and unresolved.[13]

The year 1945 marks a convenient point at which to begin a closer examination of the legal patterns of co-operation. In many ways it was a significant year for fisheries' history: The UN was founded, incorporating into it the new Food and Agriculture Organization; fisheries, which had been neglected during the war, were subjected to the beginnings of an exploitation rate unknown before the war; and maritime power was redistributed and more widely shared.

The most sensational event was the "Truman Proclamation," which was actually two proclamations made in September 1945. The operative declarations are brief enough to quote in full: [14]

> . . . Having concern for the urgency of conserving and prudently utilizing its natural resources, the Government of the United States regards the natural resources of the subsoil and sea bed of

[12] See Sir Cecil J. B. Hurst, "Whose is the Bed of the Sea? Sedentary Fisheries Outside the Three Mile Limit," *British Year Book of International Law,* Vol. 4 (1923–24), pp. 34–43, and M. W. Mouton, *The Continental Shelf* (The Hague: Martinus Nijhoff, 1952), pp. 149 ff.

[13] See Gilbert Gidel, *Le Droit International Public de la Mer,* Vol. 1 (Recueil Sirey), Paris, 1932, pp. 488 ff., as discussed by Mouton, *op. cit.,* pp. 138–61.

[14] See text and bibliography in W. W. Bishop, Jr., *International Law* (2d ed.; Boston: Little, Brown & Co., 1962), pp. 535–42.

the continental shelf beneath the high seas but contiguous to the coasts of the United States as appertaining to the United States, subject to its jurisdiction and control. In cases where the continental shelf extends to the shores of another State, or is shared with an adjacent State, the boundary shall be determined by the United States and the State concerned in accordance with equitable principles. The character as high seas of the waters above the continental shelf and the right to their free and unimpeded navigation are in no way thus affected. (2667)

. . . In view of the pressing need for conservation and protection of fishery resources, the Government of the United States regards it as proper to establish conservation zones in those areas of the high seas contiguous to the coasts of the United States wherein fishing activities have been or in the future may be developed and maintained on a substantial scale. Where such activities have been or shall hereafter be developed and maintained by its nationals alone, the United States regards it as proper to establish explicitly bounded conservation zones in which fishing activities shall be subject to the regulation and control of the United States. Where such activities have been or shall hereafter be legitimately developed and maintained jointly by nationals of the United States and nationals of other States, explicitly bounded conservation zones may be established under agreements between the United States and such other States; and all fishing activities in such zones shall be subject to regulation and control as provided in such agreements. The right of any state to establish conservation zones off its shores in accordance with the above principles is conceded, provided that corresponding recognition is given to any fishing interests of nationals of the United States which may exist in such areas. The character as high seas of the areas in which such conservation zones are established and the right to their free and unimpeded navigation are in no way thus affected. (2668)

These proclamations were unexpected and widely misinterpreted. The fisheries' part (2668), in retrospect, seems to have been only an assertion of the importance of making and respecting treaties concerning high seas fisheries regulation and conservation. Unfortunately, it was confused by many with the first proclamation, concerning the continental shelf.[15]

In retrospect, again, this first declaration (2667) seems to have

15 See Josef L. Kunz, "Continental Shelf and International Law: Confusion and Abuse," *American Journal of International Law,* Vol. 50 (1956), pp. 828–53.

merely modified the position taken in the Anglo-Venezuelan Treaty of 1942 that submarine resources in the shelf could and might be appropriated by neighboring states. It should not be forgotten that at the time the United States was involved in an internal dispute over its offshore (tideland) oil reserves; the Proclamation can therefore be seen as an element in the strategy of the federal government in claiming the rights over these resources. Its effects, however, were world-wide.

The continental shelf proclamation precipitated a series of somewhat similar proclamations by other states.[16] These can be put into three groups. The first group was primarily concerned with sedentary fisheries, such as pearl and oyster. An important example is the Australian proclamation in 1953 of sovereignty over seabed and subsoil contiguous to any part of the coast for the purpose of exploring and exploiting the natural resources of that seabed and subsoil; [17] legislation was passed to regulate their use by foreigners,[18] resulting in a dispute with Japan.[19]

A second group of proclamations appeared to be concerned primarily with mineral resources, chiefly oil. Most of these asserted rights similar to those claimed by the United States. In the Middle East, they cleared the way for the complete division of the floor of the Persian Gulf.[20]

A third group of proclamations claimed the rights not only to the shelf, but also to the use of the seas above it. Mexico and Argentina made such claims but, apart from fisheries, did not claim a right to interfere with free navigation. Other South American states went further, combining the two elements in the

[16] Generally, see S. Oda, "The Continental Shelf," *Japanese Annual of International Law*, Vol. 1 (1957), pp. 15–37.

[17] *1953 Commonwealth of Australia Gazette No. 56*, September 11, 1953, p. 2563.

[18] Pearl Fisheries Act (No. 2), 1953, Act No. 38, 1953; and see L. F. E. Goldie, "Australia's Continental Shelf: Legislation and Proclamations," *International & Comparative Law Quarterly*, Vol. 3 (1954), pp. 535–75; D. P. O'Connell, "Sedentary Fisheries and the Australian Continental Shelf," *American Journal of International Law*, Vol. 49 (1955), pp. 185–209; "Australia and the Continental Shelf," *Australian Law Journal*, Vol. 27 (1953), p. 458.

[19] The case has been submitted to the International Court of Justice and a provisional regime has been agreed upon in the interim: see 191 UN Treaty Series (1954), p. 125.

[20] P. C. L. Anninos, *The Continental Shelf and Public International Law* (The Hague: H. P. DeSwart & Fils, S.A., 1953), pp. 22 ff.

Truman declaration and claiming full rights over the shelf and the seas above it. (One claimed also the air space above.) Chile, Ecuador, and Peru (the CEP states) having no shelf off their coast, claimed "exclusive sovereignty and jurisdiction over the [200 nautical mile] zone" and "exclusive sovereignty and jurisdiction over the seabed and subsoil." [21]

The CEP states have not completely closed their fisheries to other nations, but rather have placed restrictions and costs on their use. So far there has been no test of their claims in the international court.

In 1952, South Korea proclaimed the so-called Rhee line, which in effect closed to Japan fisheries up to 250 miles from Korea. Then Russia in 1956 stated that the Sea of Okhotsk would be closed to Japanese salmon fishermen. This claim, however, was dropped when Russia and Japan signed the Northwest Pacific Fisheries Treaty which has led to regulations on seasons, gear, and amount of catch. In 1957, over the protests of Japan, the United States, the United Kingdom, and other nations, Russia closed the Peter the Great Bay (near Vladivostok) to all foreign vessels and aircraft.[22]

In 1957 Indonesia closed about half a million square miles within her archipelago as internal waters by using the headland system for drawing straight base lines, and also claimed a twelve-mile territorial sea. The Philippines have acted similarly.[23]

No account of law and practice of fisheries would be complete without mentioning the claims by Iceland and Norway,[24] which gave rise to disputes with Britain. The Icelandic dispute which extended from before 1952 till 1962, spanning the 1958 and 1960

[21] F. V. Garcia-Amador, *The Exploitation and Conservation of the Resources of the Sea* (2d ed.; Leyden, Netherlands: A. W. Sythoff, 1959), p. 99.

[22] S. Oda, *International Control of Sea Resources* (Leyden, Netherlands: A. W. Sythoff, 1962), pp. 28–31 and 72–76. See also "A Map Analysis of Japan's Fishery Problems," *Japanese Annual of International Law,* Vol. 3 (1959), p. 103, and Bishop, *op. cit.,* pp. 500–501.

[23] See J. Evensen, "Certain Legal Aspects Concerning the Delimitation of Archipelagos," in *Law of the Sea,* UN Doc. No. A/Conf.13/18. It would appear that these closures have not been vigorously enforced.

[24] For a recent survey of the Iceland dispute, see C. J. Colombos, *The International Law of the Sea* (5th ed. rev.; London: Longmans, Green and Co., 1962), pp. 140–43. For the Norwegian fisheries case, see Bishop, *op. cit.,* pp. 493–96; Colombos, pp. 104–13, and 163; C. H. M. Waldock, "International Law and the New Maritime Claims," *International Relations,* Vol. 1 (1956), pp. 180 ff.

Law of the Seas Conferences, was an example of an economic argument advanced by coastal states for a wide territorial sea.

When Iceland became a republic during World War II, she repudiated a 1901 agreement with Britain establishing a three-mile territorial sea, and in 1948 she asserted sovereignty over the fisheries above the continental shelf. In 1952, however, she apparently reduced her claim to a four-mile territorial sea but measured it from a system of straight base lines similar to the procedure advanced by Norway. This extension of her exclusive fishing area worked to the severe disadvantage of the British distant-water industry. It was met by a boycott of Icelandic fish landings at British ports, which lasted for several years.

When the 1958 Law of the Sea Conference failed to produce a convention on the width of the territorial sea, Iceland sought to extend her claim to exclusive fishing rights to a twelve-mile limit. Britain rejected this claim, and British gunboats patrolled to protect vessels fishing within the area. The boycott campaign of the British industry against the purchase of Icelandic fish recommenced.

When, once again, a Law of the Sea conference was called in 1960, the British government proposed to Iceland a gradual phasing-out of British fishing in the area between a six-mile limit and a twelve-mile limit, so that after about ten years Iceland would have the full twelve miles. This proposal, which came close to the United States–Canada suggestion nearly adopted by the Conference in 1960, was accepted as the basis of an agreement. But the agreement, so close in time to the Geneva conference, is hardly a source of general law; its wording stresses only that Iceland "will not object. . . ." U.K. "will not object . . ." presumably to avoid an impression that twelve miles is other than a bilateral agreement.[25]

Iceland's bargaining strength throughout this long dispute came from her international strategic position, supported by her own belief in her *economic* need for the sole use of these fisheries to strengthen her vulnerable international trade position. With little or nothing to lose, she persuaded many smaller nations of the moral rightness of her actions and aims, till the twelve-mile fishing limit, rejected at the 1960 Conference by a narrow margin, appeared the obvious solution to the conflict.

[25] For text of agreement, see Great Britain, Treaty Series No. 17 (1961), Cmnd. 1328.

It is too soon yet to conclude that Iceland's long struggle has ushered in a period of wider coastal fishing limits, and perhaps also a wider territorial sea, as a rule in international law. But it has not been without effect. In separate agreements, the United Kingdom made concessions to Denmark with respect to the Faroe Islands and to Norway.[26] The fact that British fishermen had been more or less established in the areas now claimed as national fishing zones was recognized by dividing the fishing zone into areas into some of which British fishermen might be permitted and by stretching out the process of exclusion over a period of years.[27] This recognition of past usage of a fishery is frequently referred to as "established rights" or "historic rights."

Claims to wider fishing zones or territorial seas were subsequently made by other countries. Canada and the United Kingdom have also made recent announcements of their intention to extend their limits to twelve miles.

The dispute between Britain and Norway arose over base lines. It had long been the practice both in treaties and in decisions on jurisdiction to draw a base line across the mouths of bays, harbors, narrow fjords, and river mouths having less than a certain width (such as ten miles) and to declare the waters within to be "internal waters," which, like lakes and rivers within the country, are part of the sovereign territory of the state and liable to its domestic regulations. In such waters foreign commerce has no automatic right of passage nor have foreign fishermen, but both have right of refuge in storm.

There is a considerable body of decision and expert literature on the rules for drawing these base lines: for example, the important North Atlantic arbitration of 1910 [28] and the full discussion at The Hague conference of 1930. Although the arguments for broadening the internal waters behind these lines have usually

26 For text of the United Kingdom agreements with Denmark and Norway, see Great Britain, Treaty Series No. 55 (1959), Cmnd. 776, and No. 25 (1961), Cmnd. 1352, respectively. Generally, see D. H. N. Johnson, "Developments since the Geneva Conferences of 1958 and 1960: Anglo-Scandinavian Agreements Concerning the Territorial Sea and Fishing Limits," *International & Comparative Law Quarterly*, Vol. 10 (1961), pp. 587–97.

27 *The Economist*, October 8, 1960, p. 126.

28 The Tribunal for the North Atlantic Coast Fisheries Arbitration, concerning the rights of U.S. fishermen on the Canadian and Newfoundland coasts, made certain recommendations about the position of closing lines to be drawn across bays. J. B. Scott, *Hague Court Reports*, 1916.

been based on historical reasons, there has recently been a tendency to advance economic and social reasons for awarding to the coastal states exclusive sovereignty over certain bays and gulfs. Both the historical and the social types of argument were used in the judgment in the influential Fisheries Case in 1951, concerning the legality of Norway's claimed right to draw straight base lines from headland to headland.

The northern Norwegian coastline is deeply indented and characterized by groups and chains of islands, many of them some distance from the mainland. Norway wanted to draw base lines (sometimes forty miles in length) from island headland to island headland, and thus enclose, as internal waters, vast areas which Britain claimed were the high seas. Britain, in effect, wished to draw a three-mile line around each of the outer headlands, thus giving the high seas an irregular border which would penetrate between promontories and islands surrounded by Norwegian territorial waters. The dispute came before the International Court in 1951.[29]

In its judgment the Court denied that the rule that the length of base lines between headlands be restricted to ten miles had become customary; it accepted both the Norwegian placing and shape for base lines, and generally upheld the Norwegian argument for the relevance of a long tradition in Norwegian affairs of a close link between the land and the waters under dispute.

The judgment has been widely cited and undoubtedly formed the basis of the work of the Geneva Conference on base lines.[30] The Court, however, declared that although the delimitation of internal waters (behind a straight base line) is a unilateral and domestic matter, it has an international aspect, and its validity depends upon international law,[31] that is, upon historical usage and international acceptance. This appears to be a reminder that the mere claim of a country that it is applying the Norwegian or Geneva rules is not sufficient guarantee that other countries must respect the new territorial sea and fishing zone thus created.

Thus, in the 1950's, progress had been made narrowing the high

[29] [1951] *International Court of Justice Report*, 116.

[30] At the 1958 Geneva Conference it was noted that the following countries claimed a straight baseline system: Cambodia, Finland, Iceland, Norway, and Philippines. UN Doc. No. A/Conf.13/Cl/L.11/Rev.1, Corr. 2. More recent claims to such a system have been made by Tunisia and South Africa.

[31] *Ibid.*, p. 132.

seas, both by widening some territorial waters and zones of exclusive fishing rights, and, more significantly on some coasts by establishing base lines farther out from the land. Widespread adoption of these practices by other countries would, of course, reduce the area in which the freedom of the seas applies to fishing. This was roughly the situation when the Geneva Convention on the Law of the Seas convened in 1958.

The Geneva Conventions on the Law of the Sea

All these claims influenced the delegates to the 1958 Conference on the Law of the Sea; it appeared to most of them that the old three-mile fishing limit was already on its way out. Perhaps more important even than the increasing width of the fishing zone though was the drastic shift seaward of its base line, as permitted by the 1951 Fisheries Case. On many coasts this award has no importance, but on indented coasts with many islands it will possibly have doubled or trebled the area of exclusive fishing rights enjoyed by the coastal state.

The 1958 Conference [32] was not the first to discuss the law of the sea; a conference sponsored by the League of Nations and held at The Hague in 1930 gave much time to the territorial sea. Preceded by intensive study by a Preparatory Commission, the 1930 Conference concentrated its attentions on the base line and the width of the territorial sea. Its efforts to produce a convention failed, but its labors brought three matters to wider attention: (a) the concept of a "contiguous zone" surrounding territorial waters in which the coastal state might have certain rights that were less than its rights on the same subjects within its territorial sea; (b) the continental shelf as a concept that might lead to a scientifically-justified width of the territorial sea; (c) the disparity of claims among nations on the width of their territorial seas, though three (or four) miles was the width most frequently claimed.

In 1949, the United Nations asked the International Law Commission (an associated advisory organization of fifteen members) to attempt to codify the Law of the Sea. The experts did not confine themselves to the territorial sea, but set out to deal with a va-

[32] On the 1958 conference generally, see United Nations Conference on the Law of the Sea, *Official Record,* 7 volumes, UN Doc. No. A/Conf.13, 1958.

riety of maritime problems, including the continental shelf, high seas fisheries, the conservation of fish stocks, piracy, etc. Their draft reports were revised over the years; the Anglo-Norwegian decision of 1951, for example, had an impact, as did the Icelandic contentions. In 1955 an expert administrative and scientific conference in Rome led to further revisions of the draft reports.[33]

Finally, in 1958, delegates from 86 countries went to Geneva to work over the conventions for some two months. The topics were divided into agenda for distinct committees, and, at the end, four conventions were presented for a two-thirds majority approval, and for later ratification if passed. These covered: (1) territorial seas and contiguous zones, (2) the high seas, (3) fishing and conservation of living resources of the high seas, and (4) the continental shelf. As revised by the plenary sessions of the Conference, all conventions were passed, approved by the United Nations General Assembly, and opened to ratification. Table 18 shows the situation regarding ratification as of September 24, 1964: all but the Convention on Fishing and Conservation have come into force, having received the required twenty-two ratifications.

The Convention on the Territorial Sea and the Contiguous Zone. In drafting this Convention the Conference was concerned with four main topics. First, it reviewed the base line from which the width of the sea might be drawn, coming to a decision consistent with that of the International Court in the Norwegian case. Second, it considered contiguous zones; the concept was accepted as a jurisdiction of closely-defined state authority over particular matters (such as customs and sanitation) beyond the bounds of its territorial sea. Third, it clarified the meaning of the right of "innocent passage" guaranteed foreign vessels through the territorial sea in peacetime, a right that is obviously important if the width of the sea is to be extended. Fourth, it discussed the territorial sea but failed to agree on its width. Some countries, including the Soviet Union, argued for a right to delimit up to twelve miles of coastal sea. Similar limits appealed to Iceland, the South American states, and some newly independent states. However, the principle that came closest to general acceptance was the United States proposal for a six-mile territorial sea plus an adjoining six-mile exclusive fishing belt, plus free access to nations with "historic rights"

[33] International Technical Conference on the Conservation of the Living Resources of the Sea, held at Rome from April 18 to May 10, 1955.

Table 18. Ratification, as of September 24, 1964, of Four Conventions Passed at the 1958 UN Conference on the Law of the Sea

Date ratified	Territorial seas and contiguous zones	High seas	Fishing and conservation of the living resources of the high seas	Continental shelf
April 28, 1959		Afghanistan		
March 14, 1960	U.K.	U.K.	U.K.	
March 18, 1960	Cambodia ª	Cambodia ª	Cambodia ª	Cambodia ª
March 29, 1960	Haiti	Haiti	Haiti	Haiti
Nov. 22, 1960	U.S.S.R.	U.S.S.R.		U.S.S.R.
Dec. 21, 1960	Malaysia ª	Malaysia ª	Malaysia ª	Malaysia ª
Jan. 12, 1961	Ukranian S.S.R.	Ukranian S.S.R.		Ukranian S.S.R.
Feb. 27, 1961	Byelorussian S.S.R.	Byelorussian S.S.R.		Byelorussian S.S.R.
April 12, 1961	U.S.A.	U.S.A.	U.S.A.	U.S.A.
April 25, 1961	Senegal ª	Senegal ª	Senegal ª	Senegal ª
June 26, 1961	Nigeria ª	Nigeria ª	Nigeria ª	
Aug. 10, 1961		Indonesia		
Aug. 15, 1961	Venezuela ª	Venezuela ª		Venezuela ª
Aug. 31, 1961	Czechoslovakia	Czechoslovakia		Czechoslovakia
Sept. 6, 1961	Israel	Israel		Israel
Nov. 27, 1961		Guatemala		Guatemala
Dec. 6, 1961	Hungary	Hungary		
Dec. 12, 1961	Romania	Romania		Romania ª
Jan. 8, 1962				Colombia
March 13, 1962	Sierra Leone ª	Sierra Leone ª	Sierra Leone ª	
June 29, 1962		Poland		Poland
July 31, 1962	Madagascar ª	Madagascar ª	Madagascar ª	Madagascar ª
Aug. 31, 1962	Bulgaria	Bulgaria		Bulgaria ª
Oct. 15, 1962		Central African Republic ª		
Dec. 28, 1962		Nepal		
Jan. 3, 1963			Colombia	
Jan. 8, 1963	Portugal	Portugal	Portugal	Portugal
April 9, 1963	South Africa ª	South Africa ª	South Africa ª	South Africa ª
May 14, 1963	Australia	Australia	Australia	Australia
June 12, 1963				Denmark
July 10, 1963			Venezuela	
April 16, 1964			Jamaica ª	
May 11, 1964				U.K.
Aug. 11, 1964	Dominican Republic	Dominican Republic	Dominican Republic	Dominican Republic
Sept. 14, 1964	Uganda ª	Uganda ª	Uganda ª	Uganda ª

ª By accession.

Source: *Status of Multilateral Conventions,* U.N. Doc. No. ST/LEG/3, Rev. 1, as of September 24, 1964.

in the fisheries newly enclosed. The United Kingdom, the United States, and Canada had all entered the Conference attempting to hold the territorial sea at three miles. At the end, however, the United Kingdom supported the United States "six plus six plus historic rights" proposal, while Canada and other countries favored a simple "six plus six." The Conference that met in 1960 [34] was also unable to reach a two-thirds majority on any particular breadth, and the Convention therefore does not deal with the width of the territorial sea.

The Convention on the High Seas is largely a codification of accepted laws of navigation and the permitted behavior of ships with respect to piracy, smuggling, collision, the protection of cables, and so forth. Rather more important to the fisheries is its provision that there must be a "genuine link" between a state and ships flying its flag—a decision that may weaken the attractiveness of certain flags as "flags of convenience." [35] It also states that countries may enforce their laws applicable in contiguous zones (and, presumably, in fishing zones) by "hot pursuit" of violators into the high seas.

The Convention on the Continental Shelf carried into international law the spirit of the Anglo-Venezuelan Agreement, the Truman declaration, and the assertions of the Persian Gulf states by assigning to the coastal state the seabed and submarine resources out to a depth of 200 meters—or beyond, where the state is capable of exploiting the natural resources there. The "natural resources" are defined in Article 2.4 as of the seabed or subsoil, minerals, and "sedentary" species on the seabed, defined to comprise fish which "at the harvestable stage, either are immobile on or under the seabed or are unable to move except in constant physical contact with the seabed or the subsoil." The Convention expressly denies the coastal state the waters above the continental shelf outside the territorial zone. Its meaning for minerals seems quite clear; but for fish which are swimming or floating part of their life, and sedentary at the harvestable stage, there appears to be a double status: they may be open-seas resources when they are young but under the coastal state's sovereignty when they are harvestable, without significantly moving from the same part of

[34] See Second United Nations Conference on the Law of the Sea, *Official Record*, UN Doc. No. A/Conf.19, 1960.
[35] See footnote 38 below.

the seas. It is possible that this situation might make it difficult either to regulate the total ecology of high-seas waters, or to manage satisfactorily a shellfish population harvested by the coastal state.

In 1963, there was an energetic exchange between France and Brazil over the lobsters living on the Brazilian continental shelf.[36] More recently, the United States and the Soviet Union have signed an agreement (February 5, 1965) that defines the king crab as a resource of the continental shelf over which the coastal state has sovereign rights. Under this agreement, a form of "historic rights" clause gives the Soviet Union the right to continue their crabbing activities on the U.S. shelf under the Bering Sea for two years at a reduced level.[37] The Japanese, however, while agreeing to reduce their catch of king crabs as a conservation measure, do not accept the claim that the crabs are a resource belonging to the coastal state.

The Convention on Fishing and on the Conservation of the Living Resources of the High Seas goes beyond anything that might be described as international law before 1958. It is an example of deliberate international law-making by an international body to deal with problems foreseen rather than experienced (a characteristic it perhaps shares with the Convention on the Continental Shelf). In this respect it has a family resemblance to land-tenure laws worked out for new territories in advance of their opening up for settlement.

It should first of all be stressed that we are now considering the high seas. In the absence of this Convention, the freedom of the seas for fishing holds, subject only to a few general rules of behavior for vessels on the high seas, domestic laws governing nationals on the high seas, and whatever treaties a vessel's home state [38] had

---

[36] *New York Times*, 1963, February 25, p. 4, col. 4; February 26, p. 3, col. 1; March 2, p. 2, col. 6; April 3, p. 2, col. 7.

[37] *Commercial Fisheries Review*, Vol. 27 (April, 1965), pp. 46–47.

[38] The Convention on the High Seas required that there be a "genuine link" between the vessel and the state whose nationality it claimed. There is much dispute about the possibility of interpreting this requirement; see Myres S. McDougal and William T. Burke, *The Public Order of the Oceans* (New Haven: Yale University Press, 1962), Chapter 8, especially pp. 1013–35. It is generally assumed to apply chiefly to merchant shipping.

The Fishing Convention, however, is more lenient: Article 14 suggests that the Convention applies to ". . . craft of any size having the nationality of the state concerned, according to the law of that state, irrespective of the nation-

subscribed to. The continental shelf has no meaning for the jurisdiction of a coastal state over ordinary fisheries; the territorial sea
gives a coastal state jurisdiction over high-seas fish only when they
have migrated or strayed over the territorial-sea limit or the
fishing-zone limit, if there is one.

There were two rather special reasons for the fishing powers encouraging the drafting and adopting of this Convention. First,
some nations felt that the pressure from coastal states to extend the
three-mile limit in order to protect neighboring fisheries from
overexploitation would be lessened if this danger could be dealt
with otherwise. Second, the states already participating in agreements on particular fish stocks were anxious to see their treaties
recognized and supported in the Convention. Consequently, the
drafting of this Convention was inspired by nationalistic motives
as well as by farsighted world statesmanship.

This Convention starts with a reaffirmation of the freedom of
fishing on the high seas, subject to some special rights of coastal
states and to the main articles of the Convention.[39] These articles
deal with a new "duty" of all states to conserve the living resources of the high seas, conservation meaning the measures to
achieve "the optimum sustainable yield from these resources so
as to secure a maximum supply of food. . . ." A stock exploited
by a single state must be so protected. And where a stock is exploited by more than one state, those participating in the fishery
must enter into conservation agreements, if one of them so suggests. The coastal state must always be included in these arrangements, even if it is not using the stock; the conservation measures
must not be antithetical to the measures followed by the coastal
state (presumably within its territorial waters); the coastal state
may in emergency take the initiative and prescribe measures to be
followed by the other fishing states. Article 9 sets forth a "settle-

---

ality of the members of their crews." Hence (quite apart from the possibility
of conflict between the two conventions for states that have in some way
recognized both of them, or states dealing with countries that have done so)
it would appear that the fishing convention accepts the possibility that craft
may seek a "flag of convenience" either to escape restrictions of fishing on
the high seas, or to gain the benefits of rights to fishing, under a treaty.
L. F. E. Goldie has mentioned the first of these possibilities to us in corre-
spondence. See McDougal and Burke, pp. 1076–78.

[39] For discussion of this convention, see W. W. Bishop, Jr., "The 1958
Geneva Convention on Fishing and the Conservation of the Living Resources
of the High Seas," *Columbia Law Review*, Vol. 62 (1962), pp. 1206–29.

ment" procedure for resolving the disputes arising when these compulsory provisions are invoked, which seems essentially to amount to recourse to an approximation to an arbitration board. All conservation measures must be shown to be based upon scientific findings of need and practicability, and must not discriminate against fishermen of any particular state.

Most discussions of the main articles of the Convention have dealt with the special position of the coastal state. It is alleged by critics that the requirement that conservation measures must not clash with those adopted by the "adjacent" coastal state is too loose and that the convention concedes too much to a state that may be hundreds of miles from the fishing ground. It is also argued that to allow a coastal state to participate in regulation-making even if it is not using the stock to be conserved is to allow it to prescribe regulations for others which are not operative against itself.[40]

An important principle *not* written into the Convention is the abstention principle, advanced by the United States with Canadian support, in the spirit of their agreement wth Japan in the North Pacific Treaty.[41] This principle asserts that those states that have invested time, effort, and money in a stock, and have restrained their fishermen so as to increase the productivity of that stock, should have the exclusive use of the stock if it is fully utilized. The conserving states having refrained from destruction of the stock, new states should abstain from catching its yield. This was suggested as a principle similar to that embodied in setting up the special rights of coastal states. It would have enabled states already fishing to refuse a new state entry to a treaty; but it did not finally appear in the Convention.

In brief, this Convention, taken with the others, sets up a system by which a structure of treaties might be erected that would preserve many of the world's most important fish stocks—although as a practical matter, the width of territorial seas must first be agreed upon. The Convention does so in a way that should allow all nations to participate, and provides machinery for the settlement of disputes. It has, however, two possible weaknesses: it envisages treaties based on stocks of fish rather than on regions, thus giving little encouragement to arrangements that might *change* the

[40] See D. H. N. Johnson, "The Geneva Conference on the Law of the Sea," *The Year Book of World Affairs,* Vol. 13 (1959), pp. 90–91.

[41] International Convention for the High Seas Fisheries of the North Pacific Ocean, Article III (1) (a).

dominant stock of a certain region; and it appears to make it possible for the coastal state to frustrate the full use of the Convention's procedure for bringing about optimum utilization. The validity of the latter contention is so far untested; and whether the former is an important criticism depends upon research in adapting and improving the uses of the oceans beyond preying upon stocks provided by nature. Both questions, which are urgently in need of further research, are discussed in later chapters.

This concludes our review of international law as it concerns the resources of the seas. The strides since 1945 have been great. Of the four Geneva Conventions, three have come into force. The Norwegian claims to straight base lines have been sanctioned by the International Court of Justice. Further, the unilateral claims of the governments of Iceland, Korea, Indonesia, and the CEP states to extended territorial seas or fishing limits appear to be tolerated by some other states. These other claims may therefore become recognized in international law at some future date, and a general extended authority for the coastal state may become established. The declarations of various states with regard to the continental shelf and the Geneva Convention on the Continental Shelf seem close to identifying a new international rule.

Chapter 10

Competing Doctrines of International Law of the Sea

㲀. 㲀.

IN tracing the development of the international law applicable to fisheries and other marine resources, we drew attention to the slogans and doctrines invoked by the various states. These slogans and doctrines have been frequently used in domestic discussion, litigation, learned writing, and international conferences. Indeed, they have been so frequently expressed that it might appear to a cynical observer that the interested states are simultaneously committed to policies that may be in conflict with each other.

The purpose of this chapter is to examine five of these doctrines: keeping the seas free, looking after the special interests of coastal states, paying respect to historic rights, conserving fish stocks, and abstaining from fishing where other states are fully utilizing and managing a fishery.[1] This examination does not deal in detail with the source, employment, and chronology of usage

[1] A much longer list of slogans and phrases will be found in Myres S. McDougal and William T. Burke, *The Public Order of the Oceans* (New Haven: Yale University Press, 1962), pp. 41–48. They, too, mention the list of "labels" only to dismiss it in favor of their own highly productive approach, in which they examine the law of the sea and the process by which it becomes established in terms of its relevance to what they believe are the real problems and aims of the international community. For a brief illustration of an approach similar to McDougal's, see M. A. Kaplan and N. de B. Katzenbach, *The Political Foundations of International Law* (New York: John Wiley and Sons, 1961), p. 153.

and decision of each of these principles.[2] Instead, it is confined primarily to a search for the goals which are, or might be, imputed to those who invoke them. And it leads to the suggestion that other, more basic aims must also be considered in the formulation of policy.

We believe that the five principles which are so frequently invoked cannot serve as a productive framework for shaping future international arrangements for the uses of the oceans. For one reason, they describe the outcome of past disputes and agreements, or the objective of past claims, but do not express the process which led to these results nor the assumptions made about fundamental national or international goals. For another reason, the rapidly increasing competition and congestion on the seas described in earlier chapters indicates that descriptions of the outcomes of past disputes offer little guidance to the settling of the problems of the future.

In addition, it is important to point out that rules for the high seas are linked to national strategies that may be based on interests other than marine resources. These links are important in two respects. First, agreements and concessions concerning fisheries may be made between nations in order to win other reciprocal advantages, both on the high seas and in other spheres of international politics. Second, nations may proceed even more indirectly and make demands (e.g., for coastal territorial rights) as matter of strategy, so as to have strength for making concessions in subsequent negotiations on the same or on different matters.

Our examination of the principles concentrates primarily on what "ought" to be, rather than what "is." This approach differs from that of the great majority of international lawyers who have

[2] For a good account of the sources of international law, and the processes by which it develops, see J. L. Brierly, *The Law of Nations* (5th ed.; London: Oxford University Press, 1955); L. Oppenheim, *International Law*, ed. H. Lauterpacht (8th ed.; London: Longmans, Green and Co., 1955); W. W. Bishop, Jr., *International Law—Cases and Materials* (2d ed.; Boston: Little, Brown and Co., 1962), in their opening chapters. An interesting recent treatment will be found in Kaplan and Katzenbach, *op. cit.* For the approach of Myres S. McDougal, see McDougal and Burke, *op. cit.*, pp. 1–63. A similar approach is used by D. M. Johnston in two papers entitled "The International Law of Fisheries: A Policy-Oriented Inquiry in Outline," in *Current Law and Social Problems*, Vol. 1, ed. MacDonald (Toronto, 1960), pp. 19–67, and Vol. 3, ed. E. E. Palmer (Toronto, 1963), pp. 146–237.

made theirs a positive discipline rather than one for speculation and prescription on ethical and welfare grounds.[3]

The Freedom of the Seas

The first "legal" principle to be considered is that of the freedom of the seas. It does not, of course, apply only to fishing, but to all maritime traffic and commerce. In this wider context its traditional importance has been stated by Lauterpacht to involve ". . . perfect freedom of navigation for vessels of all nations; it involves absence of compulsory maritime ceremonials; it involves freedom of innocent passage through the maritime belt [territorial sea] for merchantmen and warships where the maritime belt forms a part of the highway for international traffic." [4]

In its narrower application to fisheries, Lauterpacht states that this freedom means that the open sea is not and never can be under the sovereignty of any state.[5] From this it follows that since it is not the territory of any state, the open sea cannot be the subject of any state's legislation, administration, or jurisdiction. Nor can it be acquired by any state through occupation or prescription.

This absence of national rights is the foundation for all claims of freedom to fish on the high seas. Recent doctrines and principles are stated, not as contradictions but merely as modifications to

---

[3] However, in a recent attack on those who would treat international law, quite consistently with positivism, as a body of inherited rules ". . . unaffected by the power and other social processes in which they are prescribed and applied . . . ," Professor Myres McDougal detects a normative trace. His own efforts to find the common interests of people and to recommend alternatives in future decisions more in accord with what he believes to be the common interests of people have been referred to as "realistic," or "rationalistic." This more recent split over method and assumptions should not be confused with the earlier rejection of natural law (and reason) for positivism, though there are surely grounds for suggesting that some reference to the earlier approach is being made. See Kaplan and Katzenbach, *op. cit.*, p. 75; and an exchange between Professor S. V. Anderson and Professor McDougal: "A Critique of Professor Myres S. McDougal's Doctrine of Interpretation by Major Purposes," *American Journal of International Law,* Vol. 57 (1963), pp. 378–84.

[4] Oppenheim-Lauterpacht, *op cit.*, 7th ed., p. 591. (A slightly revised statement appears in the 8th edition, p. 591.)

[5] *Ibid.*, p. 589, footnote 1.

the fundamental freedom of the seas. For example, Article I of the Geneva Convention on Fishing and Conservation of the Living Resources of the High Seas begins: "All States have the right to engage in fishing on the high seas, subject to. . . ."

Because it is based on absence of national jurisdiction, freedom of the seas can only be negative in its approach. As Professor Gidel has noted, it cannot provide a basis for more than equal access to the resources of the seas.[6] In this respect, therefore, it must be sharply distinguished from recent proposals to "internationalize" the exploitation of the sea. Both the "freedom" and "internationalization" approaches stress the invalidity of national claims. But the latter might justly be called a positive approach, implying co-operative use by many nations, while the former is negative, stressing only that nations are powerless to interfere with each other.

Furthermore, while the "international" approach has a universal or humanitarian ethos underlying it, the freedom of the seas is merely an anticipatory example of laissez-faire philosophy. It is humanitarian or liberal only to the extent that it recognizes the desirability of an acceptable rule of law rather than the maritime anarchy or monopoly that would presumably take its place.

Those who invoke the "freedom of the seas" today frequently make two serious errors. One is the belief that it is a "freedom" like those of the Atlantic Charter.[7] This is erroneous because the doctrine is not a statement of a fundamental human right, but merely a consequence of lack of jurisdiction or national right. The second is the belief that this "freedom" applies to national waters, as in the claim that Canadian or American fishermen have a basic right to use their territorial seas unimpeded. This, too, is wrong because whatever freedom they have to use their national waters is derived from their national constitutions and laws; the freedom of the seas as a basic principle applies only to international waters.

In arguing that the seas could belong to no one, Grotius and his

[6] Gilbert Gidel, *Le Droit International Public de la Mer*, Vol. 1 (Recueil Sirey), Paris, 1932. Discussion of Professor Gidel's views is found in M. W. Mouton, *The Continental Shelf* (The Hague: Martinus Nijhoff, 1952), p. 151.

[7] Indeed, President Woodrow Wilson did insert the freedom of the seas among his Fourteen Points of 1917–18; but he appears to have considered it as a means to the prevention of war rather than as a right in itself. See C. G. Fenwick, *International Law* (New York: The Century Co., 1924), p. 229, citing P. B. Potter, *The Freedom of the Seas in History, Law, and Politics* (New York: Longmans, Green and Co., 1924), pp. 242–47.

contemporaries started with the legal approach to property. Things *could* become property only if they could be appropriated or prescribed. Applied to nations, lands must be capable of being held against other states. This, they argued, could be said only of a narrow coastal strip (the territorial sea), not of the high seas, which no navy could be powerful enough to hold in the sense that an army could hold national territory. A second condition was that things *should* be property if they were apt to be exhausted unless carefully managed. Thus, farm land should become property because no one would tend it unless he could reap where he had sowed. But, Grotius said, this condition did not apply to the high seas, because their wealth was inexhaustible.

These two conditions have had a long inning. They were fully accepted by the classical political economists in their discussions of private property, and are well reviewed by John Stuart Mill in his chapter on property, which in many respects seems otherwise to be in favor of socializing or at least equalizing property in land.[8] Since freedom of the seas is but one of several principles advanced today, it is less important than it would once have been to determine accurately where—or whether at all—the conditions for property (or sovereignty) apply to the oceans. It does appear, however, that there is some doubt that the oceans are inappropriable; indeed the doctrine of the freedom of the seas itself may be one force preventing appropriation by one or another of the great powers (although undoubtedly it is to the grand strategy among the great powers that we must look for ultimate explanations of such restraints). And there is much more doubt that the oceans or their fisheries are inexhaustible. While it may be impossible to destroy some species of fish by today's fishing methods, it is possible to deplete a species; and it is certainly possible to raise the productivity of the seas by means analogous to those which have justified private property in land. Consequently, it is not surprising that to many people the freedom of the seas, no longer based on unassailable assumptions, is something less than an article of faith.

But to most early legal scholars, the assumptions were valid and the principle of freedom of the seas was workable. Most important for this discussion, the principle proved to be increasingly convenient for the great naval powers. First Holland and later Britain found it a convenient legal prop for their naval and mercantile

---

[8] John Stuart Mill, *Principles of Political Economy*, ed. W. J. Ashley (London: Longmans, Green and Co., 1909).

ambitions on the high seas.⁹ And, after her older rivals had been subdued, Britain maintained it against newcomers both large and small. In this she was joined by the nineteenth-century naval powers, all of whom sought to keep open the high seas, valuable fishing grounds, narrow straits, and strategic routes for their naval forces and merchant and fishing fleets.

The freedom of the seas, therefore, was defended most strenuously by the larger European nations. They had now developed a vested interest in the right to use the high seas almost as freely as they did their own territorial waters. As a corollary, they fought hard to keep narrow the internal waters from which they might be excluded, and to limit severely the legal conditions under which they might be denied the use of the territorial sea.

However, the increasing use of the high seas by a large number of nations, many of whom could by no stretch of imagination be called great naval powers, has gradually given the "freedom of the seas" the *effect* of protecting the rights of individuals, or at least of small individual states. Thus from an earlier argument that the seas belong to no one has emerged today's principle that the seas belong to all. This may be said to provide a jumping-off point for recent claims that the seas ought to be used for the *benefit* of all. But the two ideas are not the same, and there remains a gap between them as wide perhaps as the gap between the exponents of the two ideas.

On the one hand, the freedom of the seas is defended by those who feel its realization will benefit their fishing industry and other national interests. They claim a community interest in the seas because they seek, as particular members of that community, free access to marine resources.¹⁰

On the other hand, there are those who appeal explicitly to humanitarianism and egalitarianism. Starting with human needs for food and materials, and noting the increasing world population, they claim that the bounty of the seas *should* be made available to those in great need. Or, starting with the seas, they wish as

⁹ However, A. Pearce Higgins and C. J. Colombos, *The International Law of the Sea* (3d ed.; London: Longmans, Green and Co., 1954), p. 53, does cite Selden as saying in 1618 that a State had a "duty to humanity" to keep its seas open to other people.

¹⁰ This terminology owes much to McDougal and Burke, *op. cit.;* see especially pp. 51–56, 561–63 and 747–51. We referred to this as a vested interest of the larger nineteenth century states in our discussion a few paragraphs above.

economists and technicians to "maximize and generalize" the benefits from marine resources.[11] Presumably, those most concerned with the fairest distribution of the wealth of the seas might go further, urging to each according to his needs: those who hunger have a *greater* right to the seas than those who are otherwise well off. Carried so far, of course, this last formulation might even be used to claim that the width of fishing zones should depend upon the measured needs of the claimants. By now, the gap between the traditional interpretation of freedom of the seas and the idea of generalized benefit has become a yawning gulf. Because, as a practical proposition, this generalized approach to human benefit has been applied mainly to the claim for wider seas for coastal states, it is considered in more detail below.

One of the best-known views on this topic is that of McDougal and Burke.[12] Identifying national egoism (not only selfishness in appropriating resources for use, but also for non-use) with any decision or regime that excludes the greater part of the world community from access to resources, they approve of decisions to *include* all nations. Leaving aside the problem of fisheries depletion that might result from complete laissez-faire (which they discuss), they favor freedom of the seas in most situations, as allowing widespread, international, and complete utilization (though not, it should be emphasized, merely because the freedom of the seas is an historic principle). It is impossible to do justice here to the breadth of their argument,[13] but it may be observed that their policy would be likely to bring widespread benefits to those nations that already take a large share of the fish. This result may be consistent with their concept of world goals [14] but not with everyone's.

Similar disagreements occur with respect to the so-called absten-

[11] This terminology we owe to Giulio Pontecorvo.

[12] See their "Crisis in the Law of the Sea: Community Perspectives versus National Egoism," *Yale Law Journal*, Vol. 67 (1958), pp. 539–89.

[13] See *The Public Order of the Oceans, op. cit.*, pp. 499–520, especially p. 514, where a possible means of dealing with the poorer states' needs is suggested. But the apparent objective of the cited section is to demonstrate the gains for world ("community") production and efficiency from restricting the breadth of exclusive fishing zones.

An interesting discussion of the twin problems of the production of fish and its distribution among states is to be found in D.M. Johnston, in *Current Law and Social Problems*, Vol. 1 (1960), pp. 62–67.

[14] See *The Public Order of the Oceans, op. cit.*, pp. 17–19.

tion principle, according to which fisheries that are already fully used (and managed, though that condition is irrelevant here) by first-comers should be closed to late-comers.

We shall see in later chapters that the idea of widespread benefit may even require the intervention of an international body for its realization. But the point at this stage is merely this: freedom of the seas both in its source as a doctrine and its practice has little relation to an idea that may easily be confused with it: the idea that the benefits of the seas should be made available (not merely legally accessible) to all.

Both the doctrine of the freedom of the seas and the idea of internationalization of the uses of the seas are "inclusive," taking into account the "community interest" rather than the "exclusive" interest of individual states. But it must be reiterated that until very recently no one who invoked the freedom of the seas had in mind any notion more grandiose than freedom of opportunity.

With respect to fishing, this freedom to participate has already led to excessive investment in new vessels and excessive recruitment of fishermen, and it will continue to have expensive consequences. The fishermen themselves are anxious to enter to reap the profits of newly-opened high-seas fisheries, and their eagerness is often encouraged and subsidized by governments keen to maintain their national share of international stocks. Thus, freedom of the seas may well become freedom to waste labor and capital.

Conservationists have not been slow to point out that freedom of the seas may also mean freedom to deplete fish stocks to the level of unprofitability (or even, in the case of some vulnerable species, to extinction). This point of view is implicit in the fisheries' agreements (provided for in the Geneva Conventions) some of which are listed in the next chapter.

The Special Position of the Coastal State

The principle dealing with the special position of the coastal state [15] is in many ways opposed to the principle of freedom of the seas. In Article 6.1 of the Conservation Convention, the matter is

[15] F. V. Garcia-Amador, *The Exploitation and Conservation of the Resources of the Sea* (2d ed.; Leyden, Netherlands: A. W. Sythoff, 1959), pp. 201 ff.; *The Public Order of the Oceans, op. cit.,* Chapter 5.

put thus: "A Coastal State has a special interest in the maintenance of the living resources in any area of the high seas adjacent to
its waters." We have already seen that the CEP states and Iceland
have acted on this principle. Iceland's proposal to the Law of the
Sea Conference on the coastal state's "preferential rights" to
adjacent high seas stocks begins: "Where a people is overwhelm-
ingly dependent upon its coastal fisheries for its livelihood or
economic development, and. . . ." Naturally enough such ideas [16]
have been advanced chiefly by those representing interested
coastal states. But to some writers they have a positive virtue, aiding and encouraging the development of the ocean's wealth as
against the purely permissive, negative virtues of the freedom of
the seas. In recent international law meetings, this principle has
found expression in two claims: it has been the basis of the argument that territorial seas ought, with the full powers of sovereignty, to be broadened; and it has been behind a strong campaign
to give the coastal states "exclusive" or preferential fishing rights
over adjacent seas. To ward off the first claim, many states have
supported the second.

The claim to the "exclusive" use of waters by the neighboring
coastal state has had a number of arguments advanced to support
it. We have identified five [17] of these, especially connected with
fisheries, which are present in varying combinations in the arguments and motives of each coastal state.

(a) A simple desire to extend the frontiers of the country.
Some nations seem primarily to regard an increase in the territorial sea as a means of increasing their territory and their potential wealth. In a sense, this might be described as an "imperialistic" motive.

(b) Resentment of the free fishing of other countries off their
coasts. Some nations have voiced resentment of the rights of the
older and more developed nations to use the waters bordering on
the newer countries. This might be described as an "anti-
imperialistic" motive. It is sometimes coupled with the thought
that the older countries, having mismanaged and depleted their
own fisheries, now are in the process of spoiling others'.

[16] S. Oda, "The 1958 Geneva Convention on the Fisheries," *Die Friedenswarte*, Vol. 55 (1960), pp. 321–25.

[17] For another list, see C. M. Franklin, *Law of the Sea; Some Recent Developments*, U.S. Naval War College, International Law Studies, 1959–60
(Washington: U.S. Government Printing Office, 1961), pp. 116–19.

(c) The coastal state needs the employment offered by fishing to occupy its large labor force.

(d) The coastal state needs the food. Various states have pointed to the low standard of living, particularly the low protein intake, of their people as an argument for their being conceded the exclusive use of the adjacent high seas.

(e) The coastal state depends upon the income from the fishery.

This list can be subdivided into groups according to various points of view. Three are of special interest.

First, from a legal point of view, there is a difference in the degree of control over fisheries needed to achieve these ends. The last four probably require only some sort of exclusive fishing zone, but the satisfaction of the first reason would require full sovereignty over territorial waters.

Second, the last three arguments are essentially economic. Their validity depends upon alternative opportunities for the labor force and upon alternative sources of food. For a country whose labor force has few other opportunities than fishing and which depends heavily upon fish for food or for a source of income through exports, all three arguments may apply. But when an economy is diversified, and coastal populations are not isolated, only one or two of the three may apply. It should be pointed out that coastal populations often have special political influence on their national policymakers, greater than their proportion of the national economy, labor force, or voting population.

Third, classifying from the point of view of the nature of the argument, we may observe that the first two arguments have been a powerful incentive to assert a special *right* of the coastal state to fisheries; the last three, however, concentrate on their special *needs*.

Consequently, the entire set of arguments has very little internal consistency, except that all have force in leading coastal states to make the same claim.

Every fishing nation is, of course, a coastal state, and may be under economic or political pressure to protect its inshore fisheries from foreign use. Canada, for example, distrusts Russian ships on the Grand Banks; the United States fears Canadian trawlers on Georges Bank; Great Britain fears continental fishermen in waters near Scotland; Russia distrusts Japanese salmon fishermen; and so forth. Because nearly every important fishing nation has fisheries in both distant and near waters there are relatively few among them who are whole-hearted opponents of the so-called coastal state argument. But there is a large number of new nations with small inshore fleets and few prospects of distant-water fishing. On a mere counting of heads, therefore, the coastal-state position is becoming steadily stronger. Buttressed by the nationalism of the new states and by the humanitarian attractions of supplying food for underdeveloped countries, it has proved too strong for the older freedom-of-the-seas nations. There was, therefore, little effort made at the 1960 Law of the Sea Conference to establish the three-mile territorial sea. (Although we are dealing here with fisheries, the reader should bear in mind that many other considerations were frequently more important in determining national positions. The width of the territorial sea, for example, determines the area of neutral waters within which enemy ships may find shelter.)

The coastal principle can also get some scientific support from the argument that the coastal seas and the neighboring land environment are in fact a single ecology. It is asserted for example that the richness of the continental shelf and the adjacent high seas fisheries depend largely upon estuarial influences, which can be modified or damaged by human action. A multitude of terrestrial actions can affect ocean productivity. Consequently, it is argued, it is advisable that those who control the fishery be those who control the land.[18] It can be seen that this argument approaches the "abstinence principle" for species such as salmon.

It goes without saying that a much stronger ecological argument can be advanced *against* the widening of the fishing zone of the coastal state. Since fish are no respecters of boundary lines, and since any width of the fishing zone is bound to cut across the habitat of some stocks, it follows that such lines should not be drawn any fixed number of miles from the coast.

Rather, so it is urged, the fish stocks themselves ought to be put under some sort of management that takes into account the control of their entire life cycle and ecology. If this is not done, fisheries that are only partially within the zone held by a coastal state, or are within it for only a part of their life, will be damaged or destroyed by fishermen not under that state's authority.

[18] However, there is a contrary point of view: the coastal waters in many areas may gain their productivity and otherwise be affected by influences coming chiefly from the deeper waters of the ocean. This point of view, of course, diminishes the argument for coastal state control.

This was the lesson that the Geneva Conference seems to have learned from the report of the experts at the Rome Conference on the Living Resources of the Sea in 1955: management should be based on stocks, not on miles. And, partly for this reason, they attempted to help coastal states by asserting that these states had a special right to be included and considered in the making of conservation agreements, rather than by agreeing to an extensive broadening of the exclusive rights of coastal states. Such conservation arguments would probably go against a case for an arbitrary broadening of the width of the fishing zone by a small number of miles, but might support a case for putting a stock under the management of the most "convenient" nation.[19]

On the whole, however, it is clear that the other types of argument are more relevant and more influential than that for conservation. Strong opposition to a wider fishing zone has come from two sources: those countries who see the principle as working against their own maritime interests and those who believe that to leave the coasts *exclusively* to the coastal states would mean that much of the wealth of the seas would go "to waste."

The limited applicability of this principle must be recognized. It has little to say about the future uses of most of the high seas for fisheries. But for the special purposes of the coastal states, the principle has been highly successful. Scientific opinion and explicit opposition have had little effect against the cumulative strength of these states. They have a particularized claim to make; they are on the ground, and have been, often, for centuries; as underdeveloped African and Asian nations they support each other both in their claims to *rights* and their demand for more food and materials. The concessions made by the Japanese to the U.S.S.R., Canada, the United States, and others, by the British to Iceland, the Faroe Islands, and Norway, and by other great fishing nations to coastal states (for a variety of immediate reasons) have all strengthened the general position of the coastal states. In the Law of the Sea Conferences, coastal states have gained their continental shelves and the mineral resources beneath. The delimitation of territorial seas measured from straight base lines thus creating new, and extending old, internal waters has been countenanced by

[19] But note McDougal and Burke, who point out the difficulty of identifying a coastal state with a particular stock, *The Public Order of the Oceans, op. cit.*, pp. 458–60, and D. M. Johnston, in *Current Law and Social Problems*, Vol. 3 (1962), p. 208.

the International Court of Justice and incorporated into the 1958 Geneva Convention on the Territorial Sea and Contiguous Zone. The extraordinary claims to a minimum of 200-mile territorial seas by Chile, Ecuador, and Peru have been only feebly challenged. Thus this "exclusive" principle would appear to be winning the day.

In fact, the concessions won have very little relevance to the principles by which the high seas might be governed. A few miles one way or the other are important to the distribution of the coastal productivity among the nations, but not to the question of the method of the ocean's uses. It is important that the "special position of the coastal state" be recognized as a principle advanced for the allocation of the wealth of the coastal waters only—not of the high seas.

The Abstention Principle

The abstention principle,[20] which was *omitted* from the Convention on Fishing and Conservation, reverses the Grotian argument about the impossibility of exhaustion (and therefore the unprofitability of investment to prevent it). It argues that if investment has taken place, and exhaustion has been prevented, then property ought to be conceded. The Grotius point might be stated: "if no investment then no property," whereas the abstention argument is "if investment then property." The two are clearly not the same, especially when it is seen that the exponents of the abstention principle want *exclusive* property in a fish stock. There are clearly many degrees of private property, from the small "equity" Canada has in the seal fishery, to sole ownership. It has not yet been fully argued that investment via regulation and expenditure requires complete ownership as its reward, though some incentive is of course necessary.

Indeed, there has been surprisingly little discussion of the basic premises behind the abstention principle, which has been pro-

---

[20] For statements, see W. C. Herrington, "Comments on the Principle of Abstention," *Papers Presented at the International Technical Conference on the Conservation of the Living Resources of the Sea, Rome, 1955*, UN Doc. No. A/Conf.10/7, pp. 344–49; and R. van Cleve, "The Economic and Scientific Basis of the Principle of Abstention," in *Law of the Sea, Official Record*, Vol. 1, UN Doc. No. A/Conf.13/3, pp. 47–63.

posed by some of the western fishing powers, and which was accepted by Japan in the original North Pacific Treaty. The principle was rejected by the Law of the Sea Conference in 1958, without much published comment.

Historic Rights

Fourthly, we turn to the idea of "historic rights," [21] a catch-all phrase which, in fisheries, refers to a claim that states have acquired rights where they have long fished, even if a broadened territorial sea, a new fishing zone, or a new treaty regime puts that fishery under the management of other states. In the Geneva Conventions, historic rights are implicitly deferred to at several points. For example, in spite of the new "special rights" of the coastal state, the nations already fishing a high-seas stock are entitled to join a regulatory agreement without discrimination (unless the stock lies within a new zone of exclusive jurisdiction).

On the other hand, the historic rights principle was not popular with many of the newer states at the 1958 and 1960 conferences. A United States proposal to create a six-mile belt beyond the territorial sea with exclusive coastal fishing rights subject only to the historic rights of those states fishing there for more than a certain period was much less well supported than a subsequent Canadian proposal abandoning this form of historic rights. The many delegates favoring very broad limits for the territorial sea seemed to view it as a virtue that this regime would cut off the "historic rights" of older nations in their adjacent coastal seas. Within the past twenty years, Britain seems to have lost her "historic rights" to fish off the coast of Iceland and the Faroe Islands, as has Japan in the waters near Korea and in the Sea of Okhotsk.[22]

In general, this principle is an international manifestation of first-come, first-served. It is easy to understand and to administer, but it is obviously unpopular with latecomers.

Conservation

"Conservation" is essentially a recently-enshrined principle of international law. Although it was built into fisheries' treaties in

[21] Garcia-Amador, *op. cit.*, p. 209.
[22] See pp. 163–65.

the nineteenth century, and had become a clear objective of many national fisheries' administrations, it was not until the Law of the Sea Conferences in 1958 and 1960 (and their preliminaries in the decade preceding) that it played a part in the mysterious process by which international law is distilled. Its rapid acceptance is easy to explain. Conservation had become part of the prevailing intellectual climate among fisheries' experts. And, as it was the only clear common aim of countries grappling with the problem of fishing,[23] it was eagerly adopted in a situation where more basic aims had not been explored or defined.

The importance of careful use of the seas and skillful management of fish stocks needs no emphasis. But fisheries conservation does not constitute a satisfying philosophy so long as it is merely defined as maximum physical yield from a given stock. Conservation *per se* produces no gain in welfare for man or fish. It is true that there will be more fish caught, but more labor and capital must be expended in rearing and catching them. Men may become better, or worse off. True again, there will be more fish of the favored stock, but most of them will be killed by fishermen; and there will be fewer fish of competing stocks. Unless evaluated by economic criteria, conservation is merely a state of nature.

Conclusion

It must be conceded that many of these rules have emerged from disputes in which fisheries, or even the more important uses of the oceans such as navigation, have actually been of minor importance. The strategy of the great powers in achieving what they feel to be their national interests has not always been conducted in terms directly relevant to the questions with which we are concerned. Nations have had to balance matters of defense and security against commercial and social benefits and costs. And frequently claims have been made as part of a process of bargaining—for example, a state may assert rights or needs to protect itself from mak-

[23] The Convention on Fishing, however, is not drafted in the most precise, unambiguous terms and therefore is subject to various interpretations; those delegates voting for the same provisions were not necessarily voting for the same interpretations. It should also be noted that the Convention can be used as a means for reaching various fisheries' goals. Thus there was perhaps little consensus at the Conference on the real meaning of "Conservation" or the proper means of implementing it. See S. Oda, *op. cit.*, p. 317; and McDougal and Burke, *The Public Order of the Oceans*, pp. 972–73 and 975.

ing concessions or to win reciprocal concessions from its neighbors.

Nevertheless, we feel that the invocation of these principles can be of real disservice to those who wish to understand the immediate issues in the high seas fisheries. To recapitulate, the doctrines we have dealt with are: (a) the freedom of the seas; (b) the special position of the coastal state; (c) the abstention principle; (d) historic rights; and (e) the conservation principle. The first of these began as a shield for special interests, but it may become transformed into a genuinely "inclusive" doctrine. Of the rest, all but the last are clearly vested-interest doctrines, and even the conservation principle may be often invoked for domestic interests. This last principle is, at root, completely technocratic: it sets out a physical objective as a substitute for conflicting social ends. None of the doctrines discussed are based on comprehensive social objectives, though arguments can be advanced that each of them benefits the world community. In particular, there is no scope for economic efficiency or other general economic ends for the fishery as a whole.

Such "economic" criteria need a little explanation here, though we shall discuss them at greater length in later chapters. The term "economic" has two kinds of meaning in this context. One which we have referred to several times is commonly encountered in the legal literature; it refers to the economic gain of one country over others, by obtaining rights to fish, use ports, or sell fish in a certain market. In most fisheries discussions, the term is used in this sense and refers to the *distribution* of the income and wealth from the fishery between countries.

The general economist,[24] however, uses the word economic to describe a second type of problem: that of economic efficiency. Briefly, this may be stated as the search for a system in which not only fishery resources, but also manpower and capital are used, and allocated, as between all industries and products, to produce the largest present value of all outputs over a long period of time. It is true that the distribution question mentioned in the above paragraph must in practice be dealt with at the same time: what states are to get the economic benefit of this efficiency? Further, as will be discussed later, the *definition* of maximum output or least cost depends upon some understanding about the distribution of

[24] And others; see McDougal and Burke, *The Public Order of the Oceans*, pp. 499–520.

wealth and income. Nevertheless the search for economic efficiency can be sufficiently well defined to be dealt with alone.

In this second sense we may ask how fish can be caught at the least cost; how a waste in duplication of vessels and crews can be avoided; how long hauls to distant ports can be avoided; how the more valuable fish can be preferred in fishing to "trash" and predators; how two, three, or more valuable species can be grown and caught together; how the costs of seasonality can be reduced; and to what extent it is worthwhile to protect and "plant" valuable fish. These questions arise in the simplest local fishery; more important, they also arise in the great fisheries on the high seas, where congestion and conflict are threatening to become the rule.

These problems suggest that it is necessary to find rules by which the high seas can be managed in the interest of the world community. The principles discussed in this chapter whereby one state seeks to gain advantages over another do not meet this test, nor do they meet the test of efficiency, which is discussed in Chapters 2 and 12.

Chapter 11

Fishery Treaties and Commissions

🐜. 🐜. 🐜. 🐜. 🐜. 🐜. 🐜. 🐜. 🐜. 🐜. 🐜 🐜. 🐜. 🐜. 🐜. 🐜. 🐜. 🐜. 🐜. 🐜. 🐜.

IN this chapter, we turn from general principles to the specific "contracts" of international law; to the bilateral and multilateral agreements that affect the use and development of ocean fisheries. These agreements arise in response to indications of trouble, such as controversy over rights to a fishery area, problems of congestion, or the awareness of the depletion of the resource. The increasing severity of these troubles indicates the pressing need for understanding more about the courses and opportunities for resolution by international agreement. Indeed, while there is a multitude of fishery treaties and conventions, there is a virtual absence of published information other than formal declarations and reports.[1]

[1] For information see: W. C. Herrington and J. L. Kask, "International Conservation Problems, and Solutions in Existing Conventions," in *Papers Presented at the International Technical Conference on the Conservation of the Living Resources of the Sea, Rome, April 18 to May 10, 1955,* UN Doc. No. A/Conf.10/7, 1956, pp. 145–66; FAO, Legislation Research Branch, *Comparison and Abstracts of Selected Conventions Establishing Fisheries Commissions,* Rome, 1962. See also the second of two papers by D. M. Johnston, "The International Law of Fisheries," in ed. E. E. Palmer, *Current Law and Social Problems,* Vol. 3, Toronto, 1963, pp. 146–237, and an article in two parts by S. Oda, "New Trends in the Regime of the Seas: A Consideration of the Problems of Conservation and Distribution of Marine Resources," *Zeitschrift für Ausländisches Öffentliches Recht und Völkerrecht,* Vol. 18 (1957), pp 61–102 and 261–86. For Pacific treaties up to about 1940, see J. Tomasevich, *International Agreements on Conservation of Marine Resources* (Stanford: Food Research Institute, Stanford University Press, 1943).

This chapter is an initial and preliminary effort to compare and contrast some of the attempts that nations have made to co-operate in the research and exploitation of fisheries. We begin by classifying and describing, very briefly, the different kinds of agreements —those that are concerned with the division of rights to fishing areas, those that are primarily of a research nature, and those that attempt management, either of a particular stock or of a fishery region. It is important to point out that there are also wide differences among the treaty commissions in the degree of autonomy that they can exercise, or in the provision for new entrants. These points, together with the objectives and different methods for reaching objectives, are also raised in the following pages.

There is a great deal to be learned about the process of reaching agreements on fishery treaties, about the viability of different treaty commissions, and about the prospects for future arrangements. Specialists in foreign relations, public administration, economics, and international law, all have much to contribute. About the most that we can do at this stage is to raise questions. How do the commissions vote? What pressures do they feel, and how do they respond? To what extent do they take into account economic and social considerations that are not written into their terms of reference? Why are some commissions autonomous and others dependent? How do commission members from different nations resolve conflicts between the interests of their nations and the interests of the world community? What is the role of independent "outside" forces when the shape of the treaties or the decisions of the commissions are being determined? What are the various ways of obtaining co-operation from member governments in enforcing regulations, issuing permits, commissioning research, providing funds? It seems to us that answers to these questions can help, not only in resolving conflict in fisheries, but also in furthering the understanding of methods for achieving greater international co-operation in all spheres of interest.

Fishing Rights Treaties

Quantitatively, the most important group of treaties deals with the concession of rights to fish certain waters; rights to land fish; rights to obtain supplies, especially bait; and similar matters. For particular states, such rights are likely to be far more important than co-operative research or management agreements, since they make the resource available for exploitation. Arrangements of this kind are the maritime equivalent of boundary agreements, or bilateral trade agreements—indeed, they often form a part of treaties dealing with other matters, especially treaties concluding a war. Few, if any, of them require a Commission or other treaty organization.

Treaties of this kind could be spotted all around the globe. The Treaty of Washington (1871), which is best known for its disposal of the *Alabama* claims arising out of the Civil War, was important to both New England and to Canada in that it confirmed Canada's right to her territorial waters while permitting American fishermen to continue fishing there. Similarly, in a century of treaties Great Britain and her neighbors have defined and redefined the area open to their fishermen, notably in the North Sea Convention of 1882, "to regulate the police of the fisheries in the North Sea outside territorial waters," and incidentally to define each state's territorial water closed to the fishermen of the other signatories. This series culminated in recent agreements with Iceland,[2] Norway,[3] and Denmark with respect to the Faroe Islands.[4] Italy and Yugoslavia have agreed since 1958 on the fishing rights in the Adriatic.[5] Finland and the U.S.S.R. have had an agreement on seal fishing since 1959.[6]

These treaties, though important, are of secondary interest here because they deal only with the question of *who* is to fish and not with *how* fishing is to be organized.

Research and Management ("Conservation") Treaties

This group comprises international agreements on the "conservation" of fisheries. For convenience, they have been classified into two groups: (a) research, and (b) stock and regional regulatory treaties. This classification, however, is by no means watertight; all

[2] Great Britain Treaty Series No. 17 (1961), Cmnd. 1328.
[3] Great Britain Treaty Series No. 25 (1961), Cmnd. 1352.
[4] 337 UN Treaty Series (1959), 416; Great Britain Treaty Series No. 55 (1959), Cmnd. 776.
[5] 379 UN Treaty Series (1960) 23.
[6] 338 UN Treaty Series (1959) 3.

treaties make some provision for obtaining scientific information, include some reference to the particular stocks of fish to be conserved, and state the regions of the sea to which they apply.

RESEARCH TREATIES

These agreements comprise arrangements for the collection, coordination, and distribution of information about particular regions of the sea, or about particular stocks of fish. They rarely provide for management or regulation, but in some instances it is clear that they are regarded by some of their members as the first step toward more active co-operation in the harvesting of ocean resources.

Senior of these in age, and probably in accomplishment, is the International Council for the Exploration of the Sea (ICES). Formed in 1902 by nine Baltic and North Sea states, ICES has concentrated on detailed investigation of hydrographic and biologic conditions of these two seas. It has a long and distinguished list of publications, and has taken the lead in co-ordinating the collection and standardization of fisheries statistics and the biologic research by the interested nations. In recent decades it has also functioned as the research arm of *the North Seas mesh convention,* referred to below, thus fulfilling the aim expressed in its first report: ". . . to prepare for the rational exploitation of the sea on a scientific basis. . . ."

Most of the other purely research or exploration agreements have been set up under the sponsorship of FAO, which has acted as organizer and has provided facilities and personnel for meetings.[7] The Indo-Pacific Fisheries Council [8] was formed in 1948, and the General Fisheries Council for the Mediterranean in 1949.[9] Two further bodies are now close to formation, one for the West African coast and the other for the South East Atlantic. Similar in form to ICES, each of these four bodies suggests, co-ordinates, and publishes the results of national research and of routine statistical inquiries.

---

[7] It should be pointed out that, in contrast to FAO's agricultural division, fisheries biologists have not confined their work to the development of individual fisheries, but have also undertaken some significant basic research relevant to all fisheries.

[8] 120 UN Treaty Series (1952) 59.

[9] 126 UN Treaty Series (1952) 236.

STOCK REGULATORY TREATIES

Research is only the first step toward an agreement on the management of fisheries. What the next step will be depends upon the particular problem and how the nations decide to deal with it. They have a choice between agreeing to conserve a particular fish stock or species and agreeing to apply conservation to a particular region of the ocean.

In view of the extensive history [10] of protecting animals such as deer and game birds, and the lengthy experience of the "fishing classes" of Europe in protecting certain sport fish, it is not surprising that the first important fisheries management agreement took the form of a "stock" treaty. This was the Fur Seal Treaty, between Russia, Japan, the United States, and Great Britain (later, Canada). Signed in 1911 and revised at various times (the latest being 1957),[11] it is unique among all conservation treaties in that it appoints two "agents"—the United States and Russia—to carry out the management and harvesting of the herds on their islands. Pelagic sealing is prohibited, and provision is made for sharing the proceeds among the signatories. In effect, the agreement creates sole ownership in each of the two areas. The task of the Commission, therefore, is merely to ensure that the best methods of research and of harvesting are being pursued. With respect to most decisions, its unanimous recommendations are, in effect, direct instructions to the U.S.S.R. and the United States.

The second treaty to incorporate regulatory features was the Pacific Halibut Convention between United States and Canada. In 1923, the two countries set up an international commission to study the halibut fisheries and agreed to close the fisheries during three winter months. In 1930, when the convention was renegotiated, the commission was given the power to regulate as well as to conduct research. The commission was given authority to set up areas, to close and open seasons and areas, regulate gear, and to establish quotas for each area for each season. It was also given powers to enforce these objectives; it can, for example, prohibit the departure of a vessel for a closed area. Finally, it was given an independent and influential research arm. The regulatory powers have the force of law of each country, subject only to the possible

[10] See A. D. Scott, *Natural Resources: The Economics of Conservation* (Toronto: University of Toronto Press, 1955), Chapter 3.
[11] Canada Treaty Series No. 26 (1957).

disapproval of the respective governments.[12] The total quotas, which apply to the nationals of these countries, both in national waters and on the high seas, are not divided into national quotas.[13] The strength and breadth of this authority over a stock of fish and the conditions of its harvesting set a most important standard for subsequent international agreements.

In the early 1930's, the League of Nations' Economic Committee managed to secure agreement among some of the main whaling nations (but not Japan) on steps to protect the growth and reproduction of the baleen whale stock. Similar, informal steps were taken by the Norwegian-British "cartel" between 1931 and 1934.[14] A treaty covering more species and closing the whaling season after a certain number of weeks was signed in 1937 by nine countries, but neither this treaty nor one signed in 1938 achieved success in limiting the total number of whales to be killed. A basic difficulty in securing agreement on a total quota seems to have stemmed from concern over how it would be allocated: some countries would not sign, and the signatories could not agree among themselves on the relative size of national quotas. It was not until 1944 that a total quota for Antarctic whales was first agreed upon.[15] A subsequent agreement in 1946 [16] set a pattern by specifying its regulations in its text and schedule. The job of the International Whaling Commission is not only to administer the regulations but also to debate possible amendments. Recommendations accepted by a three-quarters majority become amend-

[12] FAO, *Comparison and Abstracts, op. cit.,* p. 18, seems to be misinformed on this matter; see the text of the Convention reproduced on p. 61 of the FAO study.

[13] For a history, see *Report of the International Pacific Halibut Commission,* No. 25 (1956), pp. 5–6.

[14] The main reference for the prewar period is Karl Brandt, *Whale Oil: An Economic Analysis,* Fats and Oils Studies, Vol. 7 (Stanford: Food Research Institute, Stanford University Press, 1940). See also Tomasevich, *op. cit.,* pp. 275–87.

[15] See R. Kellogg, "The International Whaling Commission," *Papers Presented at the International Technical Conference on the Conservation of the Living Resources of the Sea, Rome, 1955,* UN Doc. No. A/Conf.10/7, pp. 256–61. See also S. Oda, *International Control of Sea Resources* (Leyden, Netherlands: A. W. Sythoff, 1963), pp. 78–82. The literature on whaling law, treaties and regulation is surprisingly small, although the situation is touched on in many general works. For a bibliography, see McDougal and Burke, *The Public Order of the Ocean* (New Haven: Yale University Press, 1962), pp. 943 ff.

[16] 161 UN Treaty Series (1953) 72; Canada Treaty Series No. 54 (1946).

ments to the treaty unless rejected by members within a ninety-day period.

The regulations call for the protection of whales of various species and size, the setting of a total annual quota, the placing by each government of an inspector on each of its factory ships, and the submission of a large amount of information on the kill to a central office in Norway. For many years, the nations that actually participated in whaling attempted to reach agreements on shares of the total quota that each nation's fleets could take. In 1961, the whaling nations agreed to allocate the total permissible kill as follows: 20 per cent to the U.S.S.R., 33 per cent to Japan, 32 per cent to Norway, 9 per cent to the United Kingdom, and 6 per cent to the Netherlands.[17] Since then, both the United Kingdom and the Netherlands have sold their whaling fleets to the Japanese, and with the fleets went their shares of the total take.

During the last few years, however, the scientific recommendations of a total quota that would permit the rehabilitation of the whale stocks have been ignored by the whaling nations. For the 1964/65 season, Japan, U.S.S.R., and Norway tentatively agreed upon a quota about twice that recommended by the scientists. The continued depletion of the whale stocks of the Antarctic appears inevitable.

The Pacific Salmon Convention between the United States and Canada—preceded by a convention in 1908 and by another in 1918, which were not adopted—was signed in 1930 and eventually ratified in 1937. With only two members and easier enforcement than the whaling treaty, it was immediately effective.[18] It provided both for research activities and for stock management of the sockeye salmon (pink salmon were added in 1956). Canadians and Americans each fish their own territorial waters. The International Pacific Salmon Fisheries Commission is empowered to make rules about gear and open days so as to equalize the catch of both members, as well as to maximize the yield. The Commission is also responsible for developing fishways that ease salmon migration to and from the inland spawning beds.

Two infrequently-mentioned agreements were also made in the prewar years. In 1929, five Baltic countries signed a convention to set trawl meshes in the Baltic plaice and flounder fisheries; and in

[17] Oda, *op. cit.*, p. 81.
[18] See Consolidated Convention in *Annual Report of the International Pacific Salmon Fisheries Commission* (1957), pp. 5–9.

1937, a similar treaty was signed by the countries along the Skagerrak, the Kattegat, and the Sound to regulate mesh on plaice trawls.

After the war, some of the fisheries agreements were revised and strengthened, and new ones were made. In 1949, a new convention was signed by the United States and Costa Rica to establish the Inter-American Tropical Tuna Commission, with responsibilities for yellowfin tuna, skipjack, and bait fish in the eastern Pacific.[19] Panama, Ecuador, and Colombia later joined. During its first decade, the Tuna Commission established an impressive permanent organization which has planned research and published reports on the findings. Studies have been made with regard to tuna, the relevant bait species, and the environment of both, as well as the relationship between fishing effort and abundance. In recent years there has been discussion of recommending to the member states a catch limit for yellowfin to offset the depleting effects of the rise in total effort.[20] There has also been some talk of national quotas, by which the members could allocate the annual limited catch. But the determination of national quotas would not be the business of the Commission (or of any other treaty commission [21] we have studied); it would be a matter for direct diplomatic negotiation.

These first treaties were concerned mainly with a stock of fish, rather than with fish in a certain body of water. This was due, partly at least, to alarm about the drop in the catch per unit of effort or the decline in the catch total of either the main species or its bait. Some of the stocks brought under the protection of these treaties are of the vulnerable species: mammals, anadromous fish, and some other species that are either slow to reproduce and grow or that seem unable to escape in sufficient numbers from the efficient fishing effort that has been attracted by their high commercial value. The apparent exhaustion of stocks that are both valuable and vulnerable has touched off measures designed to deal with the emergency in a particular stock.

It would be wrong to argue that the research and conservation activities resulting from the stock treaties have neglected the environment and food of the selected species. The salmon treaty, for

[19] 80 UN Treaty Series (1951) 3.

[20] See the recent reports of the Commission, for example, 1960, pp. 4 and 19, and 1961, p. 4.

[21] In the Salmon Convention, the Commission is entrusted with the allocation of half the catch to each member.

example, has been largely occupied with the improvement of the Fraser River route to the spawning grounds, and the tuna treaty with the environment of bait fish. But there is nevertheless a real difference of degree between the design and object of the treaties mentioned so far and those following, which might be designated regional treaties. In the drafting of a stock treaty, the members may eventually be led by the requirements of their fisheries' scientists to make provision for the study of that stock's environment, whereas in the drafting of a regional treaty the members begin with the entire body of water and may expect ultimately to examine all its potentialities and mysteries.

REGIONAL REGULATORY TREATIES

In a typical regional conservation treaty, the problems are much broader, dictating a more deliberate pace. The sense of urgency may be lacking, and the emergency attitude will be replaced by a more methodical step-by-step approach. For example, expert conferences had considered the gradual decline of North Atlantic catches for decades, but little was done. For one thing, the decline was slow, and it was not believed that the basic stocks were in danger of disappearance. Furthermore, the decline was less disastrous for some countries than for others. Finally, there were more countries involved. Consequently, measures to rehabilitate the many stocks in the region were very slow to gain agreement.

The earliest of the regional regulatory treaties was stimulated by a British prohibition on the use of small mesh for fish caught by British nationals in the North Sea, an action that became the basis of the international Convention for the Regulation of the Meshes of Fishing Nets and the Size Limits of Fish in 1937.[22] Suspended during the war years, it was revived in 1946 [23] and became effective in 1954 in a large area roughly bounded on the north by a line drawn from the tip of Greenland to the North Cape of Norway, and on the south by the southern waters of Britain and Ireland. The single basic regulation (concerning mesh size [24] and size of fish caught) [25] was written into the agreement, and could be changed only by unanimous agreement of the signatories.[26]

[22] Not to be confused with the earlier North Sea "police" and fishing-rights convention mentioned in Chapter 6.
[23] Great Britain Treaty Series No. 8 (1956), Cmnd. 9704.
[24] *Ibid.,* Annex I.
[25] *Ibid.,* Annex II.
[26] *Ibid.,* Art. 12 (10).

This Convention has been supplanted by the North East Atlantic Fisheries Convention,[27] signed in 1959. It is more extensive than its predecessor in two ways: it takes in Baltic and southern-European Atlantic waters; and it is empowered to deal with a much wider variety of regulations and topics. In this and many other respects it is like or goes beyond the International Convention for the Northwest Atlantic Fisheries and its membership overlaps that of ICNAF.

The International Convention for the Northwest Atlantic Fisheries [28] became effective in 1950, and now has thirteen North American and European members, including the Soviet Union. The Commission, which has a small staff and no real research facilities, must depend like all regional treaties on the facilities of member countries. It has pioneered a new technique whereby the Convention area (which is bounded approximately by the latitude of New York to the south, the tip of Greenland to the east, and the North American coast to the west) is divided into 23 areas characterized by more or less distinct stocks of demersal fish, and each area is studied by a panel made up of the nations exploiting it. The panel proposes regulatory measures (based on its studies) to the Commission, which reviews the recommendations and refers them, in turn, to the member governments for joint action. If accepted by the member governments of the appropriate panel, the regulations become binding on all the contracting governments when their nationals fish in these areas.

The South Pacific Convention,[29] signed in 1952 by Chile, Peru, and Ecuador—properly the Permanent Commission for the Exploitation and Conservation of the Maritime Resources of the South Pacific—takes a quite different form. It covers at least a 200-mile belt off the coasts of its members. Little has come of this very comprehensive agreement for joint exploitation and protection of fisheries.

Different again, is the North Pacific Fisheries Convention,[30] also signed in 1952, which covers an area roughly between the international date line and the North American coast (including the Bering Sea). The activities of the Commission take the form of

[27] Great Britain Parliament, Miscellaneous No. 3 (1959), Cmnd. 659.

[28] 157 UN Treaty Series (1953) 157.

[29] United Nations Legislative Series, *Laws and Regulations on the Regime of the Territorial Sea* (New York: United Nations, 1957), pp. 723–35.

[30] 4 U.S. Treaties 380; International North Pacific Fisheries Commission, Report of First Meeting (1954), pp. 11–17.

commissioning research, and from its results recommending regulations for the joint fisheries and, more important, determining the application of the "abstention" principle.[31] The signatories, Japan, Canada, and the United States, have agreed that where a stock is shown to be under management, and fully utilized by one or more members [32] the other member or members will abstain from fishing that stock within the treaty area. To fulfill its tasks, the Commission has been led into intensive examination of the migratory habits of salmon (to determine the boundaries of the Canadian and American stocks, which are fully used and managed), and into studies of the distribution and utilization of halibut, herring, and crab stocks.

This agreement is currently being renegotiated. It has been determined that salmon originating in the Bristol Bay rivers spend part of their lives to the west of the present treaty boundary and therefore can be taken freely by the Japanese under the terms of the original agreement. The United States fishermen wish to extend the treaty area to cover this stock. The Japanese, however, are unwilling to have their rights to high seas salmon diminished.

Parenthetically, it is interesting to note the attitude toward fishing agreements that has been adopted by Japan and Russia, the powers with the largest international fishing fleets. Japan's freedom to fish in coastal waters near various states has been resented and feared. Consequently, Japan has found it politic to participate in fishing agreements, and she is a member of the Whaling Convention, The North Pacific Fur Seal Convention, the Provisional Regime to Regulate Pearling by Japanese Nationals (with Australia), and the Japan-Soviet Northwest Pacific Fisheries Convention. Not unnaturally, she regards these treaties as arrangements by which she buys the right to fish by accepting certain regulations. She wants the fishing rights, but is not very enthusiastic about the conservation aspects of the conventions. Russia, on the other hand, has a divided interest. In the Atlantic, the Bering Sea, and mid-Pacific, Russia is in somewhat the same position as Japan—increasing her fishing effort in waters already used by other states. Hence Russia has maintained her membership in the seal treaties, the International Whaling Convention, and ICNAF, and is a signatory to the North-East Atlantic Fisheries Convention. Also, recent items in the press have sug-

---

[31] *Ibid.*, Article III.
[32] *Ibid.*, Article IV (1) (b).

gested she might not be averse to joining the North Pacific Fisheries Convention.

On the Asian coast, however, Russia has salmon and other fisheries which she occasionally claims as her own, and there she acts like a coastal state fending off intruders. Agreements between Russia and Japan dealing with the coast of Siberia and the salmon fishery date back to the close of the Russo-Japanese war in 1905.[33] The latest, the 1956 Northwest Pacific Fisheries Convention,[34] covers the northwest Pacific generally west of 175° West and north of 45° North latitude, including the Sea of Okhotsk, parts of the Sea of Japan and the Bering Sea.[35] Japan and Russia agree to the size limits on herring and crab; but the main emphasis of the treaty seems to be the protection of the salmon and the extent of Japanese fishing in the Sea of Okhotsk. This convention states its regulations in its text and provides for a joint commission, one of whose tasks is to revise the regulations, on the basis of scientific considerations, in respect of the total catch of salmon, the amount of the mixed catches of small herring and female and small crabs and the mesh size of crab nets.[36]

Observations

What conclusions can be drawn from the fishing agreements outlined above? Because there is such a wide range in the adminis-

[33] See Z. Ohira, "Fishery Problems between Soviet Russia and Japan," *Japanese Annual of International Law,* Vol. 2 (1958), p. 1; Gordon Ireland, "The North Pacific Fisheries," *American Journal of International Law,* Vol. 36 (1942), pp. 416–22; and S. Oda, "New Trends in the Regime of the Seas," *op. cit.,* pp. 80–83. There is a brief discussion in Tomasevich, *op. cit.,* pp. 27–28 and 228–30; and in D. M. Johnston, "The International Law of Fisheries," *Current Law and Social Problems,* Vol. 3 (1963), p. 163.

[34] For an unofficial translation, see *American Journal of International Law,* Vol. 53 (1959), pp. 763–73.

[35] The eastern boundary of this convention area is the same as the western boundary of the North Pacific Convention (mentioned above) under which the Japanese have abstained from fishing for salmon. As noted above, some of the salmon of the Bristol Bay streams spend a part of their lives west of this line and therefore within the area that is regulated by the Soviet-Japanese Commission. If the United States is successful in extending the controls of the North Pacific Convention westward to cover the migrations of the Bristol Bay salmon, the two commissions would then have overlapping responsibilities.

[36] See S. Oda, "Japan and the International Fisheries," *Japanese Annual of International Law,* Vol. 4 (1960), p. 53.

trative arrangements and organizations of the treaty commissions, clear patterns and trends are not readily discernible. However, certain general observations can be made with respect to the autonomy of the commissions, the organization of research effort, and the different objectives and goals. From the discussion of these that follows, three major problems for the future are isolated and identified. The first is the method by which non-signatory nations can accede or become a party to the treaties. The second is the question of the equitable sharing of the resource where the catch is limited. And the third is the possibility and problems of establishing central international authorities to operate the fisheries.

THE AUTONOMY OF TREATY COMMISSIONS

The greatest autonomy both in making regulations and in commissioning or carrying out research is possessed by commissions appointed by countries that are willing to sign away a little power. This willingness is enhanced where co-operation can clearly work to the benefit of the participating nations. Such was the case with respect to Pacific salmon and halibut. The United States and Canada have given the commissions dealing with these resources such a high degree of autonomy that the tasks of the two governments have been less to be advised by the commissions than to confirm their decisions.

But co-operation between nations frequently involves the bearing of inequitable costs. The North Sea mesh-size regulations make this difficulty clear. Here one minimum mesh size is bound to be more effective for some stocks than for others: an extreme expression would be that the growth of catch from some stocks is being sacrificed for the growth of others. In turn, this choice favors the fishing techniques, areas, or markets of some nations more than others. Thus, the participating nations are unwilling to grant a great deal of independence to the commission.

When a commission lacks independence, it becomes a sort of permanent international conference, devoted to a single topic. Little more is accomplished than could be accomplished by *ad hoc* international conferences that are called to set up international institutions and rules, and then disbanded until a new decision is required. This, of course, is too pessimistic. The commissions have staffs and permanent secretaries; experience and confidence do accumulate; and commission recommendations do tend to pass from the channels of diplomacy into the paths of departmental routine. A good example is provided by ICNAF, which has a large and disparate membership. We may expect that experience in co-operation, clarification of objectives, greater biological knowledge, and success in regulation may combine gradually to strengthen the Commission and render more automatic the approval of the member states to proposed measures. In fact, the members, aware of continued declines in catch per unit of effort, have given the Commission the task of making a broad study of alternative methods of fishery regulation, including the technique of limiting entry.

The degree of autonomy granted to a commission does not appear to depend upon the nature of the treaty, i.e., whether it is concerned with a stock or a region. But it is clear that a regional treaty commission needs more autonomy, for it must go beyond the study of each of the stocks in its area. The wider the scope of its activities and the greater the extent of its knowledge, the more it will be under pressure to make (or recommend) choices: for example, between the size of catch in adjoining areas fished by the same fleets, or between ecologically competing stocks in the same or adjoining areas. Such choices will inevitably become more and more technical and are likely to give the commission a greater degree of responsibility.

In addition, the very fact that a nation is a member of a regional treaty implies an acceptance of the economic and biological complexity and integrity of the entire oceanic region. This, in turn, implies a recognition of the fact that some region-wide decisions must be made, which both protect the interests of the various contracting parties and, in some sense, advance the common conservation objective. If there is any trend, we expect that it will be toward the establishment of more regional commissions and toward the granting of a greater degree of autonomy.

THE ORGANIZATION OF RESEARCH

We turn now to "the research question," the problem of how best to acquire technical, biological, oceanographical, and marketing information on which to base decisions about catch, seasons, and areas.

It was made clear by all the technical writers in the papers for the Rome Conference on the Living Resources of the Sea [37] that

---

[37] United Nations, *Papers Presented at the International Technical Conference on the Conservation of the Living Resources of the Sea, op. cit.*

the biological approach to conservation measures should be firmly based on studies of species in their physical and ecological environments. Obtaining this knowledge is slow and expensive, requiring the establishment of marine biological stations and oceanographical laboratories, the dispatching of research vessels, and the collection and analysis of masses of statistics.

The different circumstances of the nations and fisheries involved have dictated two types of decision about research facilities: dependence upon the various national research organizations, or establishment of a separate permanent research organization. The first course is encouraged by the following considerations: the expense of new establishments can be saved by increasing the capacity of existing ones; the experts in the existing establishments may be jealous or suspicious of a new establishment; and countries without existing facilities may be assisted [38] to acquire them in the process of satisfying the research requirements of convention membership. The second course, a new establishment, will be permitted or encouraged if the members now have no facilities and would prefer pooling their resources to making separate research investments; if the members are all comparatively wealthy and can afford to duplicate their national facilities; or if their national facilities are required for tasks not covered by the convention.

Whatever the reasons in particular cases, the trend has been to depend on existing national facilities. It is true that the three most effective stock treaties—those dealing with salmon, halibut, and tuna—have their own research organizations. But the North Sea Mesh-Size Convention has always depended on ICES, which in turn has depended on the facilities of its members. And the same holds for all the rest: the tendency for both stock and regional treaties has been to set up a directorate or secretariat, with one or two highly competent scientists acting as international civil servants to take care of the co-ordination and publishing of national research efforts bearing on matters of concern to the commission. Their staff is usually clerical; they have neither laboratories nor research vessels.

An additional factor that may be important in determining the form of research organization may be the degree of emergency that accompanies the establishment of the commission. All conventions

[38] D. M. Johnston, *op. cit.*, p. 226.

have, as it were, been set up in advance of full knowledge. In the case of the stock treaties in particular, it seems that the emergency leading to the treaties also stimulated the imposition of regulations that might in some instances be considered premature. In order to quell opposition to the regulations, provisions have been made for setting up relatively elaborate research facilities, as in the case of the commissions for halibut and salmon. The less urgent circumstances and greater complexities of the regional treaties have permitted the adoption of a more leisurely approach to conservation measures and, there has been willingness to wait while the research questions were farmed out to national institutions. Of course, if the waiting period is too long, serious overfishing can occur.

It is not clear which approach is better—dependence of the commission upon national research efforts or the creation of the commission's own research staff and facilities. In the former case, researchers, employed by member governments, may be forced to adopt roles favorable to the objectives of their country. It is argued that this undesirable situation is ended when commissions can instruct and depend on their own staff of experts, who are then free of the pressures to plead their own country's case.

The alternative point of view states that a commission research staff will act as an independent bureaucracy, tending to develop a vested interest in its own point of view, becoming overly defensive of its own past decisions, and using its claim to impartiality as a shield against criticism. It is claimed that the free argument and contention among scientists from different nations leads to constructive criticism and perhaps to better results in the long run.

Like the question of commission autonomy raised above, this controversy cannot be decided by mere discussion. In many ways it is similar to the familiar problem of industrial research: should business and government undertake their own research, or are business and national interests favored when projects are farmed out to specialized institutions, universities, and firms? It is also similar to the question sometimes raised about American oceanographic and fisheries research: Is it desirable to have so many separate small stations, many of them carrying out portions of a larger research program without any clear view of the total question? International fisheries research, it seems to us, is a useful question for further investigation by social scientists.

OBJECTIVES OF TREATY COMMISSIONS

Among all these agreements there are few articles that empower commissions or their advisors to take account of such economic aims as increased efficiency in the use of labor and capital (either by reducing the cost of a given catch, or by increasing the value of catch for a given cost). Just as the Law of the Sea Convention on Fishing and Conservation specified the purely physical goal of conserving the resources of the oceans, so the various treaties seem to compel their commissioners to maximize the sustainable catch and nothing more.[39]

There are, of course, important qualifications to this statement. The Halibut Commission, among others, is free to confer with industry in setting its regulations and apparently attempts to minimize the burden of these regulations on the fleet. And furthermore, the regulations themselves are obviously compromises between the implementation of immediate catch maximization measures and the losses that may be experienced when meshes are first increased, quotas first imposed, or areas first closed. Where particular economic considerations have been given serious weight in deciding upon the extent and timing of conservation measures, it has usually been in deference to industrial demands rather than in response to general national and international economic goals. There has been complete neglect of what most economists believe to be the basic causes of low incomes and low productivity in the fishery: resistance to new technology, common property, and free entry to the fishery.

Resistance to new technology is not typical of all fisheries,[40] but there is no doubt that "nautical luddism"—the prevention of innovation by the banning of especially effective fishing systems—has been a powerful force in many national fisheries and some international agreements. Here the force of industry pressure on administrators and international commissions is divided. Some own-

[39] "It is self-evident that the primary purpose of the powers granted to the Commissions is to permit maximum sustained catches, although this point is not always explicitly stated in the Conventions." FAO, *Comparison and Abstracts, op. cit.,* p. 14.

[40] The extremely competitive conditions of some new fisheries may encourage a rate of innovation faster than that desirable for the best use of the capital required. See A. D. Scott, "The Economics of Regulating Fisheries," *Economic Effects of Fishery Regulation,* FAO Fisheries Reports No. 5, Rome, 1962, pp. 25–61.

ers urge freedom to use the new techniques. But the majority, usually, is concerned to protect its investment in the old apparatus by condemning the new for its destructiveness. It is not surprising that the majority has had its way in many fisheries, for banning new methods protects many jobs and the value of many people's personal wealth.

International conventions do not instruct commissioners actively to seek the best use of the seas by encouraging the introduction of new methods. Their job is held to have ended when they have made available to member nations' fleets the maximum annual yield. How wastefully, relative to possible costs, this yield may be caught is of no concern to them.

Similarly, the conventions do not make it possible to reduce the input of labor and capital required to take the catch. The limitation of entry is in every case a national matter. By raising the annual yield and increasing the information available, the conventions may in fact encourage an increased effort to take a catch that could be caught without it. In this negative sense, the conventions encourage increased entry, until the participants no longer benefit from the larger yield, but are driven once more to longer hours, harder fishing, and lower shares and profits.

NATIONAL QUOTAS AND THE LIMITATION OF ENTRY

In some of the agreements, the total permissible take is apportioned among the participating nations. Canada and the United States, for example, share equally the catch of salmon within the treaty area. And in the Antarctic, Japan, Norway, and Russia now divide what's left of the whales. Where such national quotas are in effect, it is possible, at least theoretically, for each nation to decide how best to catch the given amount of fish. This step amounts to making each nation's industry independent of the actions of others. The industry can make its own deliberate plan for economically taking its quota, since it cannot be forestalled by the vessels of other nations. The government is similarly free to restrict the number of fishermen or indeed to select a given firm or syndicate to act as that country's chosen instrument in that fishery.

In practice, however, national quotas are not without difficulties. And it is not even clear that they are a useful step toward eliminating the waste of labor and capital by each nation. Uncertainty might well create an incentive for each member-nation's industry to try to take its quota early, in case the year's total catch should turn out to be smaller than expected. This incentive in turn may justify a nation's having a larger fleet than is economically required to bring in the quota. In effect, the members will race each other to bring in their respective quotas, and the need for racing will discourage restricting the size of fleets and encourage over-capacity and short, early seasons.

The national-quota idea may also entail other difficulties. One is that in regional treaties national quotas would probably have to be split up for subregions and local stocks. The problem would then stem from the limited productivity and costliness of each subarea, rather than from the uncertainty of predicting the total catch—a difficulty typical of stock treaties concerned with pelagic species. First-comers on each small ground would do better than those fishing their quota at a more leisurely pace, and an incentive to have larger and swifter fleets would once again be created.

Consequently, it appears that national quotas are unlikely to eliminate the expensive competition for the total catch that now is typical of both national and international fisheries. Such economizing would result only from some single authority, with the firms or member nations acting in complete concert.

In addition to the problems of improving economic efficiency, the establishment of national quotas raises problems about the distribution of the seas' wealth. A national quota is, in essence, a property right in a resource, similar in many respects to property rights acquired by coastal states when they extend their exclusive fishing limits. It has been argued that such rights have monopoly characteristics and that they might serve to retard the rate of technological innovation or to prevent more efficient producers from using the resource.[41] As to the rate of technological innovation, the most desirable outcome is not clear. It may be, as mentioned before, that free competition in undivided fisheries stimulates a too-rapid innovation. The users of the outmoded equipment cannot afford to wait until they have amortized their equipment because to do so means letting the innovators take a greater share of the resource. Hence, a slower rate of improvement in national-quota fisheries may actually constitute a better use of capital and national savings.

Also, the establishment of national quotas or the extension of coastal limits may, or may not, exclude more efficient producers

[41] McDougal and Burke, *op. cit.,* pp. 508–10.

from using the resource. Such rights can be (and have been) sold, leased, or licensed to fishermen from other nations. The Dutch and the English, for example, sold their quotas in the Antarctic whaling industry when they sold their fleets to the Japanese. By retiring excessive inputs, the economic efficiency of the industry could be greatly improved.

Some Problems for Research

The international fishery commissions are subject to great economic pressure, but they are not really empowered to make decisions on common economic grounds. To what extent might they do so under present treaties? To what criteria should they appeal when members live under different levels of cost and price? Could they, without further discussion, now encourage the restriction of fishing effort and the adoption of new techniques, or do these objectives, too, await the development of new criteria?

We cannot neglect the fact that most participants today evidently care less about questions of "how" and "why" to conserve fisheries than about the question "for whom." Obviously, the Law of the Sea Conferences were divided over the regimes and over the width of the territorial sea just because nations would be affected unequally by each proposal. So it is with treaties. In particular, there are three questions which need research and the exchange of views.

First of these is the method of adherence. How are non-signatory nations to be prevented from spoiling the work of the treaty organizations by fishing outside the framework of their regulations and measures? Or, how are older fishing nations to be prevented from permanently appropriating high-seas resources merely because they were there a few decades earlier? These two questions, obviously posed by different sets of people, are two sides of the same coin.

It is true that they were dealt with in the Fishing and Conservation of the Living Resources of the High Seas Convention. In rejecting the "abstention principle" and paying little attention to "historic rights" on the fishing zone and territorial sea problem, the conference seems to have relied on the negotiation-and-adjudication technique to find a method for new entrants to participate in fisheries already under convention management. But it gives the arbitration boards few, if any, principles on which to act in settling these matters.[42]

Large fishing nations like the United States, Russia, and Japan must respect international arrangements now existing because they form a part of the delicate distribution of resources, territory, wealth, and power. This balance has, of course, been implicit in the acceptance of the freedom-of-the-seas regime. However, it is an unstable equilibrium, subject to changes in the views and the values of the great powers to whom fisheries may be a relatively unimportant element in global strategy. This balance must be respected in determining how quickly to move toward different international fisheries arrangements; but it need not be considered as unchangeable.

Some of the older stock treaties, such as those for seal, halibut, and salmon, make no provision for new adherents. Other treaties (e.g., the North East Atlantic and ICNAF) seem flexible and designed to make provision for the changing distribution of fishing power. But this is achieved simply by providing the freedom of opportunity to compete by throwing in ever larger lumps of labor and capital. Arrangements must be found that facilitate adaptation to changes in the distribution of effort and, at the same time, prevent the wasteful application of productive inputs.

A second question requiring investigation is the setting of equitable quotas for fishing nations. The extent of historical involvement, however large and inefficient, is obviously important in arriving at agreements on the distribution of resources. New countries, with small fleets and short histories, however, will quite naturally complain of the unfairness of this approach. These different views must be balanced as well as combined with general agreements on an equitable distribution of resources and with principles of conservation and economic efficiency. Here, it seems to us, is a field to be thoroughly examined and discussed in advance of conflict.

A third question arising from the examination of the treaties and commissions is that of the possibility of establishing a central international authority for managing ocean fisheries. Such an approach has been implied in many of our comments. Internationalization has many different meanings and the advantages and

---

[42] "The closest these [Geneva] conferences came to providing the rationale for a system of shared conservation authority was in stressing the universal responsibility to conserve." Johnston, *op. cit.*, p. 220. (In the succeeding paragraphs he goes on to suggest his own "rationale.")

disadvantages are difficult to anticipate clearly. Further discussion of this approach is offered in succeeding chapters but it should be listed here along with the other questions calling for intensive research.

Conclusions

The general drift of the development of the international law of the sea fisheries is difficult to ascertain. For years international law has been built largely on a compromise between the concept of the freedom of the seas and the special interests of the coastal states. But today the balance between these forces is shifting and, at the same time, new concepts and pressures are emerging. The world-wide extension of the fishing efforts of some nations is bringing foreign fleets into waters that have been utilized only by domestic fishermen for many years. Such distant-water fishermen are anxious to maintain the openness of the seas and the privilege of fishing close to foreign shores. There is also a growing number of small nations, with little current investment in fishing industries, that would like to "protect" the resources in their coastal waters, and seek to do so by claiming greater limits of exclusive rights.

These contrasting forces reflect the economic pressures that are associated with the growing demand for fishery products and the increasing scarcity of the resources. For many of these resources, the economic scarcity is compounded by depletion. The desirability of overcoming depletion, or of conserving and managing the resource, is an additional element that should be considered in reformulations of international law. The necessity for this is further indicated by anticipating future technological innovations that will create remarkably efficient harvesting devices or make possible the culture of the seas. In addition to these forces, the concept of the utilization of the seas for the good of the world community is receiving increased emphasis.

The Law of the Sea Conventions in 1958 and 1960 made some effort to deal with some of these different forces and concepts. Indeed, they formulated some aspects of a regime well in advance of contemporary practice. However, it is doubtful that these formulations will be sufficient to accommodate, without conflict, the new technical problems, economic forces, and political pressures that are daily growing stronger and stronger.

Side by side with the practice and principles of international law are the agreements and treaties on fisheries worked out over the past sixty years. Beginning with the most vulnerable fish stocks, the most valuable species, and the most friendly nations, they have gradually been extended to cover, however loosely, whole regions of the seas. This emerging regional approach has certain advantages over the stock type of treaty in that it can make, or recommend, choices on a wider variety of problems, including selection among competing areas, stocks, and fleets.[43] However, the regional approach is regarded by some critics as an unrealistic compromise between a world-wide approach and a stock-by-stock approach, both because certain valuable species do not confine themselves to one region and because biologically-relevant regions do not conform to economically—or politically—suitable regional groupings of states and industries.[44] Certainly the apparent advocacy of the regional approach by some international experts before the Law of the Sea Conferences made little headway with the national representatives. Nevertheless, the trend toward regional management of fishery resources is important and will inevitably have a significant effect on the kinds of future regimes that are established for the sea.

We feel that it is extremely important to give adequate consideration to these many different thrusts that will affect the international utilization of ocean fisheries. Future arrangements will have to be quite different from those that are in existence today if the international utilization is to be harmonious and beneficial to the world community. Some of the criteria that should be considered in the reformulations of the law of the sea are discussed in the next chapter.

[43] See J. L. McHugh, "Can We Manage Our Atlantic Coastal Fishery Resources," *Transactions of the American Fisheries Society,* Vol. 88 (1959), pp. 105–10, for a discussion of the costs of concentrating on a single stock.

[44] Both the desirability of a regional approach and the political difficulties have been noted by D. M. Johnston in his notes on the Russo-Japanese Northwest Pacific Convention: "It seems that better results could be expected in the joint conservation of these two controversial species if the convention were to include the stocks inhabiting Russian waters, so that a comprehensive programme for the conservation of the entire species in the region could be accomplished, but it is possible that this would merely widen the rift by inviting controversy over the nature of the coastal state's special interest." Johnston, *op. cit.,* pp. 211–12.

Chapter 12

Objectives for Fisheries Management

꩜. ꩜. ꩜. ꩜. ꩜. ꩜. ꩜. ꩜. ꩜. ꩜. ꩜ ꩜. ꩜. ꩜. ꩜. ꩜. ꩜. ꩜. ꩜. ꩜. ꩜.

IN this chapter we turn to the objectives for the management and administration of international fisheries, focusing on questions about the production of the wealth of the seas rather than its distribution. In our previous discussion on legal principles and treaty commissions, it became clear that most of the forces at work relate to the appropriation of ocean resources. The principle of the "freedom of the seas," for example, benefits those countries that already have large, developed fleets and industries. The arguments of the coastal states, on the other hand, are more exclusive and would, if fully accepted and extended, result in dividing the wealth of world fisheries among separate nations. Similar benefits are sought by those who advocate the doctrines of abstention or of historic rights. Even the principle of conservation, which is the only one that appears to be free of these claims to wealth, is frequently advanced by countries that can see some special advantage to themselves in the adoption of certain conservation regulations.

The questions of the distribution of the seas' wealth cannot be entirely divorced from those of its production. The two are interdependent and must eventually be brought together. For example, it is important to know what countries are involved when determining how to achieve the best use of the seas.

The two principal objectives discussed are variants of the idea of the maximization of production from the oceans, regardless of the nationality of the user. The first, proposed chiefly by scientists, is that the world should attempt to maximize the long-run contribution of the oceans to the world supply of food and materials. The second, advanced by economists, is that the benefits from the ocean in excess of the costs of exploitation should be maximized. The first objective therefore emphasizes the physical volume of production and the second emphasizes the rent or the economic surplus of the seas' exploitation.

Before beginning the discussion, and by way of apology for oversimplification, we do not mean to imply that all biologists advocate the physical goal without regard for economic criteria. Nor do we mean to aver that economic objectives are the only objectives that society should consider. Many of the most respected biologists who have been involved in negotiations for the management of the seas have long argued that the ultimate decisions on policy must take economic efficiency considerations into account, have used economic arguments to support actual policies, or have discouraged conservation policies that have no clear economic support.[1] But, beguiled by the apparent simplicity of the physical goal and impressed by the difficulties of including economic criteria, those who negotiate fisheries treaties and law have found it easier to agree on maximizing sustainable output than economic rent.

But, of course, there are other goals than these that society may seek from the exploitation and utilization of international fisheries. The role of the biologist and economist is not so much to prescribe policy as to point out the ramifications of the decisions that are being made. They should work in concert in the investigation of the size and incidence of the costs and the gains of alternative systems for using the seas' productivity. They should exam-

[1] The list is a long one. For recent examples, see M. B. Schaefer, "Biological and Economic Aspects of the Management of Marine Fisheries," *Transactions of the American Fisheries Society,* Vol. 88 (1959), pp. 100–104; R. Beverton and S. J. Holt, *On the Dynamics of Exploited Fish Populations* (London: HMSO, 1957), pp. 376 ff.; "The Theory of Fishing," *Sea Fisheries: Their Investigation in the United Kingdom,* Michael Graham, ed. (London: Edward Arnold, Ltd., 1956), pp. 372–441, especially pp. 416–18; and many of the biologists represented, for example, in the FAO *Economic Effects of Fishery Regulations,* Fisheries Reports No. 5, Rome, 1962. This attitude is noted by McDougal and Burke, *The Public Order of the Oceans* (New Haven: Yale University Press, 1962), pp. 472 ff., and by D. M. Johnston, "The International Law of Fisheries," *Current Law and Social Problems,* Vol. 3 (1963), p. 218. Also see F. H. Bell, "Economic Aspects of Regulation of the Pacific Halibut Fishery," *Biological and Economic Aspects of Fisheries Management,* ed. J. A. Crutchfield, Seattle, 1959, pp. 51–75.

ine fully the economic and social consequences of different schemes and they should search out different management and regulatory devices that could achieve society's goals.

Maximize the Product of the Oceans

The most frequently stated objective is to maximize the useful product of the oceans. For example, Garcia-Amador, before developing his thesis that coastal states have special rights to adjacent fisheries, paraphrased the recommendations of the International Law Commission to the 1958 Law of the Sea Conference thus: ". . . the object of a conservation measure or programme is indeed to obtain the 'maximum sustained yield' of the one or more species exploited. . . ." [2] Conservation is invoked here because the Conference eventually drafted the Convention on Fishing and Conservation of the Living Resources of the High Seas. Though the phrase "optimum sustainable yield" was eventually substituted for "maximum sustainable yield," it was tied to the objective of securing a "maximum supply of food and other marine products." Hence, it can be said that the participants in the conference, like many who have written about the uses of the sea, stated the objective to be the maximum product from the sea.

Those who advocate this aim do so for a variety of reasons. Some foresee such large future demands for food that they feel the ocean should be exploited to the utmost, or they feel that the resources of the seas are practically inexhaustible and therefore should be utilized as substitutes for scarce land resources.[3] Others are concerned about the apparent waste that they find both in the overfishing of some species and in the lack of utilization of so-called trash fish. In effect, they want to maximize production because they want to mimimize these wastes. In a rough-and-ready fashion,

[2] F. V. Garcia-Amador, *The Exploitation and Conservation of the Resources of the Sea* (2d ed.; Leyden, Netherlands: A. W. Sythoff, 1959).

[3] See R. C. Cowen, *Frontiers of the Sea* (New York: Doubleday and Co., 1960), ch. 10; F. G. Walton and Henry Chapin, *The Sun, the Sea and Tomorrow* (New York: Scribner Co., 1954), *passim;* Lionel A. Walford, *Living Resources of the Sea* (New York: The Ronald Press Co. for the Conservation Foundation, 1958), pp. 289–95. See also descriptions of conservationists' approaches to waste and physical inefficiency in Harold J. Barnett and Chandler Morse, *Scarcity and Growth* (Baltimore: The Johns Hopkins Press for Resources for the Future, 1963), p. 81.

"maximum sustainable yield" provides an easily understandable goal for agreement and law-making, particularly when only one species of fish is being considered. But this facility is deceptive.

There are several aspects to the economists' objections to the choice of maximum sustainable yield as a goal for fisheries management. In the first place, it is not entirely clear that this is an acceptable goal for all nations. As pointed out below, countries may vary widely in their attitudes towards the rate of exploitation of fisheries.

Some countries may be willing to incur the costs of waiting while depleted stocks are allowed to grow to more productive amounts. They may also be willing to accept sustained or steady yields. Other countries, however, may be more impatient and set higher values on today's output than on the yields they can expect in the future. For example, a rapid exploitation and depletion of a stock may provide them with capital that they can invest in other, more productive enterprises. Or they may anticipate a decline in the relative price of the marine product. For these countries, sustainable yields would have little appeal.[4]

The same conclusion might be reached from quite a different point of view, one that is evidently held by some Japanese scientists. They appear to reject the sustained yield objective, as applied to a particular species, on the grounds that (a) stocks of most species can be diminished but not destroyed, (b) in many fishing areas, the reduction in size of population of one species will be compensated for by an increase in population of another species, and (c) the new species may be as valuable to the fishermen as its predecessor.

A variation of this difficulty occurs where nations are fishing for

[4] See H. Scott Gordon, "Obstacles to Agreement on Control in the Fishing Industry," in R. Turvey and J. Wiseman, eds., *The Economics of Fisheries* (Rome: FAO, 1957), p. 73. The above paragraphs apply chiefly to fisheries. As to other ocean uses, it is unlikely that countries setting out to exploit minerals or to use the oceans for transportation would find the same difficulties. Dissolved, ocean-floor, or underground minerals can be used at different rates by different nations, in accordance with their own price structures. Two countries using the same marine oil or gas field, however, might have the same difficulties as two countries attempting to agree on the use of a fish stock. But because oil technology is much less sensitive to local labor costs and local prices than are fisheries, it would be much easier to agree on a "unitized" field management. In any case, we would expect that some rule of discovery or of national or international rights would apply to minerals, which are much easier to appropriate, describe, and defend than are the mobile, unbounded fish resources.

two or more species that are ecologically interdependent. The fishermen of one country may place a higher valuation on species A than on species B, while the fishermen of another country may prefer B to A. If these different species compete for the same source of food, or if one is the predator of the other, agreement on which species to manage for a maximum sustained yield becomes difficult, because one country would be required to give up its preference for that of another country. Agreement could be reached on a combination of less than maximum sustainable yields from the two species, but, to do this, money valuations should be placed on the various quantities of output of the two fish; i.e., there should be a common denominator that would show both countries what they stand to lose or gain by agreement.

Further difficulties with the objective of maximizing sustainable yield are apparent when examined from the point of view of the fishermen. In an unregulated fishery, the fishermen do not seek a collective goal, but operate as individuals, entering a fishery as long as there are profits to be shared and leaving when the profits fall off. The result is that the aggregate amount of effort tends to come into equilibrium where the costs of the average fisherman are just covered by his revenue. If the revenue and the cost curves change (in response to changes in demand, technological innovation, etc.) a new point of equilibrium will be established, but as long as there are no controls on the amount of effort, the same result will occur. Average costs will equal average revenues, there will be an excessive number of producers, and the economic rent will be dissipated.

The decision to maximize sustainable yields must be made collectively. No individual fisherman will restrict his level or rate of output unless all others take the same measures, for, to the individual, restraint means loss of harvest not deferment. Various kinds of regulations are employed to achieve increases in sustained catch. In most cases, these regulations serve to increase the costs of fishing or, at least, to prevent reduction in costs. Prohibitions against technologically efficient gear, restrictions on areas in which fishing can take place, the imposition of size limits, all make it more difficult and costly for the fishermen to reach a given level of output. Such measures could, conceivably, raise the cost curve so that it will intersect the revenue curve at the point where the maximum sustained yield is obtained. But this is a haphazard technique at best and one that leads to greater costs to society.

If the fishermen should settle on a collective goal, they are likely to choose the maximum *total* revenue, not the maximum tonnage or number of fish.

But as the fishermen collectively adjust the amount of fishing so as to approach the maximum total revenue, the increase in yield resulting from a given increase in fishing will become smaller. Finally, the increase in revenue yield will be so small that it will not be worth the increase in cost that is required to catch it. Only in exceptional cases—for example, where the extra costs are zero—would any collective operation be justified in trying for the maximum revenue. Instead, it would be content with that yield whose extra value was just balanced by its extra cost (where the slope of the revenue curve becomes equal to the slope of the cost curve as in Figure 1, p. 8 at *OA*). This turns out to be the yield of maximum economic rent and the point at which a collective effort, controlling the factors of production, would be likely to operate.

Other difficulties with the goal of maximizing sustained physical yields could be itemized, but the main point should be clear. Maximum yield is not a good ideal for policy-making because it gives no guidance when choices between rates, species, areas, or products must be made. Nor is it a goal that is socially desirable. It is not the maximum physical yield of fish that gives the greatest revenue, the greatest profit, or the greatest employment. There is no logical connection [5] between the number that represents the largest possible catch and the catch that is most desirable.[6]

As demands increase throughout the world, conflicts between nations and industries will become more severe. Choices must be made. But the instruction to "maximize sustained yield" cannot serve as a useful criterion in making these choices; we can think of no sense in which this maximum is an optimum, except by coinci-

[5] Just as there is no obvious social value in research to produce an automobile with the "maximum" speed, or a building with the "maximum" height.

[6] Ralph Turvey has argued that under certain circumstances regulation of fisheries, which will enlarge the catch, will always be more valuable than the absence of regulation. The matter is complex, but it can be said that there is no contradiction between his contention in the circumstances in which it holds (particularly, that regulation should produce no great increase in fishing cost) and that made in the text above. See Turvey, "Optimization and Suboptimization in Fishery Regulation," *American Economic Review*, Vol. 54, No. 2, Part I, March, 1964. On a similar topic, Schaefer has argued that in an overfished fishery, a restriction of effort till the catch is maximized will produce a rent that is closer to the optimum than is the previous overfished state. This argument is clearly compatible with what is said above. See Schaefer, *op. cit.*

dence with some other objective. An alternative criterion is considered below.

Maximize the Rent of the Sea

This criterion has frequently been invoked by economists when discussing the common-property nature of ocean fisheries. They have observed that although rich and productive fisheries at first [7] produce a large rent—the surplus of the value of the annual catch over the total costs of labor and capital used in the fishery—this rent tends to fall and to be dissipated among an increasing number of fishermen. Costs increase by larger amounts than the value of the catch, until in the extreme, the rent disappears altogether. The situation may be aggravated further by a fall in the steady total catch.

Although in a competitive economy all profits tend eventually to vanish, the rents of valuable land and other scarce property remain. The managers of these scarce lands attempt to build up their rents by adding machinery and other capital to them, and by employing workers, till their extra costs just balance their extra gross revenues. In this process, the rent of every property is maximized. The unmanaged common-property fishery, on the other hand, tending to zero rent, absorbs too many capital goods and workers. The absence of rent [8] is an indication that the common-property fishery has caused an inefficient allocation of resources. Economists assume that this is an undesirable state of affairs, though their views are not always representative of society's point of view.

This objective of rent-maximization, or economic efficiency, is not vulnerable to the criticism leveled at the physical-maximum goal. In the first place, adherence to it prevents the waste of labor and capital. In the second place, it can in principle resolve problems of choice between different but ecologically related species of fish and their related competing areas, nations, and industries.

[7] See G. L. Kesteven and Sydney J. Holt, "Classification of International Conservation Problems," *Papers Presented at the International Technical Conference on the Conservation of the Living Resources of the Sea, Rome, 1955,* UN Doc. No. A/Conf.10/7, p. 350.

[8] To the rational fishery-owner. It is assumed the waters have no alternative use. Thus surplus over cost in fishing is equal to the amount that could be paid to the owner for the use of the waters.

When values are placed on each kind of fish and costs ascribed to each kind of fishing (including costs of abstinence and protection), the best combination of fishing activities is precisely the combination that maximizes rent.

In principle at least, it is possible also to take into account non-commercial or intangible benefits and costs in arriving at the best use of the region. Those who are so minded could, for example, put a value on certain kinds of "food" that is greater than the price obtainable in the market; similar adjustments could be made to register the social desire to provide a livelihood for certain groups of workers. Rent can be a social concept, and the instruction to "maximize rent" can be a route to an ethically-defensible optimum.

There are two kinds of technical difficulty with the achievement of this objective. One is transitional and would occur in fisheries that have already attracted excessive capital and labor. In order to maximize rent, some of the excess factors of production would have to be excluded. It may, for example, be necessary to reduce the number of vessels and fishermen by a third or a half. In advocating policies that would require this, economists assume (a) that the gain to the industry would be great enough to compensate all those who lost and that such compensation would actually be paid, or (b) that compensation would not be necessary because society would swiftly and painlessly transfer those who lost to equally attractive jobs elsewhere. It is easy to see that these assumptions may not be fully realized in actual cases. In an economic sense, society may still be better off because of improved efficiency, but politically or socially, the imposition of such hardships, even of a transitional nature, may be difficult to bear.[9]

An additional difficulty in achieving the goal of maximizing

---

[9] Some of these difficulties can be ameliorated not only by compensating those who are excluded from the fishery but also by encouraging a gradual reduction in the number of participants. This might be done by licensing all those presently involved and recalling the licenses of those who retire, shift to other jobs, or die. It could also be accomplished by establishing, and gradually increasing, taxes or entry fees. For a review of some of the advantages and disadvantages of such schemes, see the papers in R. Hamlisch, ed., *The Economic Effects of Fishery Regulations,* FAO Fisheries Reports No. 5 (Rome: FAO, 1962). See also Hiroshi Kasahara, "Japanese Fisheries and Fishery Regulations," in California Museum of Science and Industry, *California and the World Ocean,* 1964.

economic rent lies in the administration of the rule in international waters. Two countries contemplating the same fishery may rightly make different choices about the intensity and combination of fishing activities. Given the same knowledge of the oceans and their biology, one country may decide, for example, that to catch a large volume of small fish will maximize the rent of the region; another may favor a smaller volume of larger fish, or perhaps another species that might be ecologically competitive. Such a situation can arise whenever the two countries differ in the relative valuations they place on labor, capital, and each of the possible types of fish. In Japan, for example, the cost of labor relative to the cost of vessels and equipment is less than it is in North America. Again, the Japanese valuation of cod relative to that of halibut exceeds the North American. It is not surprising that Japanese ideas about the best use of the Bering Sea and the Gulf of Alaska are at odds with those of Canada and the United States.

These different valuations are ultimately the result of the obstacles to the movement of factors from one economy to another. More directly, they result from differences in population, national income, and tastes. It is a commonplace of the theory of comparative costs that the same industry may use a different technique in each country, depending on the structure of wages and prices in each place. But it has never, to our knowledge, been pointed out that the ocean is the main locale where these structures clash. The international competition for ocean freights, for air traffic, and for the use of the fisheries are all examples.

Of course, it is possible to exaggerate these discrepancies. Forces outside the fisheries tend to bring the national wage and price structure into line, through the movement of goods and the sale of services. And within the fishery itself the increasing international trade in fish, the adoption of highly-capitalized equipment, and indeed international trade in this equipment, all tend to press toward a uniform set of labor-capital-fish price-ratios. But these equilibrating forces are constantly being disturbed: changes in national income, tastes, and population operate on particular demands, and new fisheries and fluctuations in yield work on the supply side.

Consequently, one can foresee differences arising between the directors of some international fishing authorities. The various participating nations have to argue over much more than the divi-

sion of costs and benefits: they will be in basic and continual disagreement about size, species, and amount of catch, and about the
amount of expenditure on inputs.

This point may be made clearer by reference to the world trade
in farm products and to a hypothetical example in which it is
assumed that two countries, A and B, hold part of their lands
jointly. That is, these lands are common property, as in the case of
fisheries. It is further assumed that the factors of production are
immobile. The ratios of wage rates to product prices and to the
cost of equipment are referred to as the "wage/price structure." If
the wage/price structures are identical, the two nations could
agree on a combination of the products (say forest products and
grain) to be produced jointly and on the range of proportionate
shares of the total costs and yields that would be advantageous to
them both. But if their wage/price structures were different, they
would have difficulty agreeing either on what was to be produced
or on the manner of its production. This is the source of basic disagreement on fisheries problems.

There are two different solutions to this hypothetical problem.
Assuming that there is a world market for the products that could
be produced on the common lands, the two countries could agree
to unified management of these lands. They could, on the basis of
world prices and costs, decide upon the proportion of the two
products to be produced and exported and they could then divide
the net revenues in such a way that each would be better off than
in the absence of unified management. There is no reason why two
or more countries sharing a fishery cannot behave in the same way.
Indeed, the fur seal treaty approximates some features of this unified approach in that the furs are produced under single management and the proceeds are split among the signatory nations.

If the unified approach is impossible, the countries may resolve
their difficulties by dividing the common lands between them and
removing the characteristics of common property. This division of
area is precisely what is so difficult and undesirable on the high
seas. Each stock wanders to some extent from one area to another.
Furthermore, stocks are intermingled, compete with each other
for food, and are caught together. For these and similar reasons,
nations concerned about the management of fisheries, and concerned about the diminution in their numbers, size, or quality,
must agree on joint management of an entire stock area.

Thus countries with different price structures are forced into agreement on fisheries management. Because, however, there are barriers to trade and to factor movements, they have widely differing ideas about the optimum use of an area or stock. The simple rule "maximize rent" (or "minimize cost" for a certain catch) offers little guidance when the significance of cost, and the value of different species, vary from one member country to another.

It is easy to exaggerate the technical difficulties in the fisheries rent-maximization criterion. In many cases all interested parties may have approximately the same price structures; for example, Canada and the United States in the salmon fishery. In other fisheries, the relevant catching or farming technology may be fairly insensitive to differences in the price structure, especially if annual yields fluctuate a great deal. Some broad approximation to the best yield may be widely accepted. Under such circumstances, the criterion seems greatly preferable to that of physical-yield maximization, which does not represent any optimum at all.

If the agreeing countries will go further, turning the region or fishery over to a single agency or country, most of these difficulties are swept aside. This situation is discussed below.

Reaching Agreement on the Maximization of Rent

The goal of maximizing the sustainable physical yield may provide a fairly clear aim for administrators if there is consensus about how the physical catch is to be measured and if there is only one stock and one method of catching. But because this objective is socially meaningless, the clarity is of no particular value. In addition, this rule provides no guidance where choices between species of fish or fishing methods are required.

The objective of maximizing the rent is much more satisfactory, but faces considerable difficulties when there are management conflicts among countries with different wage/price structures. The problem, therefore, is to make the rent-maximization criterion into a workable rule for international decision-making. There are two possible approaches.

The first approach is to work as close to consensus as possible in the choice of fishing methods, species, size of catch, and number of vessels, using arbitrary choices where the member nations differ.

In this context, "arbitrary" does not mean capricious; it means that agreements are reached on the basis of factors that are exogenous to the management of the fishery. Looked at from the point of view of social science and historical process as a whole, of course, these decisions may turn out to be fully determined and wholly explainable by social forces. They are merely beyond the three-mile limit of the economist's discipline.

In the use of the oceans there are already many such arbitrary elements. Why should the three-mile limit be the maximum limit of territorial fisheries—why not less, or more? Why should coastal states be awarded continental-shelf resources? Indeed, what is the virtue of any established ocean rule, except that the world balance of power has helped to establish it and keep it workable? The answers must always be that a wide variety of political, social, and commercial forces have acted on each other to produce the present situation—it is not necessarily an "optimum" from the economic or any other single standpoint.

We can see several problems concerned with the two objectives that probably will require "arbitrary" solutions. If, for example, the objective were maximum physical yield, as today's conservationists would have it, it would be necessary to make arbitrary decisions about which of competing species to protect and harvest, and which to suppress; and whether many fish of a small size are to be preferred to fewer fish of greater length or weight. But if, as we would hope, it is decided instead to make international agreements with the objective of maximizing rent, other "arbitrary" decisions may be necessary. It will be agreed that entry ought to be restricted, but to what level? Unless by coincidence the two nations have the same answer, the actual figure must be picked somewhere between them. Arbitrary elements therefore must still be present, though we will argue that the range for such choice can be considerably reduced. The same comment would apply to the choice of proportions among competing species and among competing techniques; the nations may disagree somewhat, but a "second-best" answer lies somewhere between their two preferred proportions.

Finally, we should point out that the division of input and output, especially output, between the two countries is bound to be arbitrary under either of the two main criteria discussed here. For example, in the salmon treaty Canada and the United States have decided to share the annual catch equally; a different principle is used in the halibut treaty; and still other principles are at work in setting the national quotas for Antarctic whales and for Siberian salmon. We have called these decisions "arbitrary."

The second approach has rarely been mentioned in fisheries-law literature,[10] though it has been thoroughly explored in writings about the international use of joint river-basins.[11]

This approach does not determine what the answer to a disputed international fisheries question *ought* to be, but it provides a means by which the countries involved can reach a settlement that (a) makes them all better off than their next-best course of action, and (b) allows each country to discern how much the other countries may gain or lose from a particular bargain or decision.

For example, assume three countries are discussing whether or not to place a stock of fish under management. Research must be undertaken to determine how the fishing industry as a whole will make out in the absence of a management treaty, and the extent to which it will prosper with the proposed measures. The difference, rent, or gain, may now be divided up among the nations in such a way that (a) each is better off than it would be if the fishery continued without management, and (b) the division of the total gain among the three countries is made explicit and put into num-

[10] See, however, an interesting discussion by D. M. Johnston: "... the test should be: *What are the economic alternatives for each of the claimants?*

"... If it can be assumed that all the claims made to the fishery are made because it provides the most economic means of supply for a particular type of fishery demand, it is relevant to compare the next most economic means of supply as a 'second-best' alternative for each claimant." Johnston's ensuing suggestions take in more considerations than an economist would think necessary, given the availability of the measuring rod of money. Further, it appears to start from the situation where one state or another has to lose something, and set out the principle that the state losing "relatively more" should get priority, though not necessarily all of the contested fishery. See Johnston, "International Law of Fisheries," in *Current Law and Social Problems*, 1960, pp. 63–67.

[11] Primarily in the work of John V. Krutilla. See "Columbia River Development: Some Problems of International Cooperation," *Land and Water: Planning for Economic Growth* (Boulder: University of Colorado Press, 1961), pp. 91–119. For a discussion reflecting the ideas of Krutilla and many other experts, see John D. Chapman, ed., *The International River Basin* (Vancouver: University of British Columbia Publications, 1963), especially Chapter II. See also A. D. Scott, "Equitable Compensation in International River Basin Development," *Water Resources and Economic Development of the West*, No. 10, 1961, pp. 103–11.

bers so that governments, fishermen, and others interested are assured that equity is being observed. If it is impossible to achieve (a), then it is probable that there is actually no total gain from the proposed treaty, so that it is not worth proceeding within its original form; it should be abandoned, or a better scheme devised.[12] Whether the gains in (b) should be divided equally, or in proportion to needs, costs, historical participation, or contribution of territorial waters remains a matter for negotiation. Although it is impossible to devise a system of division that will remove jealousy, it is possible to make everyone better off.

Note that in this example the system of division might be left unstated: having agreed on the management technique, the nations could agree to compete on the fishing grounds for the stabilized catch.[13] But because this method of division is itself very wasteful, they may decide to divide the fishery by means of national quotas, or by means of compensation (in kind or in cash) paid to members who lose or do not gain enough by members whose fishing industries gain most.

The same approach may be made to the difficult questions of selecting species or fishing techniques, or deciding upon the intensity of fishing effort. Studies must be made of catch, value, and costs with and without the projected change, and the value of the difference, or gain in rent, ascertained. When the countries have different wage/price structures, two steps must be taken. First, all calculations for the entire fishery should be carried out using each of the levels of costs and prices ruling in the member countries. In this way the system of fisheries utilization that would produce the highest rent can be found, on the assumption that a particular country, or the world market, would buy the catch and provide the effort. This step shows the members what might be gained from unified management, discussion of which is deferred to the next chapter.

[12] Economists will recognize that this is a rough international application of the Kaldor test of whether a project increases total economic well-being. See Nicholas Kaldor, "Welfare Propositions and Interpersonal Comparisons of Utility," *Economic Journal*, 1939, pp. 549 ff. For a recent discussion, see I. M. D. Little, *A Critique of Welfare Economics* (2d ed.; New York: Oxford University Press, 1957). There is wide scope for theoretical research on the application of this approach to countries instead of to persons.

[13] For a discussion of this and other bases of dividing the catch, see S. Oda, *International Control of Sea Resources* (Leyden, Netherlands: A. W. Sythoff, 1962), pp. 63–96.

If unified management is not a political possibility, the next step is to examine those combinations of national fishing effort, particular techniques, and choice of species and size that are biologically possible to find the arrangement that yields the greatest gain over the absence of agreement on these matters. This can be done by comparing the position of each country in the absence of management with its position under a number of different arrangements in order to find a final arrangement that would provide substantial and equitably divided gains for all. If some countries are irreconcilably badly off, it may be possible to compensate them in kind, in cash, or by the use of national quotas, so as to allow what is believed to be the "best" scheme to go forward while still placing each member in a better position than it would be without agreement.

In principle, this idea is familiar, since it is precisely what is done at international congresses making a general settlement after a war. While attempting to make arrangements for the general good, especially for the maintenance of peace, there must be compensations for war damage, restoration of freedom and independence, and so forth. Usually maps, statistics, and trial-and-error are the tools of analysis used. In the case of proposed fisheries agreements, it is possible to commission fairly elaborate biological studies so that the physical and economic outcomes of some of the alternative sets or combinations of policies can be predicted. It is also possible to use high-speed computers, so that at relatively minor cost a very large number of arrangements can be compared on a uniform basis.[14]

Consequently, although the maximization of rent—appropriately defined—may run into difficulties when member countries have different wage/price structures, it is still possible to make

[14] This has actually been done in the examination for the state of Washington of alternative methods of managing the salmon fishery in Puget Sound. The fishery comes under the salmon treaty, so that assumptions must also be made about the Canadian catch. In most international situations, more members would be involved, more alternatives would be suggested, and less biological information would be available. In principle, however, the approach would be the same, the gain of knowledge would be much greater. A preliminary document, making proposals about gear and about the restriction of fishing effort has been prepared using these computations as a basis; it was presented to the Washington legislature in spring, 1963: *Salmon Gear Limitation in Northern Washington Waters* (Seattle: University of Washington, 1963), Fisheries Publications, New Series, Vol. 2, No. 1.

good use of the fishery from an economic point of view. That the use is "good" can be tested by ascertaining to what extent all members are made better off than they would be in the absence of the conservation and management proposals. We would predict that, as the studies and negotiations proceed, the willingness of members to accept compensation or quotas will increase with the increase in their understanding of the fishery's potentiality.

The discussion above of "arbitrary" elements suggests that, unless the nations are willing to lose all sovereignty, and to allow the complete equalization of prices and wages everywhere, they will have to agree on certain measures and divisions on the basis of their good will or their bargaining power. This is particularly so when "appropriable" waters are being discussed. There are few social scientists who would advance principles about the "best" international allocation of undersea mineral rights; about the "proper" width of territorial seas; or about the "fairest" shares of the net product of particular stocks or fisheries. The social scientist and the lawyer may be willing to study and even to forecast the outcome of negotiations about these subjects, but never to prescribe them: they must inevitably be the outcome of the interplay of such forces as strength, generosity, and knowledge.

Chapter 13

Alternative Arrangements for the Future

꿈. 꿈.

THE choice of the goals for the exploitation of world fisheries is but one decision that faces the world community. Another set of decisions must be made with respect to the alternative arrangements for the management of fisheries. It is evident that we feel that the present consideration of future arrangements and regimes is both desirable and necessary. However, our views are not unanimously shared. Some scholars feel that the present kinds of arrangements and the present interpretations of the law of the sea are adequate to meet future challenges. Others feel that scientific knowledge is not yet sufficient for the formulation of broad international regimes and that conditions are changing so rapidly that it would be undesirable to attempt to fix future patterns of cooperation and management. The discussion of these questions in the following pages indicates some of the requirements that will have to be met by future regimes. We also discuss the developments toward regional rather than stock management of fisheries, and the implications that these will have on arrangements. And we bring into our considerations the desirability for improving economic efficiency.

Finally, with these criteria and forces in mind, we discuss three different kinds of international regimes: the extension of coastal states' rights, management by means of national quotas, and the internationalization of marine resources under a central authority or authorities.

The Adequacy of Knowledge

The world has not yet sufficient scientific knowledge to predict accurately the consequences of even small changes in the use of most parts of the oceans. Many questions have not yet been investigated thoroughly. The superficial exploration of the ocean bottom and the identification of the main currents have not been completed. Investigation of the dynamics of most fish populations has hardly been commenced. Their migrations during their life cycles are not documented. The interdependence of fish populations is merely guessed at. The ability of some fish to endure changes in temperature, food, salinity, or light is just now being recorded.

Even where fisheries have received a good deal of study, there are some disagreements about the kinds of regulatory measures that would be most effective and about the results of regulation. This is true for the quota restrictions on the Pacific halibut and about the mesh limitations in the North Sea and Northwest Atlantic.

The gaps in our knowledge of the seas are obviously great. We need, as Walford points out, to spend more time "pursuing new conceptions of full exploitation" of the marine wilderness.[1] We still do not know how we will eventually want to use the seas— whether we should concentrate on the selective management of existing stocks or plan for the establishment of farms on the high seas where fish are enclosed, managed, and harvested.

But our ignorance does not mean that we cannot begin to plan a regime for the high seas. Improvements can obviously be made in many areas, and the necessity for such improvements is clear. We feel that it would be a serious mistake to avoid taking action until a greater amount of knowledge is available. It is important, however, that any regime that is chosen be set up in such a way that it can be altered painlessly in response to new knowledge and new technologies.

[1] Lionel A. Walford, *Living Resources of the Sea* (New York: The Ronald Press Co. for the Conservation Foundation, 1958), p. 289. On oceanography, see R. C. Cowen, *Frontiers of the Sea* (New York: Doubleday & Co., 1960), ch. 10.

The Need for New Arrangements

The depletion and congestion that are occurring with increasing frequency and severity in many international waters are the consequence of the growing effort that is being applied to fisheries. The problem of depletion has been recognized in many fishing treaties and by the Convention on Fishing and the Conservation of the Living Resources of the High Seas. According to the latter, any nation may propose conservation measures if it believes that overfishing has caused a fall in the catch below some concept of "optimum."

The threat of actual exhaustion of *most* stocks on the high seas by unregulated international overfishing is no longer seriously feared because generally the profit drops out of fishing before the stock disappears. But there is more to the biological task than merely avoiding extinction; the aim is to get the optimum yield of the optimum species. This, roughly, is what at least some of the draftsmen of the 1958 Conservation Convention had in mind as their goal.

And the Convention shows that it is not difficult for international law, taken with a structure of treaties, to guide the world toward this goal. Nations can agree to regulate, study, and protect all important stocks; indeed, so long as one state is concerned about conservation it can almost force others to join it, subject to the adjudication machinery for the settlement of disputes set up by the Convention.

But saving the fish is not the same as saving on the cost of fishing. Most treaties envisage more or less free access to the grounds during the open seasons by nationals of the participating states.

As the cost of fishing falls with innovations in technology, and as demand rises with increasing population, there will be larger numbers of vessels catching each stock. Where stocks are localized, interference among vessels will become severe. Instances of this have already occurred, such as that off the coast of France where it was reported that French vessels withdrew from the herring fishery to protest the hazardous conditions of navigation caused by the large numbers of foreign vessels.[2] Other kinds of

[2] *New York Times,* November 25, 1962.

congestion occur where vessels are operating on the same grounds but for different species or for the same species but with different kinds of gear. For example, on Georges Bank Russian fishermen have been using long drift nets for herring while Americans have been dredging for scallops. And off Kodiak Island, the Russians have been trawling and the Americans pot-fishing for king crabs.

Thus, both within agreements and between agreements, there will be growing problems of congestion. Where congestion occurs, it is dramatic evidence of economic inefficiency, of the fact that there are more vessels employed than could be justified by the returns. Congestion also increases the costs of fishing, not only by requiring more maneuvering simply to avoid collision but also because of the losses of gear. Ill will, if not open conflict, is also bound to be a product of the freedom to compete in congested waters. These three aspects of congestion—inefficiency, interference, and ill will—are the costs of delaying the planning of a regime for the high seas.

Although the world is making slow progress today in setting up rules for the use of the high seas, every year something is being done. In Chapters 9–11 we have sketched the record of the achievement thus far; it is clear that the twentieth century has witnessed many agreements for research and regulation that would have been unthinkable earlier. Further, these important steps have been taken where either congestion or depletion was an actual threat and where, therefore, research could be highly productive and regulation more willingly accepted. Because every new treaty is for some party a retreat from the freedom of the seas, there is hesitation and internal dissent until the situation has become serious, and the need for regulation and research is vividly perceived to be advantageous to all parties.

The "gradualists," many of whom have been involved in seeing these agreements through national legislatures and international congresses, are aware of the absence of knowledge, the conservatism and jealousy of marine industries, and the masses of detail that must be varied to suit particular regional or national needs.

At the very least, their experience suggests yet another requisite for the regime of the high seas: it should be capable of being implemented gradually, leaving unregulated those areas or resources on which there is no pressure, yet capable of gradually assimilating these areas into the general system without having to alter what is already under agreement.

Management by Regions or Stocks

One basic choice in organizing the high seas is between a system based on regions (oceans, grounds, or areas) and one based on particular stocks of fish. What little international debate there has been on this subject has tended to end up in generalizations about ownership or rights, rather than on systems of management. In many of the international law conference discussions, for example, the implicit choice was between inclusive use of the seas, with all nations having access to the resources, and exclusive use, under which coastal states have widely extended rights. This choice is obviously critical, but it is not really relevant to the question of management by stocks or by regions. Under full internationalization of the seas, with a single unified authority responsible for management, one would still have to choose whether to adopt a regional or a stock-by-stock approach. This would be equally true under a regime that divided the oceans among coastal states.

The decision is influenced by several factors: the views on the relative importance of the stock; the significance of ecological relationships among species; the variety of species caught by the same gear; and the migratory range of the stock. In some situations, stock management has been adopted because the species have high unit values for the participating nations and because they range over large areas without easily definable and localized relationships to other kinds of economically desirable fish. This has been true for such species as salmon, tuna, and whales. In other cases, regional management has been chosen because there are many different species that are closely related and equally desirable. The Japanese, having relatively undifferentiated taste preferences, harvest all kinds of fish off their shores. Where one stock is depleted, another of similar value may take its place. On the Grand Banks in the Northwest Atlantic, regional management is desirable because the many different ground fishes are caught by the same gear and sometimes in the same haul.

It appears to us that as the seas are more widely harvested, and as vessels extend their range, greater emphasis will have to be given to regional forms of management. The Tuna Commission, for example, has found it necessary to study both tuna and bait species; the competition between seals and salmon (each managed under a separate stock treaty in the Pacific) has sometimes been suspected to be severe; salmon feed on herring, which also have commercial value; and a choice between halibut and other groundfish is steadily being forced on the North Pacific Commission. Questions as to which is the best crop to be taken from a certain area will continue to rise. It is likely that the answer would call for taking a mixture of species in certain proportions based on differences in growth rates, ecological relationships, and kinds of gear that can be used.

The Quest for International Economic Efficiency

Looking to the future, it appears to us that a general regime for high-seas fisheries should meet several requirements. It should be flexible enough to adapt to innovations in technology and to the results of new scientific research. It should also be flexible enough to assimilate new areas and kinds of fishing activity. As a corollary, the regime should be general enough to be laid out in advance of some types of knowledge and should, both in its planning and operation, create incentives for increased national and international research on the oceans. The regime should be capable of gradual implementation so that it will not damage earlier agreements on particular regions or resources. And it should facilitate management by regions rather than by stocks. To these requirements, we add an objective drawn from the previous chapter: the regime should be one that facilitates the achievement of economic efficiency.[3]

This last requirement should be interpreted very broadly. Indeed, the precise definiton of economic efficiency is complicated by the lack of internationally-acceptable values and costs of fishing activity. Instead, therefore, we suggest merely that the objective should be to obtain any given value of fish at a low sacrifice of other things; or, for a given cost of fishing activity, to obtain as high a value of fish as possible. This objective, we have argued, is greatly to be preferred to that of obtaining the maximum sustained yield.

Yet, our chapters on law and treaties have illustrated the difficulties of obtaining, or even of defining, efficiency in international

[3] The reader should bear in mind that economic efficiency is not antithetical to conservation.

treaties. In order to examine these difficulties further, this section puts forward three distinct alternatives, arranged in order of their solution to this problem.

It must be stressed that the authors do not advocate any of these, but put them forward as a method of illuminating the problems and opportunities.

The topics dealt with so far seem to suggest that agreements modeled on ICNAF rather than on the salmon or halibut treaties hold more promise for the future. But for whom are these arrangements to be made? In the present context, this question reduces to the conditions of entry: whether new fishing states, without the benefit of historic rights or the abstention principle, can freely enter agreements on particular regions. If any nation can participate in a regional agreement simply by accepting the regulations of the commission, then the catch will be apportioned among the participating states by wide-open fishing competition. But as we have shown, this outcome has two defects. First, to avoid depletion, it requires ever more stringent regulations, as the administrative job in the face of increasing effort becomes harder and harder. Second, it brings congestion: it involves increasing inefficiency—the waste on an international scale of labor and capital. We do not believe that this is a viable system, just as we do not believe that a city can agree to have an unlimited and unregulated number of taxis or buses, or that there can be unlimited use of radio frequencies.

It follows that both administrative and economic efficiency call for the restriction of entry into the fishery of the managed area. But how can there be both freedom of the seas and restricted fishing effort?

One school of thought would answer the question simply by sacrificing the freedom of the seas. Following the "exclusive" approach, its members endorse political and legal principles such as the special rights of the coastal state, historic rights, or the abstention principle to restrict the number of states exploiting a given region. This may be a realistic political approach, but it certainly does not solve the need for limited entry of vessels. Even one or two countries can have too much effort, because the participants cutting down their effort would lose the catch to those who maintained their full fishing force.

A second approach—national quotas—may solve this problem. Canada and the United States, by having salmon quotas, are each free to regulate the entry into their respective salmon fisheries. Similarly, a whaling nation can restrict entry to efficient numbers by first obtaining a national quota and then setting the number of vessels to be allowed to kill that quota.

But the whaling treaty also indicates the difficulty of the national-quota approach. We do not refer to the system of the distribution of quotas—as we have argued, the "arbitrariness" common to all international agreements can be greatly reduced by a systematic review of the benefits, costs, and alternatives of each state. We refer rather to the fact that if free entry is allowed to all nations, then either the national quotas must each become steadily smaller, or the catch steadily larger. The latter is impossible, beyond a certain limit. Hence, as quotas shrink, one nation after another finds its quota too small to justify enthusiastic participation: the optimum size of fishing expedition is larger than the quota. Thus the Norwegian whaling mother ships, specially built, are usable only a few months of the year. After the quota is exhausted, the mother ship must be turned over to other uses the rest of the year. This would be the outcome in fishing treaties as national quotas shrink; some nations will not find it worthwhile to use their quotas at all.

There are several possible consequences of this increasing unattractiveness of the open-ended treaty. One outcome might be that the members suffering from the declining quotas would act politically (either by threatening to quit the agreement and fish without restraint or by negotiating through channels unrelated to fishing matters) in such a way as to have a certain quota guaranteed to them. Such arguments as need, or historic rights in the fishery, might be advanced to support their claim.

A second outcome might be that the declining quotas held by various countries could be rented or sold to fishing enterprises from other members (or, indeed, nonmembers) until the tenant had assembled a quota adequate to the economically-efficient scale of fishing technology. In this way the actual management might remain concentrated although the "equity" or rights in the fishery would be dispersed among a growing group of members. If this occurred, the situation would approach the third possibility.

The third alternative approach is that the fishery might be fully "internationalized." Instead of giving every interested nation a right to participate, it would simply recognize the rights of nations to the results of the fishery, and, in effect, interpret the "community interest" as the right to a share in the catch (as in the seal treaty) or to an equity in the net proceeds of the entire operation (as, for example, in the French and British governments' shares in the profits of the Persian Oil consortium).[4]

This third approach need not include all the nations of the world. When shares are being distributed, any political reality or ethical principle can be recognized. At one extreme, shares could be given to the nations on a per capita basis or on a per-miles-of-coastline basis. At the other extreme, they could be discriminatingly distributed to favor coastal states, poor nations, historical fishing nations, or great powers. This question of distribution must in essence be settled by bargaining, that is, "arbitrarily" from the point of view of economic market forces. Economic analysis, however, can provide information on the degree to which participants would be better off, and, it can thus facilitate reaching a viable and lasting bargain.

Let us assume that a wide "community interest" is desired, as a continuation of the older freedom-of-the-seas, inclusive, approach. Clearly, this criterion is still general enough to lead to a wide variety of conclusions for policy-making. Several types of regime suggest themselves.

The community interest may be interpreted rather narrowly as similar to a landlord's interest in the exploitation of land. The entrepreneur locates and manages production as best he can, but a share is returned to the community as property or income tax, lease, royalty, or "regalian right." At sea, the management of fisheries in a region might be delegated to either national or co-operative international agencies, who would turn over a share of the catch, after all expenses, to the international community, represented perhaps by the United Nations.

Internationalization might be interpreted to mean that management and harvesting ought to be in the hands of a completely international authority. Probably such an institution would have to "internationalize" its inputs, acquiring its labor and capital from a balanced sample of all the nations. But, if given full authority, it would be free to buy labor and capital in the cheapest markets and

[4] There are, of course, many domestic analogues to this kind of joint participation. Perhaps the best parallel is the American unitized oil field; but little is to be gained from examining the details of such arrangements—new and different features, arising from the biological nature of fisheries, must be taken into account.

sell marine products in the dearest markets, returning its "profits" in kind or in money to the members of the international community.

This last institution seems to come closest to the economic notion of the maximization of international welfare, in that it would use as little as needed of the cheapest services, regardless of nationality, and sell where the demand was strongest. The latter condition, of course, does not mean where *need* is greatest, since demand depends upon the world distribution of purchasing power earned from the sale of other things. The distribution of the profits, however, might equally well be in accordance with an accepted ethical system, answering need and rewarding service independently of wages and prices determined in a market.

If market values were used, if the profit achieved were the largest possible, and if this could be divided in such a way as to make every country better off than it was in the absence of this institution, then the institution would come close to Nicholas Kaldor's conception of an optimum.[5] If, however, the operation of the scheme were somewhat detached from the market, and if the proceeds were distributed according to a set of ideas about justice and equity, it would be almost inconceivable to even talk about an "optimum"; the most that could be said would be that the scheme conformed to the approach to welfare maximization described originally by Abram Bergson.[6] But both these writers have dealt with hypothetical reorganization among individuals in a single economy; there is little or no theoretical work of the same type discussing redistributions among countries. Economists are still arguing about the circumstances under which it can be said that one country *is* better off; the theorists are not yet ready to *measure* the amount of compensation that a country might pay to another and still remain "better off."

It is a virtue of internationalization that, with the principal aim given, it could proceed slowly, dismantling earlier agreements, changing techniques, introducing new methods of control, and restricting entry at a pace acceptable both to the states providing the inputs and to those whose historic position in the region is being altered. This was one of our requisites.

[5] Actually, to other writers' conception of the Kaldor principle, see I. M. D. Little, *A Critique of Welfare Economics* (2d ed.; New York: Oxford University Press, 1957), and J. de V. Graaff, *Theoretical Welfare Economics* (New York: Cambridge University Press, 1957).

[6] Graaff, *op. cit.*

It is also an advantage that, with the aim of maximizing the return given, it could operate flexibly. New quantities, qualities, and species could gradually be introduced in response either to suspected market preferences or to recommendations arising from increasing knowledge of the dynamics and ecology of the various stocks in the region. Just as a western grain farmer moves easily out of wheat and into rye, having little vested interest in either crop, so a regional authority could smoothly adapt itself to make the best of its resource, inputs, and market. This flexibility was another of our requisites.

Rather arbitrary decisions would probably have to be made about many aspects of the authority's operations, especially as mentioned above about the distribution of costs and final benefits among the nations. But once these decisions have been made, the instruction to maximize the rent of the seas has the attractiveness of internal consistency. The problems of dealing with different wage/price structures among participating nations attempting to maximize rent would not arise here.

The real difficulty with this seeming efficiency is that many of the world's fisheries are not run today with any idea of maximizing economic advantage or minimizing costs. Both in mature and in backward economies, the fisheries provide jobs for isolated sectors of the labor force. This employment goal may be just as important in the legislatures as is economic efficiency or internal consistency of principles of operation. So long as this is true, an international authority may be denied the right to maximize the rent of the seas. Instead it may be given a long list of instructions about fleets and equipment to be used, types of fish to be caught, and ports to be employed. Even these elements, however, could be assimilated by an international regime.

The nationalized industries in most countries have long and complicated terms of reference that reflect the labor interests they must assist, the bankrupt predecessors whose operations they must maintain, the industries they must supply on special terms, the communities they must maintain, and the consumer interests they must serve. Serving so many masters, they serve none well; but they do struggle on. Similarly, an international oceanic authority is a step forward, even when a long list of special instructions prevents it from ruthlessly maximizing the net economic yield of the seas. The "second best" resulting from a failure to reach the optimum allocation of labor and capital to the production of fish might still be a very desirable situation; it could well be a stage on the route to the optimum itself, allowing the fishery to develop and adapt in step with the international economy of which it should form a progressive part.

This type of internationalization, however, is merely the last of our list of three possible alternatives: to adopt an "exclusive" approach to the uses of the seas; to set up a series of international agreements with national quotas; and to "internationalize" the fisheries. It can be seen that many variants and combinations of these three alternatives are also possible.

It is too soon to advocate any one of them; it is time instead to begin research on the implications of these schemes and their variants in particular situations. When research has been done, there will still be time to design a model agreement that is flexible, efficient, and equitable.

Afterword:
Suggestions for Research

ONE of our primary objectives in undertaking this study was the identification of the significant problems that impede the rational and orderly exploitation of international fisheries. We have examined these problems primarily from the point of view of the social scientist. This is not to say that other problems of a scientific or technical nature are not important. On the contrary, they are very important and much needs to be done about them, particularly, perhaps, in the area of marine ecology. However, the background of scientific research is already relatively large and comprehensive. The needs are fairly clearly understood, and research effort will continue to increase. Social science, however, has been laggard in its attention to the problems of the sea. The needs are not clearly understood and the efforts are just beginning. It has been our purpose, therefore, to help clarify the needs for social science research and to examine how and where social scientists may make a useful contribution to the problems of international fisheries.

Some of the research tasks that are mentioned in the text are recapitulated here and made more explicit. These are by no means all of the questions that require attention but they are, in our minds, among those that provide both the greatest challenge for meaningful analysis, and opportunity for early application. They are presented here within the structure of our study; the growth, conflict, and inefficiency of international fisheries.

Our list may give the impression that no social science research has been done. Our footnotes and bibliography, however, should indicate the contrary: several fine studies have been made by or for the Fisheries Division of the Food and Agriculture Organization of the United Nations, the national and state governments of the chief fishing nations, and some private organizations and industry and trade associations. We are not, however, providing complete research outlines, and have therefore omitted reference to recent research papers in the fields we mention.

The demand for fish products is increasing rapidly, but little is known about the nature of this demand—the kinds of species that will be most sought after in the future; the effects of new processing techniques upon demand; the differences in demand patterns between nations; the possibility of substitution among species and the developing of markets for neglected species. These kinds of information are necessary if we are to be able to evaluate the future thrusts and direction of intensive fishing effort.

In terms of supply, the scientists will need to provide more refined information on the location, distribution, and ecology of the species. It is important, for example, to know the extent to which populations and groups of populations fall within national boundaries. But far more than that is required. We need to know who will be the future suppliers of fish to the world; where the comparative advantages will lie; the nature of the costs and returns of the major fishing nations; and the direction of technological innovation. We must realistically anticipate the future pattern of production among nations so that discussion of international agreements will be relevant to the economic pressure and lead to arrangements that will have some chance of success.

The kinds of agreements, the trends, and the needs for international co-operation must also be more clearly understood. We have urged the inclusion of economic criteria in these decisions; but economists have not yet provided conclusive and quantitative proof of the net revenues of rationalized management, nor have other social scientists studied the ways in which international arrangements can adapt to and facilitate the techniques for improving economic efficiency. Indeed, the whole process for reaching international fisheries decisions has been almost entirely neglected by social scientists even though its outstanding record of successful co-operation may have important lessons for fostering international harmony in other contexts.

The number of conflicts over international fisheries is growing, aggravated by increasing competition on the one hand and by strong nationalistic pressures on the other. In this framework, it is difficult to reach rational decisions that will benefit the world community over the long run. But the difficulties will become greater rather than smaller. The challenge is immediate. The opportunity for useful contribution diminishes as nations become more and more inflexible in their actions and decisions affecting the laws of the sea. We now examine the list in greater detail.

Statistics

Perhaps the most fundamental need for research lies in the accumulation and distribution of accurate and well-defined statistics on the world's fishery industries. The FAO Fisheries Division has done an extremely fine job in compiling the annual *Yearbook of Fishery Statistics*. But its success has been hampered by its dependence upon the contributions of the various nations, contributions that range widely in both accuracy and coverage. The discrepancy, mentioned in the text (p. 150), between two reports on India's output (one million tons by FAO as against two and a half million tons by the United States Foreign Agricultural Service) indicates that considerable refinement is required before we can use even the simplest and most basic measures of output.

And from an economic point of view we need to know far more than quantities of production. We cannot properly evaluate the future situation of demand and supply without knowing a great deal more than we do about the allocation of capital and labor resources and the relative efficiency with which these inputs are used. We need to know the prices of the products, the amount and cost of equipment and gear, the amount and cost of labor, operating expenses, the returns to capital and labor, and much more. The immensity of this task may be indicated by the fact that even the highly developed and sophisticated United States has virtually no generally usable data on these factors of production. This is a task that all nations must attack, not only because of its importance for international decisions but also in their own interests.

Studies of the Demand for Fisheries Activity

Studies are needed that will tell us more about the incentives that ultimately lead to the investment of labor and capital in the fisheries industries. Behind the fishing effort lies a complex mix of social, political, and economic objectives. A clear understanding of their nature and extent is essential for a proper evaluation of the future intensity of effort and of the impact upon supplies.

There should, first, be a far more refined analysis of market demand for fish than has been presented in our text. It should be very detailed and critical with respect to the major fishing nations and to those with high demand. Such studies must be based upon careful compilations of consumption statistics; analyses of price and income elasticities of demand for fish products by themselves and for fish products relative to other forms of protein; analyses of market structures and of patterns of distribution. In particular, these studies should concentrate on the trends that are apparent and on changes that might reasonably be expected.

The objective of overcoming protein malnutrition in under-developed countries is of universal significance and needs more support. However, there appears to be a tendency to oversimplify the solution and to assume that a "cheap" fish protein would automatically find an adequate market among governments or dealers. This assumption should be critically examined. It is important to know just how "cheap" the product must be; to anticipate insofar as possible, the problems of acceptance, distribution, and marketing of the product. Such information should be helpful in determining how much research money to spend on the development of the product and in overcoming obstacles to distribution and utilization.

In addition, and from a different point of view, a careful analysis of "cheap protein" demand will be useful in preparing for the impact upon producers and sources of supply. It has been pointed out, for example, that the raising of "the daily animal protein consumption level of the world's developing countries above the starvation level of 7 grams per day would require the total estimated annual yield of all of the partially or wholly unutilized species of industrial fishes in the waters immediately surrounding the United States." [1] This would be more than three times the present level of catch of all fish by the United States. There would be obvious difficulties in adjusting to even a small portion of such an increase in demand.

[1] Bureau of Commercial Fisheries, *Trident, a Long Range Report of the Bureau of Commercial Fisheries,* Circular 149 (Washington: U.S. Department of the Interior, September, 1963), p. 40.

The possibility of developing a demand for species that are not fully utilized is frequently raised with respect to food fish as well as to fish for a protein concentrate. It is suggested, for example, that so-called trash fish can be caught and sold at very low prices. And there is much effort to promote the demand for new species of fish, particularly in the markets of Western nations where demand appears to be highly specific and where the "stickiness" of taste preferences impedes the substitution among species. In Japan, on the other hand, the taste pattern is relatively undifferentiated and a wide variety of species is readily consumed. The full utilization of the few species demanded by Western nations may unbalance ecological relationships, perhaps permitting the less utilized species to supplant those that are taken in large quantities. For the world as a whole, shifts in demand may help to ameliorate (even though only temporarily) the competition for some species that are presently overfished. However, there is very little understanding of the economics of consumer substitution among fish species, nor of the techniques of encouraging such substitution. There needs to be research on differences in taste preferences and the influence on demand of such characteristics as ease of preparation, boniness, firmness, etc. There also should be studies on the effects of the trends to more highly processed and manufactured fish products and the degree to which these facilitate substitution by hiding identifiable characteristics. In short, we need to be able to anticipate and perhaps to affect the future patterns of demand.

Aside from the economic demand for the end product, there are other factors that make up the incentive to work or invest in fisheries industries. One has already been mentioned: the goal of reducing protein malnutrition. Government subsidies—which may be designed to protect employment opportunities, to increase self-sufficiency in the provision of food, or to provide more knowledge or information—also affect the intensity and distribution of effort and should be considered in the evaluations of demand. In addition, they have considerable effect upon the positions that nations take with respect to agreements on the law of the sea and on the extent of exclusive fishing rights. Realistic and effective international arrangements must take these forces into consideration and either satisfy them or divert them. Research is therefore needed both to "measure" these goals and to analyze their consistency with the other goals in each nation's set of policies.

Studies of Supply

Research into several aspects of supply is of particular significance for the rational and orderly exploitation of international marine fisheries. In discussing these aspects, we think it important to drop momentarily our social science point of view and raise some of the biological and scientific problems that are critical to the decisions that are currently being made affecting the law of the sea.

The recent and continuing controversies over the extent of territorial limits have often focused on the ability of a coastal state to conserve or manage a fishery stock, or have emphasized the economic importance of the supplies to the coastal state. However, very little information is available on these points. We need to know much more about the proportion of the state's (and of the world) catch that comes from waters within territorial limits (three, twelve, or more miles) and what proportion comes from "contiguous" zones. We need to know which fish stocks are bounded by territorial limits and, conversely, what limits are required to enclose certain fish stocks.

Similar studies are required for the supplies of bottomfish on the major presently-used fishing grounds and on potential grounds. Much work has already been done in certain areas, such as the North Sea and the Northwest Atlantic, but it needs to be expanded to other areas and refined. What are the physical yields obtainable and what are the ecological relationships between species? We also need to know the extent to which the fishery grounds can be treated as single resource managements units.

More research on the ecological relationships between species would also be valuable. This might be approached by a theoretical analysis of yields from two ecologically related stocks. What is the effect of fishing one stock intensively and a competitive (or predator or prey) species not at all? What is the effect of exploiting both stocks at different rates? It would be useful to prepare a model to show transformation functions between species under different physical and economic assumptions.

An even greater need exists for *economic* research into the characteristics of supply. The statistical requirements have already been mentioned but cannot be overemphasized. Before we can conduct analyses of international fisheries, we must know, for the major fishing nations at least, the composition of the labor force and capital stocks, the returns that are expected, and those that are actually received. More particularly, we need to know the trends of investment both in fleet operation and in the development of technology.

A study should be made of the technique and economics of expanding fishery activities through the means of foreign bases. It should focus on the factors that facilitate the establishment of processing, servicing, and exporting bases; the role of capital costs and labor inputs; and the tax and regulatory relationship between a fishing nation such as Japan, for example, and the host country.

A study should be made of the economics of large-scale fleets of the kind operated by Russia—and to some extent Japan—where factory and mother ships, repair and other servicing vessels, carrier vessels, etc., are all under the control of a single economic unit.

In addition to these studies, there should be a gradual accumulation of general economic analyses of the fishing industries in different countries throughout the world. Some of these should focus on underdeveloped nations; the role of foreign capital and foreign aid; and the effect of fisheries on the economic development of the nation in terms of income, skills, jobs, and food.

It would be useful to know more about the fishing industry's unusual ability to attract and hold a labor force that is frequently well beyond an economically efficient size. The suggestion that the gambling element is an important explanation is partially borne out by the prevalence of the share system of wages. Other factors might include the immobility caused by the isolation of fishing villages and the concomitant lack of educational facilities. Government assistance programs and activities also have important effects on labor mobility. Comparisons of these factors between nations and within nations should be undertaken, with particular emphasis on changes that are occurring.

There should be an economic survey of technological research that is being undertaken by various governments throughout the world. What is the motivation for the research, what are the scientific personnel available, and what directions is the research taking? Is it primarily long-run in its orientation? To what extent does it focus on basic biological or oceanographic knowledge? What developments can be anticipated in the facilitation of the search for fish, the capture, enclosure, management?

There should be an analysis of the factors underlying the rate of adoption of technological innovations. The speed and extent of adoption varies considerably between and even within nations, and between different fisheries. Some laws and regulations actually prohibit the use of new devices, while others serve to stimulate their development and use. The roles of government, through subsidy, trade restrictions, or outright control, are also very important in determining the rate and extent of adoption. There are wide differences among fishing ports in terms of the commitments to particular forms of vessels, gear, and systems of marketing. And furthermore, both the share system for payment of crews and the common property aspect of fisheries have their own unique influences on the rate of technical change. The differential effects of these factors upon the major fishing nations should be compared in order to determine where future advantages may lie.

Both the present differences in technology between nations and the technological changes anticipated should be examined. What are the effects of technological changes on labor inputs and on the labor-capital mix? How are the changes affecting the vulnerability of stocks? What are the implications of the changes for present and future international agreements on fisheries?

In addition to the relatively conventional studies of supply mentioned above, some research should be undertaken on the questions of depletion, or possible extermination, of a fishery resource. It is frequently stated that a fish stock cannot be exterminated because, as its abundance or density decreases, the cost of harvesting increases until it reaches the "point" at which it is no longer economical to exploit the fishery. This belief should be carefully examined, particularly in the light of technological innovations that are reducing the supply costs and increasing the vulnerability of fish stocks. It is no longer axiomatic that profit will disappear before the stock reaches a critical level.

What happens to a fishing industry when the resource is almost exhausted? This can be examined, for example, by means of a case study on the Canadian and U.S. Great Lakes fishery, which went through a severe decline in the lake trout, whitefish, and blue pike resources and a replacement of these by the lower unit-value chubs and smelt. What were the effects of, and on, demand during this shift and how were the labor and capital inputs and income levels of the fishermen changed? What adjustments were made by the processing and marketing industries? What were the costs to the economy incurred by the loss of the resource? And what are the costs involved in the attempt to bring back the lake trout fishery? It would be useful if this could be carried further to include a theoretical analysis of what the effects might have been if depletion had been prevented by regulatory measures.

International Arrangements and Controls

The supply and demand studies will provide some indication of the areas where conflict may develop in the future and of the requirements for international agreements and control. The present agreements and treaties range widely in their effectiveness and in their consequences for economic efficiency. Some of these may be more readily adaptable to future situations than others, but there has been no study given to the different approaches.

Some theoretical analyses of the economic consequences of different forms of regulation and control of a fishery are already under way, and should be continued and expanded. We need to know the different effects of quotas, entry restrictions, gear restrictions, etc., on fishermen from countries with different wage/price structures. We need to know the effects of the controls upon intensity of effort, scale of operation, and rate of adoption of technological innovations. The effects of these controls, particularly of entry restrictions, should be traced through the buying and processing stages. What are the effects on the costs of competitive buyers and processors when they are forced to obtain their "share" of a given catch from a radically reduced number of vessels?

The above theoretical analysis should be supplemented by a series of case studies of the economic effects of forms of control that are already in existence. A study was recently made of the total catch quota and the Pacific halibut treaty. Others might deal with: restricted entry and the fur seal treaty; country quotas and the Antarctic whaling convention; the doctrine of abstention and the North Pacific Fisheries Convention; gear restrictions and the North Sea treaty. Each case study, besides dealing with the economic effects on the participating nations, might also include an analysis and evaluation of the processes of agreement, change, enforcement, and research.

We have emphasized the importance of restricting entry into fisheries for the purpose of improving economic efficiency. The problems of following this course, however, have not yet received significant attention. In particular, it must be clearly demonstrated how much nations may gain by joining agreements that would reduce, or prevent excessive total effort. There is a special need for a theoretical analysis of the outcome in one fishery that is being exploited simultaneously by two countries with different wage/price structures. This should be examined under different conditions of factor mobility and free trade. It should determine to what extent and how each country can benefit by different combinations of total restricted effort, and should take account of the strategies countries may follow in attempting to maximize their shares of the available economic benefits.

There should be a careful study of the process and technique for reaching international agreement by fisheries treaty councils. What are the factors considered and what are national motives or incentives behind the agreements? What is the role of economic information in the process? How, for example, have the various participants come to agree on the allocation of country quotas for whales? What are the economic pressures that are used in reaching a decision? The "diplomacy of fisheries" is carried out largely by biologists and statisticians. How does this affect the nature of the decisions? And what is the role of the diplomats, lawyers, and industry?

Since we anticipate changes in technology and in the relative importance of fishing nations, there should be some studies made of the adaptability of international agreements and treaty councils. What are the mechanisms provided for admitting new members and for renegotiating control systems or allocations of quotas? What forms of councils and agreements are most adaptable?

Biological and economic information are essential for the successful formulation and operation of treaties. The recent disagreements between Japan on the one hand, and Canada and the United States on the other, concerning the range of the salmon and the yield of the halibut stocks emphasize the need for research. Should the research efforts be undertaken by the treaty council or by the member states? If by the council, how should it be financed and staffed, and what degree of autonomy should the council have in determining the kind of research to be undertaken?

These are but a few of the many significant social science problems in the field of international fisheries. We hope that their identification will help to stimulate greater research effort and that the research will help to improve the patterns of co-operation in the development and exploitation of world fisheries.

Bibliography

A. BOOKS

ANNINOS, P. C. L. *The Continental Shelf and Public International Law.* The Hague: H. P. DeSwart & Fils, S. A., 1953.

BARNETT, HAROLD J., AND MORSE, CHANDLER. *Scarcity and Growth.* Baltimore: The Johns Hopkins Press for Resources for the Future, Inc., 1963.

BARTLEY, E. R. *The Tidelands Oil Controversy.* Austin: University of Texas Press, 1953.

BAYITCH, S. A. *Interamerican Law of Fisheries.* New York: Oceana Publications, Inc., 1957.

BEVERTON, R. J. H., AND HOLT, S. J. *On the Dynamics of Exploited Fish Populations.* London: Her Majesty's Stationery Office, 1957.

BINGHAM, J. W. *Report on the International Law of Pacific Coastal Fisheries.* Stanford: Stanford University Press, 1938.

BISHOP, W. W., JR. *International Law—Cases and Materials.* 2d ed. Boston and Toronto: Little, Brown and Co., 1962.

BLOOMFIELD, L. M. *Egypt, Israel, and the Gulf of Aquaba in International Law.* Toronto: The Carswell Co., Ltd., 1957.

BOTTEMANNE, C. J. *Principles of Fisheries Development.* Amsterdam: North Holland Publishing Co., 1959.

BRANDT, KARL. *Whale Oil: An Economic Analysis.* Fats and Oils Studies, Vol. 7. Stanford: Food Research Institute, Stanford University Press, 1940.

BRIERLY, J. L. *The Law of Nations.* 5th ed. London: Oxford University Press, 1955.

BROWN, L. F. *The Freedom of the Seas.* New York: Dutton and Co., 1919.

CHAPMAN, JOHN (ed.). *The International River Basin.* Vancouver: Institute of Pacific Relations, University of British Columbia, 1963.

CIRIACY-WANTRUP, S. V. *Resource Conservation—Economics and Policies.* Berkeley and Los Angeles: University of California Press, 1952.

CLAWSON, MARION, HELD, R. BURNELL, AND STODDARD, CHARLES H. *Land for the Future.* Baltimore: The Johns Hopkins Press for Resources for the Future, Inc., 1960.

COLOMBOS, C. J. *The International Law of the Sea.* 5th rev. ed. London, New York and Toronto: Longmans, Green and Co., 1959.

COMMITTEE OF INQUIRY INTO THE FISHING INDUSTRY. *Report.* London: Her Majesty's Stationery Office, January 1961.

COOLEY, RICHARD A. *Politics and Conservation, The Decline of the Alaska Salmon.* New York: Harper and Row, 1963.

COWEN, R. C. *Frontiers of the Sea.* New York: Doubleday and Co., Inc., 1960.

CRUTCHFIELD, J. A. (ed.). *Biological and Economic Aspects of Fisheries Management.* Seattle: University of Washington, 1959.

DANIEL, HAWTHORNE, AND MINOT, FRANCIS. *The Inexhaustible Sea.* New York: Collier Books, 1961.

DEEK, F., AND JESSUP, P. C. *A Collection of Neutrality Laws, Regulations and Treaties of Various Countries.* 2 vols. Washington: Carnegie Endowment for International Peace, 1939.

DEWHURST, J. F., *et al. Europe's Needs and Resources.* New York: Twentieth Century Fund, 1961.

ECKSTEIN, OTTO. *Water-Resource Development.* Cambridge: Harvard University Press, 1958.

FENWICK. C. G. *International Law.* New York and London: The Century Co., 1924.

FOOD AND AGRICULTURE ORGANIZATION OF THE UNITED NATIONS. *Agricultural Commodities–Projections for 1970.* Rome: FAO, 1962.

————. *Comparison and Abstracts of Selected Conventions Establishing Fisheries Commissions.* Rome: FAO, 1962.

————. *Fish in Nutrition.* London: Arthur J. Heighway Pub. Ltd., 1964.

————. *Food Supply, Time Series.* Rome: FAO, 1960.

————. *Future Developments in the Production and Utilization of Fish Meal,* Vols. 1 and 2. Report of the International Meeting on Fish Meal. Rome: FAO, 1961.

————. *Report of the Technical Meetings on Costs and Earnings of Fishing Enterprises.* London: FAO, September, 1958.

FRANKLIN, C. M. *Law of the Seas: Some Recent Developments.* U.S. Naval War College, International Law Studies, 1959–60. Washington: U.S. Government Printing Office, 1961.

FULTON, T. W. *The Sovereignty of the Sea.* Edinburgh and London: Blackwood and Sons, 1911.

GARCIA-AMADOR, F. V. *The Exploitation and Conservation of the Resources of the Sea.* 2d ed. Leyden, Netherlands: A. W. Sythoff, 1959.

GIDEL, GILBERT. *Le Droit International Public de la Mer.* Vol. 1. (Recueil Sirey) Paris, 1932.

GRAAFF, J. DE V. *Theoretical Welfare Economics.* New York: Cambridge University Press, 1957.

GRAHAM, MICHAEL. *The Fish Gate.* London: Methuen, 1941.

GROTIUS, HUGO. *The Freedom of the Seas.* Translated by Ralph Van Doman Magoffin. New York: Oxford University Press, 1916.

HAMLISCH, R. (ed.). *The Economic Effects of Fishery Regulation.* FAO Fisheries Reports No. 5. Papers presented at an Expert Meeting, Ottawa, 1961. Rome: FAO, 1962. Fle/R5.

Bibliography255

HIGGINS, A. P., AND COLOMBOS, C. J. *The International Law of the Sea.* 3d ed. London: Longmans, Green and Co., 1954.

INNIS, H. A. *The Cod Fisheries: The History of an International Economy.* New Haven: Yale University Press; Toronto: Ryerson Press, 1940.

INTER-AMERICAN TROPICAL TUNA COMMISSION. *Annual Report* (1961).

INTERNATIONAL COMMISSION FOR THE NORTHWEST ATLANTIC FISHERIES. *Annual Proceedings.* Vol. 12 (1961–62), Halifax.

———. *Statistical Bulletin.* Vol. 10 (1960), Halifax.

INTERNATIONAL NORTH PACIFIC FISHERIES COMMISSION. *Report of First Meeting* (1954).

INTERNATIONAL PACIFIC HALIBUT COMMISSION. *Annual Report.* No. 25 (1956).

INTERNATIONAL PACIFIC SALMON FISHERIES COMMISSION. *Annual Report* (1957).

KAPLAN, M. A., AND KATZENBACH, N. DEB. *The Political Foundations of International Law.* New York: John Wiley and Sons, 1961.

KRUTILLA, JOHN V., AND ECKSTEIN, OTTO. *Multiple Purpose River Development.* Baltimore: The Johns Hopkins Press for Resources for the Future, Inc., 1958.

LEONARD, L. L. *International Regulation of Fisheries.* Washington: Carnegie Endowment for International Peace, 1944.

LITTLE, I. M. D. *A Critique of Welfare Economics.* 2d ed. New York: Oxford University Press, 1957.

LYNCH, EDWARD J., DOHERTY, ROBERT M., AND DRAHEIM, GEORGE P. *The Groundfish Industries of New England and Canada: A Comparative Economic Analysis.* Circular 121. Washington: U.S. Fish and Wildlife Service, 1961.

MCDOUGAL, MYRES S., AND BURKE, WILLIAM T. *The Public Order of the Oceans: A Contemporary Law of the Sea.* New Haven and London: Yale University Press, 1962.

MCFEE, W. *The Law of the Sea.* New York and Philadelphia: T. B. Lippincott Co., 1950.

MAGOFFIN, RALPH VAN DOMAN (trans.). *Grotius on the Freedom of the Seas.* New York: Oxford University Press, 1916.

MILL, JOHN S. *Principles of Political Economy.* W. J. Ashley, ed. London: Longmans, Green and Co., 1909.

MOORE, S. A., AND MOORE, H. S. *The History and Law of Fisheries.* London: Stevens and Haynes, 1903.

MOUTON, M. W. *The Continental Shelf.* The Hague: Martinus Nijhoff, 1952.

NATIONAL ACADEMY OF SCIENCES—NATIONAL RESEARCH COUNCIL. *Oceanography 1960–70, A Report of the Committee on Oceanography.* Washington: NAS-NRC, 1959.

ODA, S. *International Control of Sea Resources.* Leyden, Netherlands: A. W. Sythoff, 1963.

OPPENHEIM, L. *International Law.* 8th ed. H. Lauterpacht, ed. London: Longmans, Green and Co., 1955.

ORGANISATION FOR EUROPEAN ECONOMIC CO-OPERATION. *Fishery Policies in Western Europe and North America.* Paris: OEEC, September, 1960.

POTTER, P. B. *The Freedom of the Seas in History, Law, and Politics.* New York: Longmans, Green and Co., 1924.

PROSKIE, JOHN. *Operations of Modern Fishing Craft, Atlantic Seaboard, 1960.* Ottawa: Economics Division, Department of Fisheries of Canada, 1962.

Bibliography

REIFF, H. *The United States and the Treaty Laws of the Sea.* Minneapolis: University of Minnesota Press, 1959.

ROYCE, WILLIAM F., et al. *Salmon Gear Limitations in Northern Washington Waters.* Fisheries Publications, New Series, Vol. 2, No. 1. Seattle: University of Washington, 1963.

SCOTT, A. D. *Natural Resources: The Economics of Conservation.* Toronto: University of Toronto Press, 1955.

SHEARD, KEITH. *The Western Australian Crayfishery.* Perth: the author, 1962.

SMITH, H. A. *The Law and Custom of the Sea.* London: Stevens and Sons, Ltd., 1959.

TAYLOR, H. F. *Survey of the Marine Fisheries of North Carolina, with a Comprehensive View of the Economics of National and World Fisheries.* Chapel Hill: The University of North Carolina Press, 1951.

TILIC, I. *Información estadistica sobre embarcaciones utilizadas en la pesca industrial en el Perú 1953–1962.* Informe No. 8. La Punta, Callao, Peru: Instituto de Investigación de los Recursos Marinos, 1963.

———. *Material estadistico sobre la industria peruana de harina de pescado.* Informe No. 14. La Punta, Callao, Peru: Instituto de Investigación de los Recursos Marinos, 1963.

TOMASEVICH, J. *International Agreements on Conservation of Marine Resources.* Stanford: Food Research Institute, Stanford University Press, 1943.

TRESSLER, D. K., AND LEMON, J. McW. *Marine Products of Commerce.* New York: Rheinhold Publishing Corp., 1951.

TROEBST, CORD CHRISTIAN. *Conquest of the Sea.* Translated from the German by Brian C. Price and Elsbeth Price. (Originally published as *Der Griff nach dem Meer.* Düsseldorf: Econ-Verlag GmbH, 1960.) New York: Harper and Row, 1962.

TURVEY, R., AND WISEMAN, J. (eds.). *The Economics of Fisheries.* Rome: FAO, 1957.

UNITED NATIONS. *Laws and Regulations on the Regime of the Territorial Sea.* New York: UN Legislative Series, 1957.

———. *Papers Presented at the International Technical Conference on the Conservation of the Living Resources of the Sea.* New York: UN, 1956. UN Doc. No. A/Conf. 10/7.

———. United Nations Conference on the Law of the Sea, *Official Record.* 7 vols. UN Doc. No. A/Conf. 13, 1958.

———. Second United Nations Conference on the Law of the Sea, *Official Record.* UN Doc. No. A/Conf. 19, 1960.

U.S. DEPARTMENT OF AGRICULTURE, FOREIGN AGRICULTURAL SERVICE. *Food Balances in Foreign Countries,* Parts I and II. FAS-M-100 and FAS-M-101. Washington: U.S. Government Printing Office, 1960.

U.S. DEPARTMENT OF THE INTERIOR, BUREAU OF COMMERCIAL FISHERIES. *Trident. A Long Range Report of the Bureau of Commercial Fisheries.* Circular 149. Washington: U.S. Department of the Interior, September, 1963.

U.S. DEPARTMENT OF THE TREASURY, BUREAU OF CUSTOMS. *Merchant Marine Statistics, 1963.* Washington: U.S. Government Printing Office, 1963.

WALFORD, LIONEL A. *Living Resources of the Sea: Opportunities for Research and Expansion.* New York: The Ronald Press Co. for the Conservation Foundation, 1958.

WALTON, F. G., AND CHAPIN, HENRY. *The Sun, the Sea and Tomorrow.* New York: Scribner Co., 1954.

YATES, P. LAMARTINE. *Food, Land, and Manpower in Western Europe.* London: Macmillan and Co., Ltd., 1960.

B. ARTICLES, ETC.

"A Map Analysis of Japan's Fishery Problems," *Japanese Annual of International Law,* Vol. 3 (1959), pp. 103–08.

ANDERSON, S. V. "A Critique of Professor Myres S. McDougal's Doctrine of Interpretation by Major Purposes," *American Journal of International Law,* Vol. 57 (1963), pp. 378–84.

"Anglo-Norwegian Fisheries Case," *International Court of Justice Reports* (1951), pp. 116–206.

"Australia and the Continental Shelf," *Australian Law Journal,* Vol. 27 (1953), p. 458.

BAILEY, K. B. "Australia and the Law of the Sea," *The Australian Institute of International Affairs,* Ninth Roy Milne Memorial Lecture, Adelaide, 1959.

BENNETT, J. "Problems of Management Decision Making: Optimum Trawler Type for U.K. Distant Water Fishery." Paper prepared for FAO UN Meeting on Business Decisions in Fishery Industries. Rome, April, 1964.

BEVERTON, R. J. H., AND HOLT, S. J. "The Theory of Fishing," *Sea Fisheries.* M. Graham, ed. London: Edward Arnold, Ltd., 1956.

BISHOP, W. W., JR. "The 1958 Geneva Convention on Fishing and the Conservation of the Living Resources of the High Seas," *Columbia Law Review,* Vol. 62 (1962), pp. 1206–29.

BRITTIN, B. H. "Article 3, Regime of the Territorial Seas," *American Journal of International Law,* Vol. 50 (1956), pp. 923–41.

BROUILLARD, K. D. "Great Lakes Commercial Fishing Regulations," *Economic Effects of Fishery Regulation,* FAO, Fle/R5.

CHRISTY, FRANCIS T., JR. "The Exploitation of a Common Property Natural Resource: The Maryland Oyster Industry." Unpublished Ph.D. Dissertation, University of Michigan, 1964.

———. "Efficiency in the Use of Marine Resources," California Museum of Science and Industry, *California and the World Ocean,* 1964.

CRUTCHFIELD, J. A., AND ZELLNER, ARNOLD. "Economic Aspects of the Pacific Halibut Fishery," *Fishery Industrial Research,* Vol. 1, No. 1 (Washington: U.S. Government Printing Office, 1963).

DAGGETT, A. P. "The Regulation of Maritime Fisheries by Treaty," *American Journal of International Law,* Vol. 28 (1934), pp. 693–717.

DEAN, A. H. "The Geneva Conference on the Law of the Sea: What was Accomplished," *American Journal of International Law,* Vol. 52 (1958), pp. 607–28.

———. "The Second Geneva Conference on the Law of the Seas," *American Journal of International Law,* Vol. 54 (1960), 751–89.

DUMONT, W. H., AND SUNDSTROM, G. T. "Commercial Fishing Gear in the

United States," Circular 109, *U.S. Fish and Wildlife Service*, Washington, 1961.

ELGUERRA, MANUEL. "A Policy for Marine Resources: Peru's Experience," California Museum of Science and Industry, *California and the World Ocean*, 1964.

EVENSEN, J. "Certain Legal Aspects Concerning the Delimitation of Archipelagos," *Law of the Sea*, UN Doc. No. A/Conf. 13/18.

FOOD AND AGRICULTURE ORGANIZATION AND WORLD HEALTH ORGANIZATION OF THE UNITED NATIONS. "A Contribution to the UN Scientific Committee on the Effects of Atomic Radiation and the Specific Questions Concerned with the Oceanography and Marine Biology in Respect to the Disposal of Radioactive Wastes," *FAO*, 57/7/4725, mimeographed.

FOOD AND AGRICULTURE ORGANIZATION OF THE UNITED NATIONS. *Yearbook of Fishery Statistics* (annually).

GIDEL, GILBERT. "The Continental Shelf," Translated by L. F. E. Goldie, *University of Western Australia Annual Law Review*, Vol. 3 (1955), pp. 87–123.

GLENN, GENE. "The Swedish-Soviet Territorial Sea Controversy in the Baltic," *American Journal of International Law*, Vol. 50 (1956), pp. 942–49.

GOLDIE, L. F. E. "Australia's Continental Shelf: Legislation and Proclamations," *International and Comparative Law Quarterly*, Vol. 3 (1954), pp. 535–75.

GORDON, H. SCOTT. "The Economic Theory of a Common Property Resource: The Fishery," *Journal of Political Economy*, Vol. 62 (1954), pp. 124–42.

GRAHAM, HERBERT W., AND EDWARDS, ROBERT L. "The World Biomass of Marine Fishes." Paper presented at the FAO International Conference on Fish in Nutrition, 1961. Rome: FAO, mimeographed.

GROSS, LEO. "The Geneva Conference on the Law of the Sea and the Right of Innocent Passage Through the Gulf of Aqaba," *American Journal of International Law*, Vol. 53 (1959), pp. 564–94.

HAMLISCH, R., AND TAYLOR, R. A. "The Demand for Fish as a Human Food." Paper No. R/v.1/1 presented at the FAO International Conference on Fish in Nutrition, 1961. Rome: FAO, mimeographed.

HERRINGTON, W. C. "Comments on the Principle of Abstention," *Papers Presented at the International Technical Conference on the Conservation of the Living Resources of the Sea, Rome, 1955*. UN Doc. No. A/Conf. 10/7, pp. 344–49.

———. "Some Methods of Fishery Management and Their Usefulness in a Management Program." *U.S. Fish and Wildlife Service Special Scientific Report No. 18*. Chicago, 1943.

———, AND KASK, J. L. "International Conservation Problems and Solutions in Existing Conventions," *Papers Presented at the International Technical Conference on the Conservation of the Living Resources of the Sea, Rome, 1955*. UN Doc. No. A/Conf. 10/7, pp. 145–66.

HURST, SIR CECIL J. B. "The Territoriality of Bays," *British Year Book of International Law*, Vol. 3 (1922–23), pp. 42–54.

———. "Whose is the Bed of the Sea?—Sedentary Fisheries Outside the Three-Mile Limit," *British Year Book of International Law*, Vol. 4 (1923–24), pp. 34–43.

IRELAND, G. "The North Pacific Fisheries," *American Journal of International Law*, Vol. 36 (1942), pp. 400–24.

JESSUP, P. C. "The Geneva Conference on the Law of the Sea," *American Journal of International Law*, Vol. 52 (1958), pp. 730–33.

JOHNSON, D. H. N. "Developments since the Geneva Conference of 1958 and 1960: Anglo-Scandinavian Agreements Concerning the Territorial Sea and Fishing Limits," *International and Comparative Law Quarterly*, Vol. 10 (1961), pp. 587–97.

———. "The Geneva Conference on the Law of the Sea," *The Yearbook of World Affairs*, Vol. 13 (1959), pp. 68–94.

———. "The Anglo-Norwegian Fisheries Case," *International and Comparative Law Quarterly*, Vol. 1 (1952), pp. 145–79.

JOHNSTON, D. M. "The International Law of Fisheries: A Policy-Oriented Inquiry in Outline," *Current Law and Social Problems*, Vol. 1 (1960), pp. 19–67, and Vol. 3 (1963), pp. 146–237.

KALDOR, N. "Welfare Propositions and Interpersonal Comparisons of Utility," *Economic Journal* (1939), pp. 549 ff.

KASAHARA, HIROSHI. "Japanese Fisheries and Fishery Regulations," California Museum of Science and Industry, *California and the World Ocean*, 1964.

KASK, J. L. "Russia: Advanced Ocean Fishing Country," *Fishing News International*, Vol. 1, No. 3 (April, 1962), pp. 9–13.

KASSELL, BERNARD M. "The Fishing Fleet of the Soviet Union," *United States Naval Institute Proceedings*, Vol. 87, No. 11 (November, 1961).

KELLOGG, R. "The International Whaling Commission," *Papers Presented at the International Technical Conference on the Conservation of the Living Resources of the Sea, Rome, 1955*. UN Doc. No. A/Conf. 10/7, pp. 256–61.

KENT, H. S. K. "The Historical Origins of the Three-Mile Limit," *American Journal of International Law*, Vol. 48 (1954), pp. 537–53.

KESTEVEN, G. L. "World Aquatic Biomass—Its Future Abundance." Paper presented at the FAO International Conference on Fish in Nutrition, 1961. Rome: FAO, mimeographed.

———, AND HOLT, S. J. "Classification of International Conservation Problems," *Papers Presented at the International Technical Conference on the Conservation of the Living Resources of the Sea, Rome, 1955*. UN₁ Doc. No. A/Conf. 10/7, pp. 350–71.

KOH, K. L. "The Continental Shelf and the International Law Commission," *Boston University Law Review*, Vol. 35 (1955), pp. 522–40.

KRUTILLA, JOHN V. "Columbia River Development: Some Problems of International Cooperation," *Land and Water: Planning for Economic Growth*. Boulder: University of Colorado Press, 1961.

KUNZ, JOSEF L. "The Continental Shelf and the International Law: Confusion and Abuse," *American Journal of International Law*, Vol. 50 (1956), pp. 828–53.

LI, CHOH-MING. "Statistics and Planning at the Hsein Level in Communist China," *The China Quarterly*, No. 9 (January–March, 1962), pp. 112 ff.

MCDOUGAL, MYRES S., AND BURKE, WILLIAM T. "Crisis in the Law of the Sea: Community Perspectives versus National Egoism," *Yale Law Journal*, Vol. 67 (1958), pp. 539–89.

McHUGH, J. L. "Can We Manage Our Atlantic Coastal Fishery Resources," *Transactions of the American Fisheries Society*, Vol. 88 (1959), pp. 105–10.

MESECK, G. "Importance of Fisheries Production and Utilization in the Food Economy." Paper No. R/I.3, presented at the FAO International Conference on Fish in Nutrition, 1961. Rome: FAO, mimeographed.

MIKHAÏLOV, S.V." On the Comparative Efficiency of Production of Some Products of the Land and Sea" (in connection with a discussion of decisions on the 22d Congress of the CPSU). *Okeanologiiâ*, Vol. 2 (1962), pp. 385–92. Translated by W. G. Van Campen, U.S. Bureau of Commercial Fisheries. Honolulu, October, 1962.

NESBIT, ROBERT A. "Biological and Economic Problems of Fishery Management," *U.S. Fish and Wildlife Service Special Scientific Report No. 18.* Chicago, 1943.

O'CONNELL, D. P. "Sedentary Fisheries and the Australian Continental Shelf," *American Journal of International Law*, Vol. 49 (1955), pp. 185–209.

ODA, S. "Japan and the International Fisheries," *Japanese Annual of International Law*, Vol. 4 (1960), pp. 50–62.

———. "Japan and the United Nations Conference on the Law of the Sea," *Japanese Annual of International Law*, Vol. 3 (1959), pp. 65–86.

———. "New Trends in the Regime of the Seas: A Consideration of the Problems of Conservation and Distribution of Marine Resources," *Zeitschrift für Ausländisches Öffentliches Recht und Völkerrecht*, Vol. 18 (1957–58), pp. 61–102 and 261–86.

———. "The 1958 Geneva Convention on the Fisheries," *Die Friedenswarte*, Vol. 55 (1960), pp. 317–39.

———. "The Concept of the Contiguous Zone," *International and Comparative Law Quarterly*, Vol. 11, Part 1 (1962), p. 131.

———. "The Continental Shelf," *Japanese Annual of International Law*, Vol. 1 (1957), pp. 15–37.

———. "The Extent of the Territorial Sea—Some Analyses of the Geneva Conferences and Recent Developments," *Japanese Annual of International Law*, Vol. 6 (1962), pp. 7–38.

OHIRA, Z. "Fishery Problems between Soviet Russia and Japan," *Japanese Annual of International Law*, Vol. 2 (1958), pp. 1–18.

———, AND KUWAHARA, T. "Fishery Problems between Japan and the People's Republic of China," *Japanese Annual of International Law*, Vol. 3 (1959), pp. 109–25.

Proceedings—Regional Meeting American Society of International Law. "Marginal Seas and Pacific Fisheries," No. 12. Seattle, June, 1956.

RANKEN, M. B. F. "Evolution probable des industries de la pêche en Europe," *La Pêche Maritime* (December, 1960).

RICKER, W. E. "Productive Capacity of Canadian Fisheries—An Outline," *Resources for Tomorrow*, Vol. 2. Ottawa: Queen's Printer and Controller of Stationery, 1961.

SCHAEFER, MILNER B. "Biological and Economic Aspects of the Management of Marine Fisheries," *Transactions of the American Fisheries Society*, Vol. 88 (1959), pp. 100–04.

———, AND REVELLE, ROGER. "Marine Resources," *Natural Resources*. Huberty and Flock, eds. New York: McGraw-Hill Co., Inc., 1959.

SCOTT, A. D. "Equitable Compensation in International River Basin Development," *Water Resources and Economic Developments of the West,* No. 10 (1961), pp. 103–11.

———. "Optimal Utilization and the Control of Fisheries." Ralph Turvey and Jack Wiseman, eds. *The Economics of Fisheries.* Rome: FAO, 1957.

———. "The Economics of Regulating Fisheries," *The Economic Effects of Fishery Regulation.* R. Hamlisch, ed. Fisheries Reports No. 5. Papers presented at an Expert Meeting, Ottawa, 1961. Rome: FAO, 1962. Fle/R5.

———. "The Fishery: The Objectives of Sole Ownership," *Journal of Political Economy,* Vol. 63 (1955), pp. 116–24.

SCOTT, J. B. *Hague Court Reports,* 1916.

SELAK, C. B. "A Consideration of the Legal Status of the Gulf of Aqaba," *American Journal of International Law,* Vol. 52 (1958), pp. 660–98.

SHEARER, A. K. "The Tidelands as a Legal and Political Battleground," *Journal of the Bar Association of the State of Kansas,* Vol. 22 (1953–54), p. 63.

SMYTHE, J. A. "World Production and Trade in Fish Meal and Oil," *Fishery Leaflet No. 507,* Bureau of Commercial Fisheries, U.S. Fish and Wildlife Service, March, 1961.

SORENSON, MAX. "The Law of the Sea," *International Conciliation No. 520,* November, 1958, pp. 195–255.

SVERDRUP, H. U. "Some Aspects of the Primary Productivity of the Sea," *FAO Fisheries Bulletin,* Vol. 5, No. 6 (November–December, 1952).

TURVEY, RALPH. "Optimization and Suboptimization in Fishery Regulation," *American Economic Review,* Vol. 54, No. 2, Part 1 (March, 1954).

"Symposium of the Texas Tidelands Case," *Baylor Law Review,* Vol. 3 (1951).

UNITED KINGDOM INFORMATION SERVICE. "The Territorial Sea." No. R. 4503 (January, 1960).

U.S. DEPARTMENT OF THE INTERIOR, FISH AND WILDLIFE SERVICE, BUREAU OF COMMERCIAL FISHERIES. *Commercial Fisheries Review* (monthly).

———. *Fishery Statistics of the United States* (annually).

U.S. SENATE, COMMITTEE ON COMMERCE. "The Postwar Expansion of Russia's Fishing Industry." (88th Cong., 2d sess.) Washington: U.S. Government Printing Office, 1964.

VAN CLEVE, R. "The Economic and Scientific Basis of the Principle of Abstention," *Law of the Sea, Official Record,* Vol. 1, UN Doc. No. A/Conf. 13/3, pp. 47–63.

WALDOCK, C. H. M. "International Law and the New Maritime Claims," *International Relations,* Vol. 1 (1956), pp. 163–94.

WALKER, W. L. "Territorial Waters: The Cannon Shot Rule," *British Year Book of International Law,* Vol. 22 (1945), pp. 210–31.

WHITEMAN, MARJORIE M. "Conference of the Law of the Sea: Convention on the Continental Shelf," *American Journal of International Law,* Vol. 52 (1958), pp. 629–59.

WINCHESTER, CLARENCE F. "Present and Future Factors that May Influence Fish Meal Demand," *Commercial Fisheries Review,* Vol. 25 (March, 1963), p. 2.

YOUNG, RICHARD. "Sedentary Fisheries and the Convention on the Continental Shelf," *American Journal of International Law,* Vol. 55 (1961), pp. 359–73.

———. "The Legal Status of Submarine Areas Beneath the High Seas," *American Journal of International Law,* Vol. 45 (1951), pp. 225–39.

Appendix A

꽄. 꽄.

FAO CLASSIFICATION OF FISH *

Definitions of groups and sub-groups of species

1 FISHES

11 *Freshwater fishes*
> The catadromous eels and all other freshwater teleosteans. (As far as possible all anadromous or the freshwater salmonids and clupeids are excluded; see groups *Salmons, trouts, smelts,* etc. and *Herrings, sardines, anchovies,* etc.) The Acipenseridae (sturgeons), bowfins, garpikes, etc.

12 *Salmons, trouts, smelts, etc.*
> The Pacific salmonids belonging to the genus *Oncorhynchus.* The Salmonidae (salmons), Osmeridae (smelts), Coregonidae (whitefishes), and Argentinidae (deep-sea smelts). (As far as possible not only the anadromous but also the freshwater species and varieties are included here.)

13 *Flounders, halibuts, soles, etc.*
> The Heterosomata (teleostean flatfishes) and therefore includes Pleuronectidae (flounders and halibuts), Soleidae (soles), and Bothidae (scoldfishes and turbots). The flattened selacheans, i.e., rays and skates, are grouped with *Sharks, rays, etc.*

14 *Cods, hakes, haddocks, etc.*
> The Gadoid fishes of the families Gadidae (cods) and Merlucidae (hakes).

* This classification is the basis for the statistics through 1962. FAO revised its classification in 1963.

Source: FAO, *Yearbook of Fishery Statistics, 1962,* Vol. XV, Rome, 1963, pp. t-6 and t-7.

15 *Herrings, sardines, anchovies, etc.*
The Clupeiform fishes, marine and freshwater, of the families Clupeidae (herrings, sardines, pilchards, menhadens, shads, etc.), Engraulidae (anchovies), Chanidae (milkfishes), Megalopidae (tarpons), Elopidae (tenpounders), and Albulidae (ladyfishes). (As far as possible not only the marine and anadromous but also the freshwater clupeids are included here.)

16 *Tunas, bonitos, mackerels, etc.*
The Thunnidae (tunas), Katsuwonidae (skipjacks), Scombridae (mackerels), Istiophoridae (sailfishes and marlins), Xiphiidae (swordfishes), Gempylidae (snake mackerels, snoek, barracoutas), Trichiuridae (hairtails, cutlassfishes), etc.

17 *Mullets, jacks, sea-basses, etc.*
The Atherinidae (silversides), Mugilidae (mullets), Sphyraenidae (barracudas), Polynemidae (threadfins).

The Carangidae (jacks), Seriolidae (yellowtails), Pomatomidae (bluefishes), Rachycentridae (sergeantfishes), Stromateidae (harvestfishes), Bramidae (pomfrets), Coryphaenidae (dolphins), Luvaridae (luvars), Zeidae (John Dories), and other related percomorph families.

The Sparidae (porgies), Sciaenidae (croakers), Serranidae (seabasses, groupers), Scorpaenidae (rockfishes), Triglidae (gurnards, sea robins), Arripidae (ruffs), Nototheniidae (Antarctic blennies), Uranoscopidae (stargazer), Lutianidae (snappers), and other related percomorph families.

The Lophiidae (anglerfishes), Ariidae (marine catfishes), Blennidae (blennies), Muraenidae (moray eels), Brotulidae (brotula), Ophidiidae (cusk eels).

18 *Sharks, rays, etc.*
The Elasmobranchii (dogfishes, sharks, skates, rays, and other Selachii); Holocephali (ratfishes and other Chimaeridae); and other cartilaginous fishes.

19 *Unsorted and unidentified fishes*
(a) Unsorted and mixed fishes not otherwise classifiable; (b) unidentified fishes; and (c) unspecified catches and landings.

2 CRUSTACEANS, MOLLUSCS AND OTHER INVERTEBRATES

21 *Crustaceans*
All aquatic (freshwater and marine) Crustacea (lobsters, rock lobster, spiny lobster, marine crawfish, freshwater crayfish,

marine and freshwater crabs, sea spiders, prawns, shrimps, barnacles, etc.). Arachnoidea (horseshoe crabs) are also included.

22 *Molluscs*

All aquatic (freshwater and marine) Mollusca, i.e., limpets, whelks, winkles, conchs, abalones, and other Gastropoda; oysters, mussels, clams, cockles, scallops, and other Pelocypoda; squids, cuttlefishes, octopi, nautili, and other Cephalopoda chitons and other Amphineura; etc.

23 *Bêche-de-mer, sea-urchins, ascidians, etc.*

The sea cucumber (bêche-de-mer) and other Holothurians; starfishes, brittle stars, sea eggs or sea urchins, and other Echinodermata; amphioxus and other Cephalocordata; ascidians (sea squirts) and other Tunicata.

3 WHALES

31 *Blue-whales, fin-whales, sperm-whales, etc.*

Balaenoptera musculus (blue-whales), *Balaenoptera physalus* (fin-whales), *Megaptera nodosa* (humpback-whales), *Balaenoptera borealis* (sei-whales), *Physeter catodon* (sperm-whales), *Eubalaena australis* (right-whales).

32 *Minke-whales, pilot-whales, etc.*

Balaenoptera acutorostrata (minke-whales), pilot-whales, baird's beaked whales, beluges or white whales, bottlenose whales, killer whales; and other Mystacoceti not included in group 31.

4 SEALS AND MISCELLANEOUS AQUATIC MAMMALS

41 *Porpoises, dolphins, etc.*

The Delphinidae (porpoises); and other Odontoceti not included in groups 31 and 32.

42 *Eared seals, hair seals, walruses, etc.*

The Otariidae (the northern, southern and tropical fur-seals and other eared seals); the Phocidae (harp seals, harbour-seals and other hair seals); the Odobaenidae (walruses).

43 *Miscellaneous aquatic mammals*

River and sea otters; manatees and dugongs and other Sirenia; all other aquatic mammals not grouped elsewhere, i.e., not included under groups 31, 32, 41 and 42.

5 MISCELLANEOUS AQUATIC ANIMALS AND RESIDUES

51 *Turtles, frogs, etc.*
> The turtles and other Reptilia; frogs and other Amphibia; aquatic birds, such as penguins, cormorants, gannets, etc.

52 *Pearls, shells, sponges, corals, etc.*
> Pearls, mother-of-pearl, the shells of the various molluscs, sponges (Porifera), corals (*Corallium* spp.) etc.; aquatic bird guano and eggs.

6 AQUATIC PLANTS

61 *Aquatic plants*
> Seaweed, kelp, Irish moss, wracks, tangles, etc.

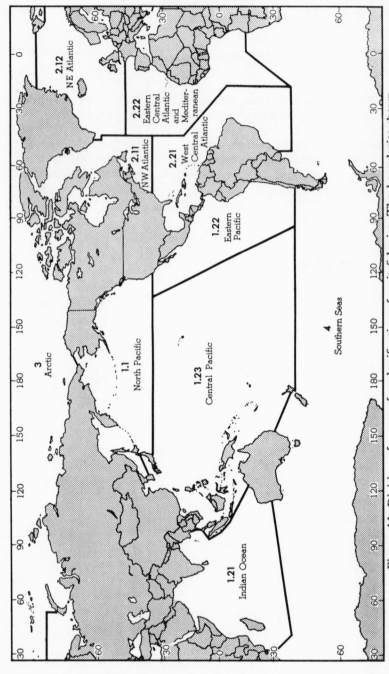

Figure A1. Division of oceans for classification of unit fisheries. The boundaries shown represent a compromise among several criteria, including oceanographic and zoogeographical factors. (*Source:* Kesteven and Holt, *op. cit.*, p. 360.)

Appendix B

Classification of Unit Fisheries

(This classification was prepared in 1955, and, while it indicates the variety of world fisheries, gear, and effort, it does not show many changes that have subsequently been made.)

Area and resource	Gear and method of fishing	Participating countries	Treaty arrangements [a]
WORLD-WIDE:			
Whales	Pelagic whaling	Denmark, Japan, Netherlands, Norway, Panama, U.S.S.R., United Kingdom	International Whaling Commission, South Pacific Commission
Whales	Shore-based whaling	Argentina, Australia, Brazil, Canada, Chile, France (for French Equatorial Africa), New Zealand, Peru, Portugal, Union of South Africa	International Whaling Commission, South Pacific Commission
Tunas, other oceanic pelagic species (swordfish, spearfish, sailfish, etc.):			
Central and South American tunas	Lines, purse-seines	Chile, Costa Rica, Ecuador, Mexico, Peru, United States	Tuna Commission
Mediterranean tunas	Traps, lines, purse-seines	Egypt, France (French territories?), Greece, Israel, Italy, Libya, Spain, Turkey	GFCM, International Commission for the Scientific Exploration of the Mediterranean Sea
Pacific tunas	Lines	Australia, China: Taiwan, Japan, Pacific territories, Philippines, United States	Indo-Pacific Fisheries Council
Tunas in other waters, not specifically referred to in treaty arrangements			
1. INDO-PACIFIC:			
1.1 North Pacific			
Salmon (five species, Oncorhynchus)	Traps, purse-seines, gill nets, lines	Canada, Japan, Korea, U.S.S.R., United States	Salmon Commission, North Pacific Commission

Area and resource	Gear and method of fishing	Participating countries	Treaty arrangements*
Sardine (<u>Sardina</u> or <u>Sardinops</u> <u>melanosticta</u>, <u>Etrumeus micro-</u><u>pus</u>, <u>Engraulis japonicus</u>)	Nets	Japan, Korea, U.S.S.R.	North Pacific Commission
Herring (<u>Clupea pallasi</u>)	Purse-seines	Canada, United States	North Pacific Commission
Mackerel (<u>Scomber japonicus</u>), jack (<u>Trachurus japonicus</u>)	Lines, nets	Japan	North Pacific Commission
Saury (mackerel), pike (<u>Cololabis saira</u>)	Dip nets, lines	Japan	North Pacific Commission
King crab (<u>Paralithodes</u> <u>camtschatica</u>)	Tangle nets, trawls	Canada, Japan, U.S.S.R., United States	North Pacific Commission
Halibut (<u>Hippoglossus</u> <u>stenolepis</u>)	Lines	Canada, United States	Halibut Commission, North Pacific Commission
Groundfish, American coast: Pleuronectids, gadoids (<u>Sebastes</u>)	Trawls, some lines	Canada, United States	North Pacific Commission
Shrimp (<u>Penaeus carinatus</u>), Yellow Sea	Trawl nets	China, Japan	Indo-Pacific Fisheries Council
Groundfish, East China Sea, Yellow Sea (<u>Pagrosomus</u> <u>major</u>, <u>Paralichthys olivaceus</u>, <u>Nibea argentata</u>)	Trawls	China, Japan, Korea	Indo-Pacific Fisheries Council
Fur seal (<u>Callorhinus ursinus</u>)	Pelagic and island fishing	Canada, Japan, U.S.S.R., United States	Fur seal agreement, 1942

1.2 Tropical Indo-Pacific;
    1.21 Indian Ocean:

Area and resource	Gear and method of fishing	Participating countries	Treaty arrangements*
Reef fish (percomorphs: Lutjanidae, Carangidae, Sciaenidae)	Lines	Madagascar, Mauritius, Reunion, Seychelles	Indo-Pacific Fisheries Council
Stolephorus species	Traps	Most Asian countries	
Groundfish (percomorphs: Lutjanidae, Carangidae, Sciaenidae)	Trawls, lines	Ceylon, India, Japan, Pakistan	Indo-Pacific Fisheries Council
Indian mackerel (<u>Rastrelliger</u> <u>kanagurta</u>)	Traps, surrounding nets	India, Indochina, Malayasia, Thailand	Indo-Pacific Fisheries Council
Indian oil sardine (<u>Sardinella</u> <u>longiceps</u>)	Surrounding nets	Southern Arabia, India, Pakistan	Indo-Pacific Fisheries Council
Clupeids, Persian Gulf (<u>Sardinella</u>, <u>Engraulis</u> species)	Various nets	Arabian countries, Iran	Indo-Pacific Fisheries Council
Groundfish, Persian Gulf (percomorphs: Lutjanidae, Carangidae, Sciaenidae)		Arabian countries, Iran	Indo-Pacific Fisheries Council
Clupeids, Red Sea	Various nets	Arabian countries, Egypt, Ethiopia, Iran	
Groundfish, Red Sea		Arabian countries, Egypt, Ethiopia, Iran	
Reef fish (percomorphs)	Traps, lines	Australia	
Rock lobster (<u>Panulirus</u> species)	Traps, lines	Australia	

1.2 Tropical Indo-Pacific;
    1.22 Eastern Pacific:

Area and resource	Gear and method of fishing	Participating countries	Treaty arrangements*
Rock lobster (<u>Jasus</u> species)		Chile	

Area and resource	Gear and method of fishing	Participating countries	Treaty arrangements[a]
Sardine (<u>Sardinops</u> sagax)[b]	Purse-seines	Chile, Ecuador, Peru	
Shrimp (peneids)	Trawls	Costa Rica, Mexico, Panama	
Groundfish, hake (<u>Merluccius</u>), pleuronectids	Trawls, lines, gill nets	Chile	
1.2 Tropical Indo-Pacific; 1.23 Central Pacific:			
Reef fish (percomorphs: Lutjanidae, Carangidae, Sciaenidae)	Lines, traps	All countries	Indo-Pacific Fisheries Council, South Pacific Commission
Flying fish (Exocoetidae)		Indonesia	Indo-Pacific Fisheries Council
Mackerel ('Kanbong, pla thu', <u>Rastrelliger kanagurta</u>)	Surrounding nets, traps	Malaya, Thailand	Indo-Pacific Fisheries Council
Groundfish (Sciaenidae, Foriniidae, <u>Stromateus</u>)	Trawls	China, Japan, Korea, U.S.S.R.	Indo-Pacific Fisheries Council
Pearl oyster	Diving	Australia, Japan	
1.1-1.22 Transition region:			
Pilchard (<u>Sardinops caerulea</u>), anchovies (<u>Engraulis mordax</u>, anchoviella species), mackerel, horse mackerel (<u>Pneumato-phorus diego</u>, <u>Trachurus symmetricus</u>)	Purse-seines	United States	
2. ATLANTIC:			
2.11 North-west Atlantic:			
Herring (<u>Clupea harengus</u>), other clupeids	Pelagic gear (weirs, seines, traps)	Canada, United States	ICNAF
Mackerel (<u>Scomber scombrus</u>), chub (<u>Pneumatophorus colias</u>)	Purse-seines	Canada, United States	ICNAF
Lobster (<u>Homarus americanus</u>)	Traps	Canada, France, Spain, United Kingdom, United States	ICNAF
Groundfish on banks (gadoids, pleuronectids, <u>Sebastes</u>)	Trawls, lines	Canada, France, Spain, United Kingdom, United States	ICNAF
Shrimp, prawn (nephrops, etc.)	Trawls	Denmark	ICNAF
2.11-2.12 Transition region:			
Groundfish (gadoids, pleuronectids)	Trawls, lines	Denmark, Iceland, Norway, Portugal, United Kingdom	ICNAF, ICES, Over-fishing convention, 1946
2.12 North-eastern Atlantic:			
Groundfish (gadoids, pleuronectids)	Trawls, demersal seines	European countries	ICES, Overfishing convention, 1946
Herring (<u>Clupea harengus</u>)	Pelagic and demersal gear (trawls, drift nets, ring nets)	European countries, U.S.S.R.	ICES, Overfishing convention, 1946
2.12-2.22 Transition region:			
Hake (<u>Merluccius merluccius</u>)	Trawls	European countries	ICES

Area and resource	Gear and method of fishing	Participating countries	Treaty arrangements [a]
2.11-2.21 Transition region:			
Menhaden (Brevoortia tyrannus)	Purse-seines	United States	
2.21 Western central Atlántic:			
Shrimp (Penaeus species)	Trawls	Cuba, Mexico, United States	
Reef fish	Lines, traps	Caribbean countries	
Groundfish	Trawls	Argentina, Brazil, Uruguay	
Reef percomorphs	Lines, seines, traps	Brazil	
2.22 Eastern central Atlantic and Mediterranean:			
Groundfish, many species	Trawls	Mediterranean countries	GFCM, ICES, International Commission for the Scientific Exploration of the Mediterranean Sea
Sardine (Sardinella aurita, Sardina pilchardus)	Surrounding nets	France, Greece, Italy, Morocco, Portugal, Spain, Yugoslavia	GFCM, ICES, International Commission for the Scientific Exploration of the Mediterranean Sea
Anchovy, horse mackerel (Engraulis encrasicholus, Trachurus trachurus), Black Sea	Ring nets	Turkey, U.S.S.R.	
Dolphin (Delphinus delphis), Black Sea	Ring nets, shooting	Turkey, U.S.S.R.	
Groundfish (percomorphs)	Lines, trawls	French, Portuguese and United Kingdom territories in Africa and southern Africa	ICES, Commission for Technical Co-operation in Africa south of the Sahara
3. ARCTIC:			
Herring (Clupea harengus)	Seines	U.S.S.R.	
Groundfish (pleuronectids)	Trawls	U.S.S.R.	
4. SOUTHERN SEAS:			
4.1 Temperate waters:			
Pilchard (Sardinops ocellata), maasbanker (Trachurus trachurus)	Purse-seines	Union of South Africa	
Groundfish (Merluccius capensis), pleuronectids (Austroglossus species), etc.	Trawls	South Africa	
Snoek (Thyrsites atun)	Jig lines	South West Africa, South Africa	
Percomorphs (Atractoscion aequidens, Johnius hololepidotus, Argyrozona argyrozona)	Hand lines	South Africa	
Sardine (Sardinops neopilchardus)	Nets	Australia	
Groundfish (Neoplatycephalus richardsoni)	Trawls	Australia	
Barracouta (Leionura atun)	Jig lines	Australia	

Area and resource	Gear and method of fishing	Participating countries	Treaty arrangements [a]
Reef fish (Chrysophrys guttatus)	Lines, traps	Australia	
Shark	Long lines	Australia	
Groundfish (percomorphs, pleuronectids)	Trawls	New Zealand	
Groundfish	Trawls	Argentina	

4.2 Antarctic:

Fur seals (Arctophalus pusillus)		Union of South Africa	

Note: In addition to the above, there are various diadromous fishes which are not at present caught on the high seas, but they spend an important part of their lives at sea. These include:

> 2.11-2.21 *Transition region:* Shad (*Alosa sapiddissima*); North America
> 1.21 *Indian Ocean:* Indian shad (Hilsa fish, *Hilsa ilisha*); India
> 1.21 *Indian Ocean:* Hilsa herring (*Hilsa reevesii*); China and Korea.

[a] Fur seal agreement, 1942: Provisional fur seal agreement between Canada and the United States, 1942.
GFCM: General Fisheries Council for the Mediterranean.
Halibut Commission: International Pacific Halibut Commission.
ICES: International Council for the Exploration of the Sea.
ICNAF: International Commission for the Northwest Atlantic Fisheries.
North Pacific Commission: International North Pacific Fisheries Commission.
Overfishing convention, 1946: Convention for the Regulation of the Meshes of Fishing Nets and the Size Limits of Fish (Overfishing conference, 1946).
Salmon Commission: International Pacific Salmon Fisheries Commission.
South Pacific Commission: Permanent Commission for the Exploitation and Conservation of the Maritime Resources of the South Pacific.
Tuna Commission: Inter-American Tropical Tuna Commission.

[b] Also basis for guano.

Source: G. L. Kesteven and S. J. Holt, "Classification of International Conservation Problems," Papers Presented at the International Technical Conference on the Conservation of the Living Resources of the Sea, Rome, April 18 to May 10, 1955, UN Doc. A/Conf. 10/7 (New York: United Nations, 1956), pp. 361–71.

Index*

Abstention principle, 185, 187, 202, 211, 215, 237; defined, 173; disagreements concerning, 181–82; and Pacific salmon industry, 102

Africa: fish consumption, 20(t), 34; fish supply, 139; food fish demand, 35(f), 39, 40(f), 41(t), 47(t)–49(t); research bodies for West coast, 195. *See also* South Africa

Agreements. *See* International agreements

Alaska: salmon traps, 15n; shrimp industry, 142

Alden, Robert, 138n

Aluminaut (vessel), 98

Anadromous fish: cultivation, 96; habitat, 75; locating, 88

Anchovies, supply outlook, 143

Anderson, S. V., 177n

Anglo-Venezuelan Treaty of 1942, 159, 162, 170

Anninos, P. C. L., 162n

Aquiculture, 70–72, 101

Argentina, supply, 140, 143

Artificial habitats, 100

Asia: fish consumption, 20(t), 21, 34; food fish demand, 39, 40(f), 41(t), 47(t)–49(t)

Atlantic Fishermen's Union, 128

Atlantic Ocean, 98; catch composition and supply outlook, 141; Japanese bases, 121; research body for, 195; supply studies, 248; zooplankton concentrations, 61, 63(f)

Attracting fish, 91; techniques, 99–100

Australia: cultivation of shrimp, 101; proclamation of 1953, continental shelf, 162

Barents Sea: catch composition and supply outlook, 141; fertility, 60; transplantation of Pacific salmon, 101

Barnett, Harold J., 217n

Base lines, 165–66, 168, 174, 186

Bases, foreign and processing, 95, 119, 120(f), 121, 249

Bell, F. H., 216n

Bering Sea: fishing treaty, Japan-Russia, 203; seal fishery treaties, 158; supply outlook, 142; U.S.–U.S.S.R. king crab agreement, 171

Bering Sea Fur Seal Arbitration of 1893, 158. *See also* Fur Seal Treaty

Beverton, R. J. H., 85, 216n

Bishop, W. W., Jr., 160n, 163n, 172n

Brandt, Karl, 197n

Brazil: dispute over lobsters on continental shelf, 171; supply, 140, 143

Brierly, J. L., 176n

Bristol Bay: salmon, 203n; supply outlook, 142

Burke, William T., 80n, 171n, 172n, 175n, 176n, 180n, 181, 186n, 190n, 197n, 210n, 216n

Bynkershoek, Cornelius van, 157

Canada: catch, 106(f), 149; change by species groups, 110(f); demand and supply outlook, 149; fishermen, 131(t); fishery industry place in national economy, 115(t); food fish demand, 40(f), 41(t), 47(t)–49(t); fur seal treaty, 85n; government role, 125; Pacific salmon and application of abstention principle, 102; salmon catch, sharing, 226; salmon fishery, 225; three-mile limit, 157; trade in fish products, 116(t); vessels and facilities, 124–25

Canned fish, consumption, 24

Cannon-shot rule, 157

Catch: annual, selected countries, 104, 105(t), 106(f), 107(f); composition shifts, 109–11; and demand projection, 37(t); diversity and specialization, 108; division by agreement, 226; by gear type, 92(t); per acre in selected fishing grounds, 68(t); percentage change, 108(f); shares, basis for allotting, 239; whales, 112, 113(f)); world total, 38(f); 104, 106(f); growth rate, 37; production potential, 68

Catching techniques. *See* Fishing techniques

Ceylon: powered vessels, 93; taste preferences, 34

Chapin, Henry, 217n

Chapman, John D., 227n

Chile: claims to territorial waters, 140, 163; supply, coastal fisheries, 140

China (Mainland): catch, 107(f); consumption, 20, 21(t); demand and supply outlook, 145–46; food fish demand, 39, 40(f), 41(t), 47(t)–49(t), 52; fresh fish catch as percentage of total, 23(t); output, 52n, 105, 145

China (Taiwan): consumption, fish and fish products, 19(t)

Christy, Francis T., Jr., 16n

Classification of fishery resource, 74–76, 262–65

Classification of unit fisheries, 267

Cleve, R. van, 187n

Coastal fisheries, supplies, 139–41

Coastal states: arguments for exclusive use of adjacent waters, 183–84, 215; special position, 182–87

* (f) refers to figure; (t) to table.

Cod: catch, 108, 109(f), 111(f); catching, 90; curing, 25; demand, 27, 39; supply outlook, 144, 151

Colombos, C. J., 163n, 180n

Commercial fishing gear. *See* Gear

Common property, characteristics of, 6–16

Competition, 4, 5, 86; factors creating increase in, 103; major fishing grounds, 141–42; problems of exclusive fishing rights claims, 140; problems of national quotas, 210

Conflict, 86; areas and sources of, 4–5, 140, 151–52, 212; study needed, 244–45

Congestion: aim of treaties dealing with, 158; and conflict over exclusive fishing rights, Strait of Dover, 140; and economic efficiency, 234, 237; future, 233–34; major fishing grounds, 141–42; and need for new arrangements, 233–34

Conservation: and freedom of the seas principle, 182; Japanese and Russian attitudes toward, 202; object of measure or program, 217; principle of, 188–89, 215; treaties dealing with, 158–59; "Truman Proclamation," 160–61. *See also* Depletion

Consumption: forms of utilization of fish, 22–27; future, 38–41; patterns of, 18–21, 26; per capita, 2, 19(t), 21(t); problems of measurement, 18; total (1957–59), by countries, regions, 20(t); total world (1958), edible fish products, 20. *See also specific species, use, or country*

Contiguous zones, defined, 168

Continental shelves: convention on, 170–71; description, 61; legal recognition, 160; national rights, 5, 160–62; natural resources defined, 170; output per acre, 68; productivity factor, 60–61; treaties relating to, 159; "Truman Proclamation," 160–62; of the world, 62(f)

Control of fishery resource, 84; depletion as factor in demand for, 14, 152; effect of lack of, 9; eumetric form of, 85–86; international arrangements and, suggestions for research, 251–52; licensing, 118, 222n; measures for, 84–86. *See also* Fishing rights; Gear, controls; Limited entry; Mesh size; Quotas; *and conventions and treaties*

Convention for the Regulation of the Meshes of Fishing Nets and Size Limits of Fish, 141n, 200–2, 206, 251

Convention on the Continental Shelf, 170–71, 174. *See also* Continental shelves

Convention of 1818, 157

Convention of 1882, 158

Convention on Fishing and Conservation of the Living Resources of the High Seas, 170, 171–74, 178, 187, 189n, 208, 211, 217, 233

Convention on the High Seas, 169, 170

Convention on Territorial Sea and Contiguous Zone, 168, 170, 187. *See also* Territorial seas

Cooley, Richard A., 16n

Costs, 233, 234; and exclusive fishing rights, 6–7; per fisherman, and revenues, 10(f); research needed, 245; and yield, revenue, effort, 7–15 *passim*, 8(f)

Cousteau, Jacques-Yves, 100

Cowen, R. C., 217n

Crab, 33, 142, 171

Crustaceans, FAO classification, 263–64

Crutchfield, James, 14n

Cultivation of fish, 96–97, 101–2. *See also* Aquiculture

Curing fish, as percentage of total utilization, 25

Currents, ocean, 58(f), 60

Daggett, A. P., 158n

Daniel, Hawthorne, 99n

Demand: effect on output levels, 82(f); elasticities of, and taste preferences, 32–34; factors affecting, 17, 28–36; food fish, estimates, 1969–71, 36(f), 38(f), 40(f), 41(t), 47(t)–49(t); fish meal, 25, 42–46, 53, 146; future, meeting, 138–52; methods for projection, 46–55; national outlooks, 145–50; for new species, developing, 247; problems of estimating, 18; projections, 36–38; research need, 244; worldwide, all purposes (1970), 2

Demand projection methods: food use of fish, 46–52; nonfood use, 53–55

Demersal fish: catch per acre, 68(t); catching device, 90; habitat, 75; locating, 88; supply outlook, 142

Denmark: consumption, fish and fish products, 19(t); fish and animal protein, income elasticity of demand, 35(f); fishing rights treaty, 194; national fishing zone claims, 165

Density of fish stock, 77; effect on output levels, 82(f)

Depletion, 3; causes of, 81; control, 14; defined, 81; economic forces affecting, 82(f), 83; effect of exploitation pattern, 8–9; and freedom of the seas principle, 182; international law, 213; and need for new arrangements, 233–34; research needed, 250; source of future conflict, 152; whale stock, 198

Distant water operations, 95–96

Distribution of fish and fish products, seasonal and geographic, 31–32

Doherty, Richard, 125n, 128

Draheim, George, 125n, 128

Dumont, William H., 90*n*
Dutch East India Company, 154

Ecology, 78–80; and the coastal state principle, 185; Cousteau's studies, 100; research needed, 248
Economic efficiency (and inefficiency): as aim in international agreements, 208; and common property characteristic of fisheries, 7; and congestion, 234; definition, 190; and eumetric form of control, 86; international, 236–42; lack of controls and, 11; and management policy, 216; and maximum sustainable yield, 14; national quotas approach, 210, 238; and restriction of effort, 16. *See also* Costs; Economic rent; Effort; Revenues
Economic rent: difficulties in reaching agreement, 225–30; and effort, 7; and eumetric form of control, 86; maximization of, 216, 221–30; provision for division in managed fishery, 227–28
Ecosystem, marine. *See* Food web
Ecuador, 24, 140, 163
Edwards, Robert L., 68
Effort, 7–15; allowed in conservation treaties, 159; controls, 84; costs per fisherman, and revenue, 10(f); defined, 84; future changes in location of, 150; intensity, determination of for managed fishery, 228; lack of control as common property characteristic, 7; national differences, 104–37; and revenue-expense relationships, haddock industry, Georges Bank, 127, 128(t); revenues, costs, and sustainable yields with respect to, 8(f); summary, 136–37; sustainable yield as a function of, 8(f); worldwide extension of, 95–96
Electric current: attracting and catching technique, 99, 100; cultivation technique, 101
Elguerra, Manuel, 146*n*, 147*n*
Employment: characteristics, 132–33; difficulties in evaluating and estimating, 130–36; and government programs, 127; inshore fisheries, 126; number of fishermen, four countries (1938, 1948, 1958), 131(t). *See also* Labor
Entry fees, 222*n*
Entry restrictions; *See* Limited entry
Established rights. *See* Historic rights
Eumetric yield theory, 8*n;* control based on, 85–86
Euphotic zone, 56
Europe: consumption (1958), 21
Europe, Eastern: food fish demand, 3, 40(f)
Europe, Western: catch, percentage decrease (1948–58), 127; consumption,

20(t), 24; demand, and future prices, 151; demand and supply, 139; employment characteristics, 133; food fish demand, 41(t), 47(t)–49(t), 50; income and forms of utilization, 33; investment in fisheries, 126; shifts in effort, 151
Evensen, J., 163*n*
Exploitation of a fishery: comparison with nonrenewable resource, 83–84; factors responsible for depletion, 82–84; pattern of, and sustainable yield, 8–9; rate of, variation in country attitudes toward, 218
Exports. *See* Trade

Factory ships, 93, 94
Family fishery operations, 132
Far East: consumption, 20(t), 21, 27, 30; food fish demand, 40(f), 41(t), 47(t)–49(t)
Faroe Islands, 159, 165
Fenwick, C. G., 178*n*
Fertility of oceans, 3; elements of, 56–61; regional differences, 63(f)
Finland: consumption, fish and fish products, 19(t); seal fishing agreement, 194
Fish, FAO classification of, 262–65
Fish flour. *See* Fish protein concentrate
Fish meal: consumption, 25; future demand, 42–46, 53; Peru, 42, 44, 146. *See also* Nonfood use of fish
Fish Meal Exporters' Organization, 44
Fish oil, consumption, 25
Fish populations, fluctuations, 77–80
Fish portions, demand, 33; production, 23
Fish protein concentrate (FPC), 25, 246; description and effects of, 30–31; and fish consumption in low-income countries, 37; future demand, 39
Fisheries, classification, 74–76, 267
Fishermen. *See* Employment; Labor
Fishery products: foreign trade, six countries, 116(t); national trade as percentage of world, eight countries, 116(t); research needed, 247
Fishing effort. *See* Effort
Fishing gear. *See* Gear
Fishing rights: exclusive, 4–7; on high seas, 171–74; historic or established rights, 165, 188, 211, 215, 237; licensing, 118, 222*n;* national claims, 140–41; treaties dealing with, 159–60, 193–94
Fishing techniques, 5, 91, 99–101, 228. *See also* Gear
Fishing zones, national limits, 5. *See also* Territorial seas; Three-mile limit; Twelve-mile fishing limit
"Flag of convenience," and fishing rights, 172*n*

Fleets: large-scale, research needed, 249; operations, 95

Florida current, 71

Food and Agriculture Organization of the United Nations, 4, 17, 18, 19, 20, 21, 33n, 35(f), 43n, 46, 49, 50, 51, 52, 53, 58, 62, 63, 64, 74, 94, 105, 106, 150, 160, 192n, 197n, 216n, 208n; classification of fish, 262–65; Fisheries Division, 135, 244, 245; research agreements, sponsorship of, 195

Food use of fish: catch and projected demand, 37(t), 38(f); demand, 38–41; demand projection, edible weight, 47(t)–49(t); demand projection methods, 46–52; national demand and supply outlooks, 145–50; world demand: distribution (1957–59, 1969–71), 40(f), 41(t), (1962, 1970), 2, percentage increase, 36(f). *See also* Consumption

Food web ("food chain"), 64(f), 65–67

Foreign bases. *See* Bases

France: competition and congestion in Strait of Dover, 140; consumption, 20(t), 21(t); fishing rights, Gulf of St. Lawrence, 159; oyster culture, 96

Franklin, C. M., 183n

Freedom of the seas, 7, 212, 213, 237; beneficiaries of the principle, 215; Grotius' view, 179; history of the principle, 154; human benefit approach, 180–81; inexhaustibility of resource, assumption, 179; internationalization approach, 178; as legal principle, 177–82; negative character of the principle, 178

Freeze-drying, 29, 30

Freshwater fish: consumption, 22–24; percentage of total catch (1962) by country, 23(t); supply, 138–39, 151; world catch, 22

Frozen fish: competition with fresh, 29–30; consumption, 22–24, 27, 29; effect on supply, 23–24; freezing on board ship, 93, 94

Fulton, T. W., 154n, 155n

Fur Seal Treaty: Arbitration of 1893, 158; control by reducing number of producers, 85n; convention, 202; regulatory nature of, 196; unified management features of, 224

Futagoishi, A., 120

Galiani, Ferdinando, 157

Garcia-Amador, F. V., 163n, 182n, 188n, 217

Gear: catch by types of (1959), 92(t); classification of, 90; conflict, 234; controls, 15, 84, 129; cost, research needed, 245; descriptions of, 89–92; efficiency, 129n; regulatory agreements, salmon, 198; treaties to resolve conflicts, 158

General Fisheries Council for the Mediterranean, 195

Geneva Conventions on the Law of the Sea, 167–74; on base lines, 166, 168; extent of territorial sea claim by nations represented (1958), 156; historic rights principle in, 188; ratification situation (1958), 168, 169(t). *See also* *specific Conventions and* Law of the Sea Conferences

Georges Bank, 127; economic inefficiency, 133; effort, revenue-expense relationships, haddock industry, 128(t); gear conflict, 234; supply outlook, 141, 142, 150

Germany, West. *See* West Germany

Gidel, Gilbert, 160, 178

Gill nets, description, 91

Goldie, L. F. E., 162n, 172n

Gordon, H. Scott, 218n

Goreux, L. M., 50

Government, support and policies in fishing enterprise, 118, 124, 125, 127, 129–30, 182, 247, 250

Graaff, J. de V., 240n

Graham, Herbert, 68

Grand Banks: concentration of fishing, 3; fertility at meeting of ocean currents, 60; management type, reason for, 235; supply outlook, 141, 142, 150. *See also* International Commission for Northwest Atlantic Fisheries

Great Britain: continental shelf rights and treaty agreement, 159; fishing rights treaties, with Denmark, 159; and freedom of the seas, 155; fur seal treaties, 158; "historic rights," losses, 188; Icelandic dispute, 164; income elasticity of demand for fish, 33; Parliament, 201n. *See also* United Kingdom

Greece: consumption, fish and fish products, 19(t)

Greenland, 60

Grotius, Hugo, 154, 155, 159, 178, 179, 187

Gulf of Alaska, supply outlook, 142

Gulf of Mexico, fishing rights in, 159

Gulf of St. Lawrence: demarsal supply, 142; device for effecting artificial nutrient upwelling, 17; French fishing rights, 159

Haddock: catching, 90; demand, 27; supply outlook, 144

Haddock industry, effort, revenue-expense relationships, Georges Bank, 128(t)

Hague Conference on the Codification of the Law of the Sea (1930): recognition the existence of continental shelf, 160; rules for drawing base lines, 165

Halibut, 236; catching, 91; demand, 27, 39; output (1930, 1950), 15; Pacific fishery under quota system, 14–15; problems complicating establishment of international agreements, 142; quotas, 197; research, 202; supply outlook, 151. *See also* International Pacific Halibut Commission

Hamlisch, R., 21, 33n, 50, 84n, 222n

Herring: Alaska catch, 129; canned, consumption, 24; conflict over fishing rights in Strait of Dover, 140; curing, 25; demand, future, 39; density and and harvesting, 77; North Sea supply, 3, 112; Norway's winter herring catch, outlook, 148; as percentage of catch, 108, 109(f), 110(f), 111(f); for reduction, 42; research, 202; supply, 142, 143–44, 151

Herring Industry Board (United Kingdom), 125

Herrington, W. C., 187n, 192n

Higgins, A. Pearce, 180n

High seas: absence of national rights, 177–78; applicability of conditions of property, 179; coastal states' preferential rights to adjacent stock, 183

Historic rights (established rights), 165, 188, 211, 237; benefits to advocates of, 215

Holt, Sydney J., 75, 85, 120, 216n, 221n

Hurst, Cecil J. B., 160n

Iceland: catch composition and supply outlook, 141; British fishing rights, 159; claim for wide territorial sea, 163–64; exclusive fishing rights claim, 140; fish meal exporter, 45; fishing rights treaty, 194; importance of fishery industry, 114; proposal to Law of the Sea Conference, 183; winter cooling as fertility element, 60

Imports. *See* Trade

Income: basic causes of low income in fishery, 208; and forms of utilization of fish, 33; and future consumption, 38–39; taste preferences, and elasticity of demand, 32–34

Income elasticity of demand, fish and animal protein, 35(f)

India: annual catch, 107(f); catch, percentage change, 108(f); species group change, 110(f); consumption, 20(t), 21(t), 27; demand and supply outlook, 150; fish culture, 97; fishery industry's place in national economy, 115(t); fresh fish catch as percentage of total, 23(t); inadequacy of consumption and production statistics, 18; taste preferences, 34; trade in fish products, 116(t)

Indonesia: catch (1963), 114n; consump-

tion, 20(t), 21(t), 27; exclusive rights claims, 163; fish culture, 97; fresh fish, catch as percentage of total, 23(t)

Indo-Pacific Fisheries Council, 195

"Innocent passage," 168

Inter-American Tropical Tuna Commission, 144, 199, 235

International agreements: conservation, 182–83, 186, 194–203; and cultivation techniques, 102; factors complicating establishment, 142; interrelationships among species and problems of, 78–79; maximization of net economic revenue as chief criterion for, 79; research needs, 244, 251–52

International Commission for the Northwest Atlantic Fisheries (ICNAF), 141, 202, 212; degree of autonomy, 205; as model, 237; technique of, 201

International Convention for the High Seas Fisheries of the North Pacific Ocean, 173n

International Council for the Exploration of the Seas, 159, 195

International Court of Justice, 174; Anglo-Norwegian base line dispute, 166; delimitation of territorial seas measured from straight base lines, 187

International Law Commission, 217; codification of law of the sea, 167

International law of the sea: codification, 167; competing doctrines, 175–91; role of, 153–74

International North Pacific Fisheries Commission, 159, 188, 201–2, 204, 227, 251

International Pacific Halibut Commission, 196, 197n, 204–5, 227, 251

International Pacific Salmon Fisheries Convention (1957), 198

International Technical Conference on the Conservation of the Living Resources of the Sea, 75, 168n

International Whaling Commission, 112, 197, 202, 238

Internationalized fishery, 238–40

Investment: private capital, 129–30; relation to problems of demand and supply, 4

Irradiation, 30

Italy: consumption, 20(t), 21(t); fresh fish catch as percentage of total, 23(t)

Japan: abstention principle, 102, 188; catch, 104, 105, 107(f); catch, increase rate of, 108(f), 114; change of catch by species groups, 110(f); consumption, 3, 19(t), 20(t), 21(t), 27, 34, 39; fish culture, 97; fish meal and oil, 26; fishermen, number of, 131; fishery industry place in national economy, 115(t); fishery operations, characteristics, 132–33, 134(t)–35; fishing agreements with, 202, 203, 212; fleet operations, 95; food fish demand, 39, 40(f), 41(t), 47(t)–49(t); foreign bases, 95, 119, 120(f), 121; Fur Seal Treaty, 85*n*, 158; government role in fishery industry, 118–19; high seas catch, 112; historic rights, losses, 188; hybridization and selective breeding, 101; investment in fishery facilities, 121; king crab fishery, 142, 171; National Fisheries Agency, 118–19, 120; and Northwest Pacific Fisheries Treaty, 163; oyster culture, 96; salmon rights, high seas, 202; scientists' view of sustained yield objective, 218; supply and demand, 139, 145 (*see also* food fish demand); taste preferences, 34; trade in fish products, 116(t), 117; use of trawls, 90, 92; vessels and facilities, 117–21; whales, 112, 113(f), 114, 198

Japan-Soviet Northwest Pacific Fisheries Convention, 163, 202–3, 214*n*

Johnson, D. H. N., 165*n*, 173*n*

Johnston, D. M., 176*n*, 181*n*, 186*n*, 192*n*, 203*n*, 206*n*, 212*n*, 214*n*, 227*n*

Kaldor, Nicholas, 228*n*, 240*n*

Kaplan, M. A., 175*n*, 176*n*, 177*n*

Kasahara, Hiroshi, 118*n*, 222*n*

Kask, J. L., 99*n*, 192*n*

Kassell, Bernard M., 121

Katzenbach, N. de B., 175*n*, 176*n*, 177*n*

Kellogg, R., 197*n*

Kent, H. S. K., 157*n*

Kesteven, G. L., 75, 120, 221*n*

King crab fishery, 142, 171

Kodiak Island, gear conflict, 234

Krutilla, John V., 227*n*

Kuntz, Josef L., 161*n*

Labor: costs, 136, 137; major fishing nations, 131; research needed, 245, 249; supply, coastal and distant-water fisheries, 136. *See also* Employment

Laevastu, T., 64

Laing, Austen, 126*n*

Latin America: consumption, 20(t), 34; food fish demand (1957–59, 1969–71), 40(f), 41(t), 47(t)–49(t)

Lauterpacht, H., 177

Law of the Sea Conferences, 156, 167–74, 208, 211, 213, 217; abstention principle, 188; conservation principle, 189; gains of coastal states, 186; Icelandic dispute, 164; preferential rights of coastal states, 183; three-mile territorial sea, 185. *See also specific conventions and* Geneva Conventions

League of Nations: Economic Committee, 197; territorial seas, 156, 167

Leonard, L. L., 159*n*

Li, Choh-ming, 52*n*

Licensing, 118, 222*n*

Limited entry, 11*n*, 85, 86; and economic efficiency, 237, 238, 251–52; Japanese system, 118, 119; level, 226; and national quotas, 209–11; research needed, 251–52

Little, I. M. D., 228*n*, 240*n*

Lobsters, demand, 33

Low-income countries: consumption patterns, 34; cultivation techniques, 103; food fish demand, 47(t)–49(t); income elasticity of demand for fish, 32, 34, 35(f); marketing organization and satisfaction of demand, 31–32; research and technology, 97–99; shrimp supply outlook, 144–45; taste preferences, 32; techniques and devices, 88–89; vessels, 93–94

Lynch, Edward, 125*n*, 128

McDougal, Myres S., 80*n*, 171*n*, 172*n*, 175*n*, 176*n*, 177*n*, 180*n*, 181, 186*n*, 190*n*, 197*n*, 210*n*, 216*n*

McHugh, J. L., 214*n*

Magoffin, Ralph Van Doman, 155*n*

Management: alternative arrangements for the future, 231–42; central international authority for, research problem, 212; and conservation, conflicting beliefs, 80–81; maximum sustainable yield as goal, economists' objections, 218–21; objectives for, 215–30; Pacific salmon industry, 102; regional approach, 200–3, 214, 235–36; three alternative approaches, 237–42; treaties, 196–203; unified, 223, 224, 225–30

Marine Research Foundation, Inc., 71

Marketing, 31–32

Maryland, restriction of power dredging of oysters, 15–16*n*

Maximum sustainable yield. *See* Yield, maximum sustainable

Menhaden: catching device, 89–90; fish meal, 26; for reduction, 42; supply outlook, 143

Meseck, G., 69, 143*n*, 145, 146

Mesh size, 27, 84, 85; conflicts over, 5; convention on, 200; costs, 204; regulatory agreements, 198–99, 200

Mexico-U.S. treaty re fishing rights in Gulf of Mexico, 159

Mikhaĭlov, S. V., 40*n*, 122, 123*n*

Mill, John Stuart, 179

Minot, Francis, 99*n*

Molluscs, 96; catch, 108, 109(f), 110(f); FAO classification, 264

Morse, Chandler, 217*n*

Mouton, M. W., 160*n*, 178*n*

Mullets, catch, 108, 109(f), 110(f), 111(f)

National Fishery Bank (Norway), 124
Nonfood use of fish: demand projection methods, 53–55; and future demand, 37(t), 41–46; national demand and supply outlooks, 145–48 *passim. See also* Fish meal
North America: consumption, 20(t), 24; employment characteristic, 133; demand and prices, 151; demand and supply, 139; food fish demand, 2, 38; investment in fisheries, 126; shifts in effort, 151
North Atlantic Coast Fisheries Arbitration (1910), Tribunal for, 165n
North Sea, 248; catch composition and supply outlook, 141; herring supply, 112; mesh-size regulations and inequitable costs, 204; supply outlook, 150; use of trawls, 90
North Sea Convention of 1882, 194
North Sea mesh convention. *See* Convention for the Regulation of the Meshes of Fishing Nets and the Size Limits of Fish
North-East Atlantic Fisheries Convention, 141n, 201, 202
Northwest Pacific Fisheries Convention, 163, 202–3, 214n
Norway: Antarctic fishing fleet, 114; -Britain dispute over base lines, 165; catch, 106(f); catch from distant waters, 112; catch, percentage change, 108(f); change of catch by species groups, 111(f); claim to territorial sea, 163–64; consumption, fish and fish products, 19(t); demand and supply outlook, 148; fish meal exporter, 45; fishing industry place in national economy, 115(t); fishing rights treaty, 194; government role, 124; national fishing zone claims, 165; number of fishermen, 131(t); specialization of catch, 109; straight base line claim, 174; trade in fish products, 116(t); vessels and facilities, 93, 124, 238; whale catch, 112, 113(f); whale quota, 198, 238; winter herring catch, 148
Norwegian Sea, catch composition and supply outlook, 141
Nutrients, upwellings of, 57–60, 58(f), 70–71

O'Connell, D. P., 162n
Ocean perch: catching, 90; demand, 27; production, 23–24
Ocean plants, 57, 59
Oceans: division for classification of unit fisheries, 266(f); false bottoms, 61; inadequacy of knowledge about, 232; productivity, 56–73

Oda, S., 162n, 163n, 183n, 192n, 197n, 198n, 203n, 228n
Ohira, Z., 203n
Oppenheim, L., 155n, 176n, 177n
Organisation for European Economic Cooperation, 127n, 131n, 141n
Output: effect of density, technology, and demand, 82(f); trends, 105–14. *See also* Catch
Oysters: culture, 96; demand, 33; techniques to increase production, 71

Pacific Ocean: Japanese bases, 121; seal fishery treaties, 158; supply, major fishing grounds, 143; supply outlook, 142; tuna regulatory agreement, 199; U.S.S.R. vessels in, 121; zooplankton concentrations, 61, 63(f)
Pacific Halibut Convention. *See* International Pacific Halibut Commission
Pakistan: consumption, 20(t), 21(t); fresh fish catch as percentage of total, 23(t); powered vessels, 93; taste preferences, 34
Pearl Fisheries Act, 162n
Pelagic fish: Antarctic catch, 113(f); catch per acre, 68(t); catching device, 88–90; habitat, 75
Perishability, effect on demand, 28–31
Permanent Commission for the Exploitation and Conservation of the Maritime Resources of the South Pacific, 201
Persian Gulf, proclamations leading to division of floor of, 162
Peru: anchoveta catch, 42(t); annual catch, 107(f); catch composition, 111; catch increase, 146; change in catch by species groups, 110(f); claims to territorial waters, 140, 163; demand outlook, 146; fertile upwellings, 59; fish meal, 26, 42, 44, 45(t); fishery industry in national economy, 115(t); nonfood fish, projected share of world demand for, 146; number of fishermen, 131, 132; output, 104, 105; reduction, projected demand, 54; supply, 139, 143–44, 146; trade in fish products, 44–45, 116(t), 117; vessels and facilities, 93, 121
Philippines: consumption, 19(t), 20(t), 21(t), 27; exclusive rights claims, 163; fresh fish catch as percentage of total, 23(t); powered vessels, 93; taste preferences, 34
Phytoplankton: estimated production, 69; in "food chain," 56, 66; requirements for growth, 57
Pontecorvo, Giulio, 181n
Pope Alexander VI, 154
Population, increase, and demand and consumption, 2, 32–33, 39
Potter, P. B., 178n

Preservation, effect on demand, 28–31
Prices: and consumption, 30, 34, 37; effect of controls, 16n; future, and demand, 151; increased, effect on yield and revenue curves, 11, 12(f); research needed, 245; and uniform set of labor-capital fish price-ratios, 223
Processing fish, transporting and, 92–96
Productivity of the sea, 56–73: estimating the potential, 66–70; means of increasing, 70–72
Proskie, John, 125n
Protein: fish and animal, income elasticity of demand, 35(f); fish as proportion of total intake, 19(t)
Protein concentrate. See Fish protein concentrate
Purse seines, description, 89–90
Puget Sound, salmon fishery, alternative management methods, 229n

Quotas: control by, 84, 85; description of system, 14–15; halibut, 197; national approach, 238; national, difficulties arising from, 209–11; national, and economic efficiency, 237–38; problems for research, 212; tuna, 199; whales, 114, 197, 198

Ranken, M. B. F., 51, 52n
Reduction of fish, 2; future demand, 42–46, 53; products of, 25–26; world catch for (1938–62, 1969–71), 38(f). See also Fish meal; Fish protein concentrate; Nonfood use
Regional arrangements, 200–3
Regional fisheries: research to develop guidelines for, 79–80; "unit," classification, 75–76, 267
Research: activity of Treaty Commissions, 202, 205–7; creation of incentives, 236; investments in, 86; in oceanography, 98; suggestions for, 211–13, 243–52; treaties, 195; treaty provisions for, 159; Tuna Commission, 199
Revenue: and costs per fisherman, 10(f); and costs, yield, effort, 7–15 passim, 8(f); effect of increased prices on yield and revenue curves, 12(f); effect of technological innovation on yield and revenue curve, 13(f); maximum total, as fishermen's collective goal, 219–20
Ricker, W. E., 149
Rome Conference on the Living Resources of the Sea, 186, 205
Russia. See Union of Soviet Socialist Republics

Salmon, 236; alternative management methods, Puget Sound, 229n; attracting techniques, 100; canned, consump-

tion, 24; catch, 109(f), 110(f), 111(f); catching, 91; demand, 27, 39; density and harvesting, 77; depletion, 3; Pacific industry, application of abstention principle, 102; regulatory agreements, 198; research, 202, 252; Russia-Japan agreements, 203; supply, 142, 144, 151; transplantation, 72, 101; traps, 15. See also International North Pacific Fisheries Commission
Sardines, 78; canned, consumption, 24; depletion (Pacific), 3
Scallops, 33, 90
Scandinavian states, claims to territorial waters, 156
Schaefer, M. B., 216n, 220n
Scott, Anthony D., 11n, 196n, 208n, 227n
Scott, J. B., 165n
Sea of Japan, 203
Seasonal limits, control by, 84
Sedentary fish, national rights, 5
Selden, John, 155, 180n
Shrimp: catching, 90; cultivation, 101; demand, 27, 39; freeze-dried, 30; frozen breaded, 23; supply outlook, 144–45, 151; U.S. Alaskan industry, 142
South Africa: catch, 112, 113(f), 114n; fish meal exporter, 45
South America: territorial seas claims of countries, 162–63
South Korea, Rhee line, 163
South Pacific Convention. See Permanent Commission for the Exploitation and Conservation of the Maritime Resources of the South Pacific
Spain: catch (1963), 114n; consumption, fish and fish products, 19(t), 20(t), 21(t)
"Standard vessel-days," 84
Statistics, suggestions for research, 245
Stocks, as a basis for management, 235: treaties regulating, 196–200
Strait of Dover, conflict over fishing rights, 140
Sundstrom, G. T., 90n
Supply: of certain species, 143–45; characteristics of, 3; coastal fisheries, 139–41; and demand, 138, 145–50; and fishing effort, 104–37; freshwater fisheries, 138–39; implications of freezing fish, 23; major fishing grounds, 141–43; research need, 244, 248–51; sources of, 138–43; trends, 105–14; world outlook, 150–51. See also Catch, Fertility, Fishing effort, Output, Productivity
Sverdrup, H. U., 57n
Sweden, consumption, fish and fish products, 19(t)

Taste preferences, 27, 28, 29, 32–34
Taylor, Clyde C., 128
Taylor, R. A., 21, 33n, 50

Technology, 97–103; consideration in reformulation of international law, 213; and depletion of resource, 9; effect of innovation on yield and revenue curves, 11, 13(f); effect on output levels, 82(f); effect on supply, 4; freeze-drying and irradiation, 29; means of increasing productivity, 70–72; rate of innovation, 210; research needed, 250; resistance to new developments, 208; vessels, 101

Territorial seas: cannon-shot rule, 157; CEP countries, claim, 187; convention on, 168, 170, 187; delimitation measured from straight base lines, 186; history of claims, 156–57; sea league tradition, 156; three-mile limit, 185, 226; origin of, 157n; twelve-mile limit, 164–65

Thailand: consumption, 19(t), 20(t), 21(t); fish culture, 97; fresh fish catch as percentage of total, 23(t); powered vessels, 94

Three-mile limit, 157n, 185, 226

Tillic, I., 44n, 121n

Tomasevich, J., 192n, 197n, 203n

Trade, fish and fish products, 115(t), 116(t), 223

Transplantation of species, 71, 101

Transporting fish, 92–96

Traps, 91

Trash fish, 23, 67, 78, 217

Trawls, 90

Treaties: alternatives for achieving economic efficiency, 237–42; before 1945, 158–60; and commissions, 192–214; conclusions, 213–14; criteria for reformulation, 215–30; fishing rights, 193–94; maximum physical yield as basis for, 14; open-ended, possible consequences, 238; primary purpose of powers granted to Commissions, 208n; problem of new adherents, 212; regional approach, 214; regional regulatory, 200–3; research and management, 195–203; stock regulatory, 196–200; three problems of concern, 158. See also names of treaties

Treaty commissions: autonomy of, 204–5; objectives of, 208–9; research organization, 205–7

Treaty of 1763 (Peace of Paris), French fishing rights, 159

Treaty of Washington (1871), 194

Troebst, Cord-Christian, 99n

"Truman Proclamation," continental shelf and conservation, 160–63, 170

Tuna: catch, 108, 109(f), 110(f), 111; catching, 89–90, 91; consumption, 24, 33; demand, 27, 39; freezing on vessels, 94; international agreement, 144, 199, 235; Japanese processing bases, 95; quotas, 199; regulatory agreements, 199; supply outlook, 144, 151

Turvey, Ralph, 16n, 220n

Twelve-mile fishing limit, 164–65

Unidentified growth factor (UGF), 43, 44, 55

Union of Soviet Socialist Republics: attitude toward fishing agreements, 202, 212; catch, 104–5, 107(f); catch, percentage change, 108(f); change in catch by species groups, 111(f); catch, rate of increase, 114; consumption, 20, 21(t); demand and supply outlook, 147; exclusive rights claims, 163; fish meal and oil, 26; fish protein and beef production, man-day requirement, 122; fishing agreements with Japan, 203; food fish demand, 3, 40(f), 41(t), 47(t); food fish production, 50–51; fresh fish catch as percentage of total, 23(t); gear conflict, 234; herring catch, 112; light-pump technique, 99; Northwest Pacific Fisheries Treaty, 163; number of fishermen, 131, 132; seal fishing agreements, 85n, 158, 194; trade in fish products, 116(t); trawl fishery in North Pacific, 142; -U.S. king crab agreement, 171; vessels and facilities, 24, 93, 94, 114, 121–23; whales, catch, quota, 112, 113(f), 198

Unit fisheries: classification of, 75–76, 267; division of oceans for, 266(f)

United Kingdom: agreement re Faroe Islands, 165; catch, 104, 106(f); catch, percentage change, 108(f); catch, specialization, 109; change of catch by species group, 111(f); consumption, 19(t), 20(t), 21(t); demand and supply outlook, 148; effect of extension of territorial seas by other governments, 148; fish meal and oil, 26; fishermen in distant water operations, 133; fishery industry in national economy, 115 (t); government role, 125–26; Herring Industry Board, 125; number of fishermen, 131(t); trade in fish products, 116(t); vessels and facilities, 93, 125–26; whales, 112, 113(f); White Fish Authority, 125. See also Great Britain

United Nations, 156n, 162n, 166n, 167n, 169, 170n, 187n, 194n, 195n, 197n, 199, 201n, 205; recipient of share of catch under internationalized approach, 239. See also Food and Agriculture Organization of; Law of the Sea Conferences

United States, 201n, 202n; Alaskan shrimp industry, 142; catch, 106(f); catch from high seas, 112; catch, percentage change, 108(f); change in catch by species groups, 110(f); claim to territorial waters, 157; competition in coastal fisheries, and exclusive fishing rights claims, 141; consumption, 20(t), 21(t); continental shelf, "Truman proclamation" re, 160–61; demand and supply outlook, 147; fish culture, 97; fish meal and oil, 26; fishery industry in national economy, 115(t); food fish demand, 40(f), 41(t), 47(t); freeze-dried shrimp, 30; fresh fish catch as percentage of total, 23(t); fur seal treaties, 85n, 158; government role, 124; income, and forms of fish utilization, 33; international agreements, necessity to respect, 212; locating fish, 89; -Mexico treaty re fishing rights in Gulf of Mexico, 159; number of fishermen, 131(t), 132, 133; ocean perch production, 23–24; oyster culture, 96; salmon, 102, 225, 226; -Soviet king crab agreement, 171; trade in fish products, 116(t), 147–48; vessels and facilities, 93, 123–24

U.S. Atomic Energy Commission, 98

U.S. Department of the Interior, Bureau of Commercial Fisheries, 92, 148n, 246

U.S. National Academy of Sciences, Committee on Oceanography, 70, 97, 98n

U.S. Senate, Committee on Commerce, 122n, 131n

U.S. Treasury Department, Bureau of Customs, 123n

Utilization of fish, forms of, 22–27, 33

Van Campen, W. G., 40n

Vessels and facilities, 117–26; construction programs, country comparisons, 126–27; effect of quota system, 15; freezing, and distant water fisheries, 24; investment and freedom of the seas principle, 182; size and power, 93–94; summary, 126–30; technology, 101; treaties to resolve conflicts, 158. *See*

also Congestion; Effort; Factory ships; Fleets

Wage-price structure: national differences as obstacle to agreement, 224; and unified fishery management, 223

Waldock, C. H. M., 163n

Walford, Lionel A., 64n, 66n, 78, 99n, 217n, 232n

Walker, W. L., 157n

Walton, F. G., 217n

Wantrup, S. V. Ciriacy-, 84n

Washington (state), alternative methods of managing salmon fishery, 229

West Germany: consumption, 20(t), 21(t); fish meal and oil, 26; fresh fish catch as percentage of total, 23(t); use of trawls, 90

Western Europe. *See* Europe, Western

Whales: agreements to protect, 112, 197, 202, 238; catch, by selected nations, 113(f); catch, total, 112, 113(f); depletion, 3, 198; FAO classification, 264; quotas, 197, 198; supply outlook, 145

Whitefish Authority (UK), 125

Wilson, Woodrow, 178n

Winchester, Clarence F., 54

Woods Hole Oceanographic Institution, 71

Yates, P. Lamartine, 46, 50n

Yield: effect of increased prices on yield and revenue curves, 12(f); effect of technological innovation on yield and revenue curves, 13(f); interrelated species, 233; sustainable and maximum sustainable, 7–15 *passim*, 8(f), 14, 81, 82, 215–21, 226

Yugoslavia, 35(f), 194

Zellner, Arnold, 14n

Zooplankton: estimation of standing crop, 63(f); importance in "food chain," 56

BARENTS SEA

SEA
OF
OKHOTSK

BERING SE

Fur Seal
Treaty

Northwest Pacific
Treaty

SEA OF
JAPAN

EAST
CHINA
SEA

EDIT. SEA

SOUTH
CHINA
SEA

PACIFIC   O

INDIAN   OCEAN

Internatio